MW00460994

*Visitation*

*Visitation*

*Resources for the Care of Souls*

EDITED BY ARTHUR A. JUST JR. AND SCOT A. KINNAMAN

CONCORDIA PUBLISHING HOUSE · SAINT LOUIS

Original prayers and adaptations of prayers contributed by Sara M. Bielby, Joshua D. Genig, Gifford A. Grobien, Marcus James Nelson, Rachel D. Thompson, and Mary Jackquelyn Veith for Concordia Publishing House.

Manufactured in the United States of America

Library of Congress Cataloging-in-Publication Data

Visitation : resources for the care of souls / edited by Arthur A. Just, Jr. and Scot A. Kinnaman.

    p. cm.
   Includes index.
   ISBN 978-0-7586-1128-4
  1. Visitations (Church work) I. Just, Arthur A., 1953– II. Kinnaman, Scot A. III. Title.
  BV4320.V55  2007
  253′.76—dc22

2007026622

1 2 3 4 5 6 7 8 9 10      17 16 15 14 13 12 11 10 09 08

# Contents

# *Foreword*

When troubles come to those we cherish, it can be an agonizing way to God's goodness. Troubles find us easily and often, but how hard, how seemingly impossible for us to go to the comfort and the joy of God! God's children turn to the Word of God because we learn that our life depends upon it. Amid all that troubles us, God's Word works understanding, puts our temporary sufferings into eternal perspective, and gives us hope centered in the resurrection of our Lord Jesus Christ.

Because we need God to keep coming to us, we need visitation. Members of the body of Christ need to go to one another and share the Word that opens our narrow hearts to all the blessings that come from the faith, hope, and love in Christ Jesus. *Visitation* serves that need and is an essential tool for comforting others in their difficult times. As Luther concluded, "Through suffering, we may finally succeed and attain this heart and cheer, joy and consolation, from Christ's resurrection" (*Sermons of Martin Luther*, John Nicolau Lenker, 2:253). May the Spirit uphold you as you guide those who suffer to the consoling Word of Christ.

Dale A. Meyer
President, Concordia Seminary, St. Louis, Missouri

# *Preface*

**But deliver us from evil.**

*What does this mean?* We pray in this petition, in summary, that our Father in heaven would rescue us from every evil of body and soul, possessions and reputation, and finally, when our last hour comes, give us a blessed end, and graciously take us from this valley of sorrow to Himself in heaven. (*Luther's Small Catechism*, Lord's Prayer, the Seventh Petition.)

IN HIS FOREWORD, Dr. Dale Meyer reminds us "troubles find us easily and often." Troubled times prove that God's Word is not the only powerful word we hear. The devil uses powerful and persuasive words to torment the mind and darken the heart. God's Word is greater still. He provides those who visit and counsel the suffering members of God's family with words that silence doubt, fear, loneliness, and guilt. *Visitation* identifies many of the common situations into which pastors, deaconesses, and even lay visitors are asked to speak that Word of hope and comfort. God's children turn to the Word of God because our very life depends upon it. Amid all that troubles us, God's Word puts our temporary sufferings into eternal perspective, giving us hope centered in the resurrection of our Lord Jesus Christ.

Visiting the distressed and the suffering, visiting the sick and the dying, speaking Jesus' words of healing, comfort, and hope into mean, ugly, and lonely situations is the blessing and challenge of those called to do God's work. Amid already full schedules, even in the middle of the night, the pastor, deaconess, or caring Christian is challenged to confess the hope that he or she has in Jesus Christ and to speak words of comfort—the very Word of God that rescues us from every evil of body and soul.

This little book has a singular focus: Holy Baptism as continuing comfort for the child of God. The essential proclamation that through Baptism we have already died with Jesus and have been given new birth born of water and the Word *is* the visitors' message of comfort. The selected Scripture readings, devotions, prayers, and hymn stanzas are ready and useful tools for the visitor. The solid and reassuring message proclaims that, as He once did in Baptism, so, too, does our Lord continue to come to us in all times.

*Visitation* is carefully designed to put immediately useful resources into the glove compartment, pocket, briefcase, or Communion kit of the visitor. Section I features twenty-eight bedside devotions based on selected psalms. Written in the first person, these brief devotions address a variety of spiritual and emotional topics. Sections II–IV offer targeted resources that can be easily accessed by the visitor to address specific issues. The devotional messages, hymns, prayers, and Scripture texts can be used as they appear, or they can serve the visitor as a way to find appropriate points of contact while composing himself or herself to speak more directly to the situation at hand. Within each section are cross-references, allowing the user to quickly see the whole range of resources available in the book. The final section contains several of the most common orders of service used by those visiting the distressed, the sick, or the dying. The orders are taken directly from *Pastoral Care Companion* and should integrate well with whatever other resource for visitation ministry that you may choose to use.

May this little book be a blessing as you minister to those waiting for the Father's rescue.

Scot A. Kinnaman
Commemoration of St. Matthias, 2007

JESUS CHRIST entered our world to release us from the diseases of our souls and to bring in a new creation. Jesus heals His creation by casting out demons, healing the sick, raising the dead, and forgiving sin. He does this by the power of His Word that creates what it says. So He rebukes the demon and says, "Be silent and come out of him," and it happens. He tells the paralytic, "Rise up and take your pallet and go to your home," and immediately the man is healed. To the widow's son at Nain, Jesus says, "Young man, I say to you, be raised," and the dead man sits up and starts speaking. And to the sinful woman at the Pharisees' Sabbath Seder, He says, "Your sins have been forgiven," and she departs in peace.

All these things come from Christ's Word as the Word made flesh. Jesus' words and His healing testify that already now in Christ, God has invaded His creation and is releasing it from the bondage of its fallenness. This freedom for the captives is real. In Jesus, all creation is undergoing a healing. He comes to bring mercy and compassion through His healing presence. But the world rejects Christ's healing by rejecting Him. At the cross all sin, sickness, and death is placed on Jesus. The world grows dark and shakes and is re-created. Healing of the whole creation by the blood of Jesus comes only after the Creator dies. Healing comes through pain, suffering, and death. Healing comes through the shedding of Jesus' blood.

Jesus visited the sick and the suffering to show them the mercy and compassion of God. We now visit the sick and suffering armed with Jesus' Word, His baptismal invocation and prayer. In our visitations we bring those we visit into communion with Jesus, Creator and Redeemer of the universe.

More than thirteen years ago, I made a comment in class that someday I would like to put together a book of lessons and prayers to assist pastors, deaconesses, and caring Christians in their visitations to the sick and the suffering. Scot Kinnaman was in that class, remembered that statement, and asked me to co-edit this book with him. Many thanks to him for making this a reality. Without his perseverance and prodding, and his wonderful insight and support, this resource would not have been possible.

I want to thank deaconess students Sara Bielby, Rachel Thompson, and Mary Veith and seminary students Joshua Genig, Gifford Grobien, and Marcus Nelson for their marvelous contributions to the devotions in Section II. I would also like to thank Pamela Boehle-Silva, parish nurse from Holy Cross Lutheran Church in Rocklin, California, for using these devotions in her visits to the sick and the suffering and for offering an honest assessment of their value in providing comfort to those who are oppressed. Finally, many thanks to Cynthia Johnson, the administrative assistant for Kramer Chapel and the deaconess program at Concordia Theological Seminary, Fort Wayne, Indiana, for her help in preparing the several drafts of the manuscript.

> May the healing medicine of the Gospel and the Sacraments put to flight the diseases of our souls that with willing hearts we may ever love and serve You.
> (Collect for the Feast of St. Luke, *LSB Altar Book*, p. 980)

Arthur A. Just Jr.
Ash Wednesday, 2007

# *Acknowledgments*

Some prayers in *Visitation* were taken from the following sources:

| | |
|---|---|
| *Daily Office* | *The Daily Office*, ed. Herbert Lindemann, copyright © 1965 Concordia Publishing House. All rights reserved. |
| *LBP* | *Lutheran Book of Prayer*, copyright © 2005 Concordia Publishing House. All rights reserved. |
| *LSB Agenda* | *Lutheran Service Book: Agenda*, copyright © 2006 Concordia Publishing House. All rights reserved. |
| *LSB Altar Book* | *Lutheran Service Book: Altar Book*, copyright © 2006 Concordia Publishing House. All rights reserved. |
| *LW* | *Lutheran Worship*, copyright © 1982 Concordia Publishing House. All rights reserved. |
| *LW Agenda* | *Lutheran Worship: Agenda*, copyright © 1984 Concordia Publishing House. All rights reserved. |
| *LW Altar Book* | *Lutheran Worship: Altar Book*, copyright © 1982 Concordia Publishing House. All rights reserved. |
| *LW Little Agenda* | *Lutheran Worship: Little Agenda*, copyright © 1985 Concordia Publishing House. All rights reserved. |
| *Occasional Services* | From *Occasional Services* copyright © 1982 AELC, LCA, ALC, ELCC. Reproduced by permission of Augsburg Fortress. |

# SECTION I

*Bedside Devotions*

# Mindful of His Own

O Lord, our Lord,
> how majestic is Your name in all the earth!
You have set Your glory above the heavens.
> Out of the mouth of babes and infants,
You have established strength because of Your foes,
> to still the enemy and the avenger.

When I look at Your heavens, the work of Your fingers,
> the moon and the stars, which You have set in place,
what is man that You are mindful of him,
> and the son of man that You care for him?

(Psalm 8:1–4)

How insignificant I am when compared to the vast universe! Does God really have time for me? He has billions of people to watch over and tens of billions of stars to keep in their appointed course. Why should He be bothered with my aches and worries?

God's Word assures me that He knows my needs and guides me with His strong but gentle hands. I can depend on Him because His faithfulness is firmer than Gibraltar. God's care is so thorough that the falling sparrow and the shooting star are not beyond His notice. Everything moves at His will.

I am more precious to God than sparrows and stars. I am so precious that God bought me back from slavery to sin and death through the blood of His own Son, Jesus, who gave His life for me to cleanse me from sin and give me life never-ending. Because of that redemption, His hands uphold me, and His heart loves me. I am God's child, now and for eternity.

Am I insignificant, frail, lost, worthless? No, for Christ has joined Himself to me, and I cling to Him as only a child can cling. God knows that I am here. God knows that I am in need of help. I know that the Lord loves me; the cross of Jesus tells me of His love. I do not need to be afraid—God cares for me.

*Prayer*

Lord God eternal, by Your grace we live, and by Your mercy we are redeemed. Look upon me in my distress and pain, and take from me the troubles of today. In Your love, let me find peace; in Your Word, hope; in Your promises, consolation. Let Your presence protect me and Your mercies remove all anxieties and cares. Graciously forgive me all my sins. Keep me in Your loving care because of Him who died that I might live: Christ Jesus, my Savior. Amen.

~

# Our Daily Delight

Let the words of my mouth
 and the meditation of my heart
 be acceptable in Your sight,
 O LORD, my rock and my redeemer. (Psalm 19:14)

Do I dare approach God, who is perfectly holy and completely righteous? Do I dare ask Him to be pleased with the words of *my* mouth and the meditations of *my* heart? Yes—because He graciously receives me into Himself. He promises to listen to me as I pour out to Him my needs and the anxieties of this trying day.

Although our sins are many and shameful, God does not turn away from anyone who comes to Him with a penitent heart, seeking peace and pardon. Because of Christ's precious blood, the Lord is our Rock and Redeemer. He blots out all our sins and remembers them no more.

God loves to hear our prayers, our problems, and our pains. He promises to make our burdens lighter and our yokes easier. His strength makes us stronger; His faithfulness makes us unafraid. He fills our hearts with peace. With His strength, faithfulness, and peace, we can rest in Him as beloved children nestle in their mother's arms.

*Prayer*

Holy, righteous, and gracious Lord, I turn to You in my

distress and pain. I beg You to be my strength, even as You are my salvation. You are my help in these trying days. I pray that Your continuing presence would give me cheer each day. Because of Jesus Christ, I know that You are my forgiving Father. Daily cleanse my soul and remove my doubt. Teach me to put my trust in You each hour. Into Your care I entrust myself and all who are troubled and distressed. In Your Son's name I pray. Amen.

~

# Under the Shepherd's Care

The LORD is my shepherd; I shall not want.
   He makes me lie down in green pastures.
He leads me beside still waters.
   He restores my soul.
He leads me in paths of righteousness
   for His name's sake.
Even though I walk
   through the valley of the shadow of death,
   I will fear no evil,
for You are with me;
   Your rod and Your staff, they comfort me.
      (Psalm 23:1–4)

Like a sheep, I am weak, frail, and often helpless. How comforting to know that I have a Shepherd who is sympathetic and understanding! He watches over *me* with His gracious care. His heart beats with love for *me*. He does not slumber or sleep; therefore, *I* can relax and be at ease.

"I shall not want." My Shepherd promises to supply all my needs. As I pass through these troubled waters, He is with me to direct my feet to the paths of safety and peace.

"He restores my soul." I am living in the sunshine of His grace, where He daily forgives sin. Through Christ's precious blood, I am united with Him. Therefore, I entrust myself to His care. No one can pluck me out of my Shepherd's hand.

"I will fear no evil." I may suffer, be in great distress, face hectic hours and irritating days, but I am still loved by my Shepherd. "Whoever believes in Him should not perish but have eternal life" (John 3:16). Because this is certain, the day is brighter and far more hopeful. I need not fight my battles alone.

I am sure of this truth: "The Lord is *my* shepherd."

### Prayer

Divine Lord, You showed Your love for me in Jesus, my Savior. Spread Your protecting wings over me. Uphold me amid suffering and pain. Give me strength to face the days with patience and the long nights with quieted nerves. Put my mind at ease as I remember Your love, which daily blots out all my sins. Keep me in Your grace. Each day give me a fuller measure of faith as I receive Your blessings through Jesus, my everlasting friend. Amen.

~

# God Cares

Turn to me and be gracious to me,
    for I am lonely and afflicted.
The troubles of my heart are enlarged;
    bring me out of my distresses.
Consider my affliction and my trouble,
    and forgive all my sins. (Psalm 25:16–18)

The world is full of people in suffering and pain, many of them afflicted far more than I. How can I be sure that God even knows about me, much less looks upon me?

"I have called you by name, you are Mine," the Lord guarantees (Isaiah 43:1). By name He called Adam, Noah, Abram, Jeremiah, Mary and Joseph, the disciples, Mary Magdalene—and He stayed by them all their days. Likewise, He promises His abiding presence to every troubled and distressed soul.

But shouldn't I hide from God because of all my rebellious thoughts, all my sins?

If it were not for Christ and His sacrificial love on Calvary, I should tremble in God's presence, for I am unholy because of my sin and my shame. But God's Son died an unholy and shameful death, becoming sin for me, that I might be holy and whole in Him. Jesus touches me with His healing hand, He draws me to His loving heart, and He blots out all my sins.

Even if the pain continues, my burden is made lighter because I am at peace with God. His love and power will see me through every difficulty and bring a ray of light into the darkest night. Therefore, I can rest and sleep; He is watching over me with His tender care every hour of my sickness.

### Prayer

Today I come to You, my God, with all the burdens of my life, both of body and of soul. In Your mercy and grace, relieve my suffering. Let me quietly rest throughout the day and sleep undisturbed this coming night.

Be with all who are sick and with those who tend to us. Restore our aching bodies to health and keep our souls in Your forgiving grace, through Jesus Christ, our Lord and Savior. Amen.

~

# The Best Security

Be gracious to me, O LORD, for I am in distress;
    my eye is wasted from grief;
    my soul and my body also.

But I trust in You, O LORD;
    I say, "You are my God."
My times are in Your hand;
    rescue me from the hand of my
    enemies and from my persecutors!
Make Your face shine on Your servant;
    save me in Your steadfast love!
O LORD, let me not be put to shame,
    for I call upon You. (Psalm 31:9, 14–17a)

For many people, life seems to be without purpose or plan, a jumble of uncertainties in which a few lucky ones get the breaks. Most people, it seems, get nothing but trouble and tears.

However, the psalmist did not believe this. "My times are in Your hand." David was sure that God, his heavenly Father, directed his life and loved him. But as I lie flat on my back in pain and distress, can I say the same thing? Does God really care about me? Is He concerned about my troubles? Does He really take care of me?

Yes. I am in Christ's hands—hands that bear the marks of His love and His suffering for me. No matter where I am, whatever I must face, I am in Christ's hands and in His safe-keeping. How comforting this is as I go staggering, stumbling, weary, tired, through a day of ordeal and pain.

"My times are in Your hand." My life is planned—planned by a loving Father who rescues us from our enemies and our persecutors through the steadfast love of His Son who trusted in Him, even unto death, on my behalf. No one can pluck me out of His hands, for He is the Almighty. Therefore, I go trustingly through the day, knowing I need not be afraid of the coming night. I can feel confident that better days lie ahead. Resting in my heavenly Father's arms, I can say with a believing heart, "Your will be done," and know that His is a good and gracious will.

### Prayer

Rock of Ages, cleft for me, let me hide securely in Your sacred wounds. Give me shelter from the fears and doubts that war against my soul. I have no other refuge; none other is able to redeem me.

Lift me to Your heart, Jesus, and heal me. Give me a stronger faith and a more hopeful outlook. Touch me with Your compassionate strength. Take from me today's pains and ills; restore me to health.

Enable those who work for my healing to perform their tasks with cheerfulness. Bless all the sick, and grant peace to each human heart through Your cross and redemption. Amen.

# Courage That Triumphs

Oh, how abundant is Your goodness,
    which You have stored up for those who fear You
and worked for those who take refuge in You,
    in the sight of the children of mankind!
In the cover of Your presence You hide them
    from the plots of men;
You store them in Your shelter
    from the strife of tongues.

Be strong, and let your heart take courage,
    all you who wait for the LORD! (Psalm 31:19–20, 24)

It takes courage to face sickness and surgery. However, none of us needs to stand alone. Jesus promises His help, and His presence makes the day cheerful and hopeful. When He touches us with His healing hand, we receive new strength—which makes for relaxed nerves and peace of mind.

The day looks brighter and the nights seem shorter as we place ourselves into the hands of the Lord. Confidence once more fills our hearts, and we can look ahead with hope. Although we cannot see beyond today, of one thing we are sure: When tomorrow comes, the Lord will be with us with His love and grace and strength to carry on.

All this is certain because it is the Lord in whom we hope. He daily forgives all our sins and grants us a fuller measure of faith, which takes Him at His word and holds Him to His promises. He keeps every agreement He has ever made with His people, His family in Christ. Truly, we can be of good courage as we live in God's family of grace.

## Prayer

Faithful Father in Christ, You who so graciously protect the children of Your family, I praise You for Your mercies, as countless as the sand. You have preserved me, comforted me, forgiven me, and touched me with Your helping hand. Continue Your blessings as the days go on, and accept the thanks of my humble heart as I acknowledge Your goodness and help. In Jesus' name I make these petitions. Amen.

~

# A Glorious Experience

Blessed is the one whose transgression is forgiven,
> whose sin is covered.
Blessed is the man against whom
> the LORD counts no iniquity,
and in whose spirit there is no deceit. (Psalm 32:1–2)

"Blessed is the one." David's most blessed experience occurred when he learned that his sins were forgiven. At peace with God, David had peace in his own soul. He knew that he did not have to be afraid of God or the future.

God has covered my sins as well. He invites me to look unafraid to Him and to the future. He opens His heart and invites me to come to Him and find rest for my soul.

I am in pain and annoyed by many irritations. However, I can calm my troubled self with the assurance that God has covered my sins, forgiven them, and remembers them no more. As God looks at me through the Calvary cross, He no longer sees my many transgressions, only my robe of righteousness, washed in Christ's precious blood.

With such a forgiving God at my side, I have the needed encouragement for each hour of the day. Tonight I can rest and sleep, for the Lord is my forgiving Father, the Keeper of my body and the Lover of my soul.

### Prayer

With humble heart I approach Your throne, Father of my Savior, Jesus. Because of Him, I dare to plead for mercy. I beg You, ease my pain and heal my body.

Although I come with all my sins, anxieties, and troubles, I leave them at Your feet. Help me to live in Your presence with a grateful heart and with continued trust. Please bring about a speedy recovery according to Your will.

I place myself entirely into Your hands, O Father of my Savior. Amen.

~

## He Knows the Way

You are a hiding place for me;
    You preserve me from trouble;
    You surround me with shouts of deliverance.

I will instruct you and teach you
    in the way you should go;
    I will counsel you with My eye upon you.
Be not like a horse or a mule, without understanding,
    which must be curbed with bit and bridle,
    or it will not stay near you.

Many are the sorrows of the wicked,
    but steadfast love surrounds the
        one who trusts in the Lord.
Be glad in the Lord, and rejoice, O righteous,
    and shout for joy, all you upright in heart!
    (Psalm 32:7–10)

Are we aimlessly stumbling through life? Many think so. But God assures us that our life is planned and directed by Him: "I will instruct you and teach you in the way you should go." To know this takes the shakiness out of our nerves and quiets our troubled spirit. Although we are in pain and distress, we can place ourselves into His everlasting arms.

How does God guide us? "Your word is a lamp to my feet and a light to my path" (Psalm 119:105). God's Word makes us wise for salvation. His promises reveal that even a sparrow does not fall to the ground without His knowledge—and we are worth more than many sparrows.

It is to humans, His children, that God opens His heart and makes known His marvelous love. To us He shows His mercy in Jesus, whose ministry of mercy reached out with healing to broken people like us and whose death on the cross healed the whole creation.

God loves us with such an amazing love that He forgives us through the blood of His own Son. Therefore, we can be certain that He is with us in our present troubles and that He touches us with His helping and healing grace. We can go through the day without fear and without worry. We can say with the psalmist, "You are a hiding place for me; You preserve me from trouble; You surround me with shouts of deliverance" (Psalm 32:7).

### Prayer

Dearest Savior, Your boundless love has redeemed me and made me an heir of eternal life. With grateful heart I acknowledge Your goodness and I praise Your mercies. Forgive my thoughtless ways and my many neglects, and make me appreciative of all Your mercies.

Reveal Yourself more and more to me through Your Word. Watch over me this day and instruct me so that no evil overtakes me. Bless me this night with a refreshing sleep. Quiet my nerves and calm my troubled spirit, most gracious Redeemer. Amen.

~

# Nothing to Fear

I sought the LORD, and He answered me
and delivered me from all my fears.

When the righteous cry for help, the LORD hears
and delivers them out of all their troubles.
The LORD is near to the brokenhearted
and saves the crushed in spirit.

The LORD redeems the life of His servants;
none of those who take refuge
in Him will be condemned.
(Psalm 34:4, 17–18, 22)

My fears—how many!—of helplessness, of continued pain, of sleepless nights. The fear that maybe God does not love me enough or that I should not bother going to Him for help and forgiveness.

All these misgivings haunted the psalmist, too, yet he did not despair. With grateful heart he announced that he had found a way to rid himself of all his fears. He sought God in prayer, and God heard him and delivered him from all his anxieties.

That's how we conquer fear as well. We go to God and discover the same thing David did: "The LORD is near to the brokenhearted and saves the crushed in spirit" (verse 18).

God loves us and does not want to punish us. Instead of punishing us for our sins, God the Father punished Jesus by pouring out His anger against our sin upon His own Son on the cross of Calvary. In Jesus, the Father is no longer angry with us because of our sin. God loves us and wants us to live—not merely for a few years or a span of life, but forever. That is why, when we come to Him in prayer, we find forgiveness and peace.

To trust God removes fear. Each hour of each day, no matter how burdensome, He is with us; He watches over us while we sleep.

### Prayer

Heavenly Father, by whose grace and goodness we live and move and have our being, hold me safe through the many uncertainties of life. I don't know what lies ahead, but of this I am certain: Your love always shines into my heart.

Enrich me with patience, hope, and trust, so I may be able to live courageously throughout today. Ease my distress, speak peace to my soul, and bless me with Your bounties in Jesus Christ. Amen.

# Under His Wings

Your steadfast love, O LORD, extends to the heavens,
    Your faithfulness to the clouds.
Your righteousness is like the mountains of God;
    Your judgments are like the great deep;
    man and beast You save, O LORD.

How precious is Your steadfast love, O God!
    The children of mankind take
        refuge in the shadow of Your wings.
They feast on the abundance of Your house,
    and You give them drink from
        the river of Your delights.
For with You is the fountain of life;
    in Your light do we see light. (Psalm 36:5–9)

Most of us complain a lot. We focus on what we do not have, and we overlook the mercies and blessings we do have. We forget that God has opened His hands throughout the years and has supplied us with everything we need for life, that He has opened His·heart to forgive the very sins with which we have offended Him.

Even if we are not among the rich and famous, our loving Father is keeping us in the shadow of His wings. He does not let us fall into a bottomless pit, but protects us as a hen protects her chicks. He gives us strength necessary for today, and He graces us with His continued help and healing.

This promise can give us a hopeful outlook, even though we are temporarily—or permanently—in distress and pain. God loves us with an everlasting love, and His kindness toward us sets our feet on a solid rock. His presence means safety, and His love protects us.

Of that we are certain, because He acts in the grace revealed and given in the cross of Jesus. On our behalf He became frail and weak because He bore our sins in His body, cleansing all of creation by His blood. Although we are frail and sinful, our union with Him washes us clean of all that pollutes us. It is well with our souls.

*Prayer*

Lord Jesus, strength of the weary, as You walked this earth among both the high and the lowly, You showed compassion to the sick and troubled and You gave help and healing to those hurt in body and mind.

Draw near to my sickbed with Your loving presence and have mercy on me. Cleanse my soul and relieve my suffering. Shorten the days of my affliction. Make me patient, free from worry and discouraging thoughts.

Bless those who seek to ease my suffering, and preserve in me the sure faith that Your love is understanding and Your help limitless. Amen.

~

# My Lord and Me

May all who seek You
　rejoice and be glad in You;
　may those who love Your salvation
　say continually, "Great is the LORD!"
As for me, I am poor and needy,
　but the Lord takes thought for me.
You are my help and my deliverer;
　do not delay, O my God! (Psalm 40:16–17)

The universe is so big, and I am so small. There are many beds in many hospitals—how can God know which one I occupy, much less hear my "poor and needy" cry for help? At times it seems as though life has no purpose; that all is luck; that if anything good does happen, misfortune is just around the corner; that behind every silver lining lurks a dark cloud.

Although David felt his life was a "pit of destruction," a "miry bog" (Psalm 40:2), he found hope in the heavenly Father. With His gracious hand, God directs both the universe and David's poor and needy life.

"The Lord takes thought for me." Therefore, I can wait patiently, knowing that God moves in His own mysterious way His wonders to perform. If He did not think on me and all humanity, how could I explain the fact that God sent His Son into this sin-sick world to save us from sin's stranglehold and eternal death? He took my sin and sickness into His own body and freed me from the eternal consequences of my own sinfulness. Jesus is my Savior and my friend, my helper and deliverer.

"The Lord takes thought for me." This puts a song in my heart, relaxes my nerves, and brings peaceful thoughts to my mind. No matter how trying the day, God's presence and blessings fill my soul with hope.

### Prayer

Merciful Lord, You have been my God at all times and have loved me in Christ Jesus, my Savior, who brought me into Your family. Receive me as I am, forgiven by Your grace, and preserve me in Your loving-kindness.

During my suffering, help me to continue to witness to all who would hear: "The Lord takes thought for me."

As Your Son's blood cleanses me from all sin, so ease my suffering and hasten the day of my recovery. Quiet my nerves, and keep me in Your grace all the days of my life because of Jesus, my Savior. Amen.

∼

# When Evening Comes, Smile

By day the LORD commands His steadfast love,
    and at night His song is with me,
    a prayer to the God of my life.
I say to God, my rock:
    "Why have You forgotten me?
Why do I go mourning
    because of the oppression of the enemy?"
As with a deadly wound in my bones,
    my adversaries taunt me,
while they say to me continually,
    "Where is your God?"

Why are you cast down, O my soul,
   and why are you in turmoil within me?
Hope in God; for I shall again praise Him,
   my salvation and my God. (Psalm 42:8–11)

Worry pushes us into a corner and encourages us to whine. It robs us of sleep and makes the nights longer. If we could only rid ourselves of the anxieties of the sickroom!

We can. "Hope in God."

"Why are you in turmoil within me?" We know why; we could make a list of the troubles that plague us. But how many of those are needless worries? Put down in writing your concerns of today, then review your list in a week or two. You will smile at how many of those were illusions.

"Why are you cast down, O my soul?" Because of my sins. Sometimes I think that this present affliction proves that God is punishing me. But if that is true, then why did God send His Son to Calvary? Because of Jesus, my soul does not need to be downcast. I do not have to wait a week or two to smile; I can do so immediately because I am at peace with God, and His help upholds me.

I do not have to be afraid. I see God's grace, and He forgives me. I bring my burdens to the Lord, and He strengthens me. I call upon Him in my day of trouble, and He delivers me. Therefore, I praise His goodness and sing of His mercy. And I smile again as He puts peace into my heart and hope into all my evenings.

### Prayer

Ever-living and ever-present Savior, who has invited all the weary and burdened to come to You for rest, hear my prayer and calm my troubled spirit. Graciously receive me, unworthy as I am. Give me a greater measure of faith, so I may cling even more firmly to Your promises and find peace and strength in Your presence. I have no other refuge. Comfort me. Stay with me today and always. Amen.

# Safely Anchored

God is our refuge and strength,
　　a very present help in trouble.
Therefore we will not fear though
　　the earth gives way,
　　though the mountains be
　　　　moved into the heart of the sea,
　　though its waters roar and foam,
　　　　though the mountains tremble
　　　　　at its swelling. (Psalm 46:1–3)

Help that comes too late is no help at all. However, God's help always comes on time—on His time. He is our refuge, our protection, and our shelter in this very hour.

The door of prayer to God's throne is always open, held open by the pierced hands of Jesus. That is one door our past sins are not strong enough to close. Because we are made acceptable to the Father by the blood of the Son, He saves us to the uttermost; His mercies last forever.

Even in our worst days, full of pain and anguish, God is our immediate help and refuge. He always gives us sufficient strength for each day; He is always equal to the situation. We do not know for sure what lies ahead, but of one thing we are certain: God is "a very present help in trouble" (verse 1).

Therefore, we can trust in Him and patiently wait for His will. He is our hiding place at all times, in every circumstance. His goodness is new every morning, and His mercy endures the day. As long as He is our refuge and very present help, we will have His strength to go on.

## Prayer

O Lord, Creator and caretaker of all things and all people, gratefully I bow before Your loving-kindness to me. You have been my help through all my days and my hope and strength in this day, in this hour.

I approach Your throne because of Christ, my Savior, confident that You neither slumber nor sleep. I plead for forgiveness and ask for protection and healing. As You have preserved my life, I entrust myself to Your safekeeping, confident that You watch over me as a child in Your family because of Jesus Christ, my shepherd and friend. Amen.

~

## Rest in a Restless Day

Give ear to my prayer, O God,
    and hide not Yourself from my
        plea for mercy!
Attend to me, and answer me;
    I am restless in my complaint
        and I moan.

My heart is in anguish within me;
    the terrors of death have fallen upon me.
Fear and trembling come upon me,
    and horror overwhelms me.
And I say, "Oh, that I had wings like a dove!
    I would fly away and be at rest;
yes, I would wander far away;
    I would lodge in the wilderness;
I would hurry to find a shelter
    from the raging wind and
        tempest." (Psalm 55:1–2, 4–8)

Have you ever wanted to fly away from the troubles and worries that descend on you?

Some have tried. Some have cut loose from everyone and live in lonely caves, hidden mountain heights, and desert wastelands. Some have turned their homes into hideaways, rarely venturing out. However, none of these people could hide from themselves or their worrisome thoughts.

No one can escape conscience and God, not even if they sail solo around the world or fly to the moon. "Where shall I flee from Your presence? If I ascend to heaven, You are there! If I make my bed in Sheol, You are there!" (Psalm 139:7b–8).

If you want peace of mind, you must fly *to* God. He opens His heart to the troubled souls that come sobbing their confessions and worries to Him. He has compassion on the sick and gives aid to the distressed.

Contentment can be found wherever you are, because God is there with you and His blessings rest upon you. Even on a sickbed, God upholds you, and His love in Christ embraces you. In Christ, your restless soul finds rest and peace today.

### Prayer

Lord of lords, my kind Father in Christ, Your divine grace is new every day. As Your child, I come to You with my burdens and anxieties. Help me to leave them all with You and to pass through the present moment with confidence and courage.

Give me a quiet and restful day and refresh my body with sleep tonight. Forgive me whenever I have murmured impatiently against You. Remove my discontent. Fulfill Your promises to me, and let Your abiding peace shine in my heart today, tomorrow, and always. Amen.

~

# Time for Prayer

But I call to God,
    and the LORD will save me.
Evening and morning and at noon
    I utter my complaint and moan,
    and He hears my voice.
He redeems my soul in safety
    from the battle that I wage,
    for many are arrayed against me.

Cast your burden on the LORD,
    and He will sustain you;
He will never permit
    the righteous to be moved. (Psalm 55:16–18, 22)

We appreciate prayer most when we are discouraged. True, the prayer of a believer changes things (James 5:16), but something else happens too: we are changed as God's Word works on our thinking. How wonderful that He has urged us to pray without ceasing!

We pray because we expect God to hear us. After all, as a part of His invitation for the prayers themselves, He promised to do so. He also promised to carry our burdens for us. Therefore, when in trusting prayer we "let" Him plan and set the best future for us and straighten out the past, our minds are put at ease and our anxieties quieted.

As this is true in sick days, so it is true every day. Prayer is an ongoing conversation with our loving Father. As we pray, His Word reminds us that He is the center of our lives and that His presence means blessings.

We give to God our burdens: sin, worry, loss, heartache, sickness. We also look to Him to supply our needs: forgiveness, increased faith, guidance, strength, relief, healing, patience, peace.

"Evening and morning and at noon I utter my complaint." The assurance that "He hears my voice" carries me through the long days and through the even longer nights.

### Prayer

Heavenly Father, gracious in Christ, once again I enter into this time of prayer with You, remembering Your mercy and goodness. I come, certain that You fulfill Your promises.

In Your grace, forgive me; in Your love, heal me. Stay with me as the days drag on, and watch over me this coming night. Bless those who serve me in my affliction, quiet my nerves, and let Your peace take full possession of my heart in Jesus Christ, my Savior. Amen.

~

# The Higher Rock

Hear my cry, O God,
    listen to my prayer;

from the end of the earth I call to You
  when my heart is faint.
Lead me to the rock
  that is higher than I,
for You have been my refuge,
  a strong tower against the
     enemy. (Psalm 61:1–3)

In this prayer we make a *humble confession*: we admit our own helplessness. We have come to our wit's end and find ourselves in a daze no matter which way we turn.

In this prayer we make a *glorious confession*: we confidently believe that all things—ourselves included—are in the hands of God. Nothing is beyond His control. He is our Rock. To Him we cling without fear. As we reach out to Him with our feeble hands, He reaches down to us and lifts us to His heart.

In this prayer we make an *earnest plea*: we ask for help. We need healing of body and cleansing of soul. We ask for peace and rest, strength and hope.

All this God gives us in Christ, our Redeemer, who on Calvary made us children of the heavenly Father and heirs of salvation. Every morning His mercies are new, and every day He gives us courage, patience, and confidence.

Therefore, we look hopefully to the future and go on, even if we cannot see beyond the next few minutes. We do not need to know what is ahead, for God sets our feet upon a rock, and He knows the way.

"Lead me to the rock that is higher than I."

"Rock of Ages, cleft for me, Let me hide myself in Thee" (*LSB* 761:1).

### Prayer

Almighty God, eternal Lord, amid the anxieties of life and the sufferings of today, I seek refuge in You. You alone can give me the strength and endurance necessary to survive the day. In Your grace protect me from all danger. Wash me thoroughly from my sin. Put a wall of love and trust around

me to protect my heart from doubt and worry. Enfold me in
Your forgiving arms because of Christ Jesus, my Savior.
Amen.

~

# Better than Life

O God, You are my God;
    earnestly I seek You;
  my soul thirsts for You;
my flesh faints for You,
  as in a dry and weary land
    where there is no water.
So I have looked upon You in the sanctuary,
  beholding Your power and glory.
Because Your steadfast love is
    better than life,
  my lips will praise You.
So I will bless You as long as I live;
  in Your name I will lift up my hands.

My soul will be satisfied as with
    fat and rich food,
  and my mouth will praise You
    with joyful lips,
when I remember You upon my bed,
  and meditate on You in the watches of the night;
for You have been my help,
  and in the shadow of Your
    wings I will sing for joy. (Psalm 63:1–7)

Mere living is not enough. A slave also has food, clothing,
and shelter, but no one wants to be a slave. I may have all the
food I need, the necessary home and clothing, yet be troubled and distressed. That which makes life worth living, that
which is better than life, is the love of God.

    God's love shows itself in His mercy. He opens His heart
and forgives my sin. Through Christ, He reconciled me to

Himself, and I find peace and hope for my soul. My mind is at ease when I come from His presence, forgiven of all sin and strengthened in faith for the days that lie ahead.

God's love shows itself in goodness. He opens His hand and supplies me with all the needs of body and life. He alone can restore me to health.

"Because Your steadfast love is better than life, my lips will praise You" day after day. I have a hope in my heart that puts a song on my lips. "For You have been my help, and in the shadow of Your wings I will sing for joy." Nestled in Your loving arms, I am not afraid.

Therefore, tonight, "I remember You upon my bed, and meditate on You in the watches of the night."

### Prayer

Lord Jesus, eternal Redeemer of my soul, I am fully aware of Your mercies. Therefore, I come to You with a grateful heart. You have forgiven all my sins, You have encouraged me to face each day with confidence, and You have given me strength to endure until the end.

Take away every disappointment and worry; instead, fill my heart and mind with peace. Today and every day, let me find hope and comfort in Your promises. Enable me to find such joy in Your saving love that my heart breaks forth in songs of praise. Amen.

~

# I Need God

How lovely is Your dwelling place,
   O LORD of hosts!
My soul longs, yes, faints
   for the courts of the LORD;
my heart and my flesh sing for joy
   to the living God. (Psalm 84:1–2)

"Is there a God?" my flesh cries out when I am in pain. "Yes!" declare the heavens. Every star in the sky, every bird that sings, every flower that blooms cries in reply, "Yes!"

Is there a God? Yes—and the Scriptures tell me who He is. He has revealed Himself through His Son, Jesus, who became flesh and died and rose that I might live.

I need God. "My soul longs, yes, faints," to be in His presence, basking in His love. I need His guidance in my life. I need to know that He has died for *me* and that *my* sin is forgiven. I need to know that He cares enough for me to untangle this web of trouble in which I find myself.

I need the courts of the Lord as a haven, a refuge. There I can go with my guilt and pain and worry—and certain knowledge that I am accepted and secure. What a comfort to know that the living God hears my flesh cry out!

My soul longs for the Lord, for His Gospel of forgiveness, for His promises, for His peace. He alone eases my troubled mind and gives healing to my body. "How lovely is Your dwelling place, O LORD of hosts!"

### Prayer

Eternal keeper of my soul, I approach Your courts to receive Your divine gifts for this day. Bless me graciously and totally with Your forgiveness for all my sin. Only then, all is well.

May Your almighty power heal me and all my fellow sufferers. In Your goodness, fill this day with hope and courage. Grant me a fuller measure of contentment and patience and cheerfulness.

For Your Son's sake, hear the cry of my heart and my flesh. Amen.

$\sim$

# The Great Discovery

Even the sparrow finds a home,
    and the swallow a nest for herself,
    where she may lay her young,
at Your altars, O LORD of hosts,
    my King and my God. (Psalm 84:3)

The sparrow had made a strange discovery, and the swallow had found it to be true: a nest built into the side of the altar of sacrifice meant safety and peace. Sacrifices were made daily at the temple and blood was flowing down from the altar as the lambs were slain, yet no one harmed the small birds nesting in that sacred place.

Oh, that I could always be as wise and as trusting as the sparrow! I, too, can be certain and sure of safety—salvation and eternal life—at God's altar on Calvary. There blood was shed as Satan and sin did their worst to the Lamb, but nothing to me. As long as faith keeps me at that altar, peace, safety, and life are mine. Nothing can harm me.

"Blessed are those who dwell in Your house," the psalmist continues, "ever singing Your praise!" (verse 4). No wonder!—for God's house is the stronghold into which hell's thief cannot break. Secure there, we are calm and unafraid. In God's courts, we are wiser than swallows and safer than sparrows. There we have salvation, peace, hope, and joy.

### Prayer

Blessed Lord and Savior, mercifully look upon me, trembling like a captured bird. Heal my troubled body and calm my anguished mind, even as You cleanse my flighty soul.

Take from me the thoughts that haunt me. Let me find refuge in Your altar, despite the dangers around me. Cause Your comforting promises to give me peace and prepare me for refreshing sleep this coming night.

Hear my prayer, precious friend and adorable Savior, and put me at ease. Amen.

~

# The Full Life

For one day in Your courts is better
   than a thousand elsewhere.
I would rather be a doorkeeper in

the house of my God
　　than dwell in the tents of wickedness.
　For the LORD God is a sun and shield;
　　the LORD bestows favor and honor.
No good thing does He withhold
　　from those who walk uprightly.
O LORD of hosts,
　　blessed is the one who trusts in
　　　　You! (Psalm 84:10–12)

Life is desirable only as we live in the sunshine of God's grace streaming into His courts. Apart from His presence, worries and anxieties depress us and remove the joy of living. God, however, pours out His blessings, and He holds us safely above the troubles of this world. Therefore, we can be hopeful and confident even in the sickbed and the invalid chair. In His presence, even a life of only one more day is the full life.

God promises us salvation forever—a promise that makes us unafraid of eternity and lets us rest in peace every day. He not only gave the promise, He accomplished it through the death and resurrection of His Son, in whom we now have the promise of eternal life. And He not only accomplished that, He put it in our hearts by His Spirit. Even in the darkest night of suffering and anguish, *salvation is ours.*

How could I long to live a thousand days anywhere else but in the courts of the Lord? Only there is my emptiness and loneliness removed. Only there are His promises for strength for the coming night. Only there can I look forward to the coming morning. Only there is the keeper and lover of my soul.

No matter what happens today, tomorrow, or any time in my life, the end is an eternity in God's heavenly court, a thousand eons in His glory. In Christ, I am already living a life that has no end. With that vision, I close my eyes and sleep.

*Prayer*

O God, You are *my* God. Your mercies are new every hour, and Your love and grace send blessings into my life from day to day. I am Your child, redeemed through the blood of Your Son, brought to faith by the power of Your Spirit.

My heart gratefully acknowledges Your goodness, for You have kept me in these hours of distress. Your Son suffered greater pain on the cross than I will ever know. He did it for me, and so I am at peace with You.

Continue to let Your healing hand rest on me, that I may recover speedily. I look forward to worshiping You once again in church and to returning to perform my daily duties to Your glory. In Your Son's name I pray. Amen.

∼

# Under His Care

Oh come, let us worship and bow down,
  let us kneel before the LORD,
    our Maker!
For He is our God,
  and we are the people of His pasture,
  and the sheep of His hand. (Psalm 95:6–7)

We are sheep in the hand of our God, a possession in which He has an interest. After all, He created me and has re-created me through the waters of my Baptism, and by His grace has brought me into His fold.

In the pasture of His love, God feeds and protects me. No matter the enemy, God does not abandon me as a hireling would. By hearing the voice of my Shepherd in His Word and receiving His holy food in Holy Communion, He creates and sustains my faith and comforts me in the hour of trial and pain.

We are "the sheep of His hand." Therefore, "He makes me lie down in green pastures. He leads me beside still waters. He restores my soul" (Psalm 23:2–3). His rod and staff comfort me. Each day I discover some blessing that encourages me and takes away the gloom and irritation of the moment.

God alone can preserve me. It is He who gives wisdom and understanding to the doctors and nurses. Through them, He takes care of me, for I am one of the people of His pasture, more precious to Him than sparrows and swallows.

Although today is full of anxiety and uneasiness, and though I may feel utterly alone, God makes His presence known to me. He will not allow anything to separate me from His eternal love.

The Lord is *my* shepherd.

### Prayer

Lord Jesus, shepherd of my soul, I come to You for rest. You know how worried I am because of the uncertainties and dilemmas that press in on all sides. If it were not for Your glorious invitation to the weary to come to You for rest, I would be crushed. I have no other place to go than into Your sheepfold.

Because of Your sacred wounds and forgiving heart, speak peace to me. Stay with me day after day. Then shall my lips praise You and my grateful heart give glory to Your name, now and always. Amen.

$\sim$

# Our Thank-Yous

Bless the LORD, O my soul;
   and all that is within me,
   bless His holy name!
Bless the LORD, O my soul,
    and forget not all His benefits,
  who forgives all your iniquity,
    who heals all your diseases,
  who redeems your life from the pit,
    who crowns you with steadfast

love and mercy,
who satisfies you with good
so that your youth is renewed
like the eagle's. (Psalm 103:1–5)

Day after day God opens His hands to bless us. His heart forgives us, and He redeems our lives from the pit. Reflecting on His mercies, the psalmist urges us to praise the goodness of the Lord.

We can be cheerful every waking hour because we know that the Lord forgives all our sins. He keeps us in His forgiving love forever.

Although we might not think that God heals all our diseases, His almighty hand helps us through the problems that distress us. Because of His power, we have the strength to survive today and rest tonight. God also "crowns you with steadfast love and mercy." Graciously, He has given you friends, neighbors, and family to enrich your life.

"Forget not all His benefits," for there are many. The sun still shines. You enjoy a cheery word. You have a bed on which to lie. Above all, you have the promises of His Word, promises to forgive your sins and to redeem your life from hell.

When you reflect on all His benefits, especially during the darkest hours of the day, you are able to thank and praise the Lord.

### Prayer

Lord, sun of my soul, I come to Your throne of grace in these days of pain and sorrow. No one is able to help me unless Your hand is with me. Shine on me with Your abundant grace that I may be restored to health and enabled to serve You in my daily tasks.

Teach me to live calmly and composed. Give me a greater measure of faith. Help me to rely on Your promises and on You, my eternal rock.

May Your presence put my mind at ease, and may the precious blood of Your Son, my Savior, cleanse me from all sin. Amen.

# God's Unlimited Grace

As a father shows compassion to his children,
   so the LORD shows compassion
      to those who fear Him.
For He knows our frame;
   He remembers that we are
      dust. (Psalm 103:13–14)

God remembers that He formed us out of the dust of the ground and that our bodies will return to that same ground because of sin. We are frail, helpless, and hopeless, yet the Lord is patient with us. Therefore, we pray daily, "forgive us our trespasses," sure that for Jesus' sake He does.

In Psalm 102, the palmist lets God know how he feels—perhaps much the same as you do: "the day of my distress" (verse 2); "my bones burn like a furnace" (verse 3); "my bones cling to my flesh" (verse 5); "I wither away like grass" (verse 11). That's why the psalmist cried to the Lord for help. In Psalm 103, the psalmist praises the Lord for help received.

The help, though, is not merely healing of body. God removes our sins as far as the east is from the west, gives a love higher than the heavens above, and redeems us from hell because of the death of His Son.

And He does more: though our bodies of dust will return to the dust, God will raise us up with an incorruptible, everlasting body. When this frail body dies, we will rise to live forever in the glory of eternity. There we will join the angels in singing praises to the Lord (verses 20–21), to the Lamb who was slain, whose blood set us free to be people of God forever.

### Prayer

Divine Savior, Your presence brings peace; Your compassion, forgiveness; Your promises, hope.

Look on me in my plight and bless me. I am tired of the struggle, confused by my doubts, angered by the irritations. Calm my heart as You quieted the Sea of Galilee.

I come to You because every other refuge fails. You must be my strength. Lift me to Your heart, blessed Savior, so I may find rest in You. Amen.

$\sim$

## The Believer's Challenge

You are my hiding place and my shield;
   I hope in Your word.
Depart from me, you evildoers,
   that I may keep the
      commandments of my God.
Uphold me according to Your promise,
      that I may live,
   and let me not be put to
      shame in my hope!
Hold me up, that I may be safe
   and have regard for Your
      statutes continually! (Psalm 119:114–117)

What a model for me! Like the psalmist, I stand before the almighty God and expect Him to keep His promises. I do so precisely because He is the Almighty, and He made those promises despite His knowledge of me. Naturally, my expectations run high!

The Lord states, "Call upon Me in the day of trouble; I will deliver you" (Psalm 50:15). So I call. I cry out of the depths of my misery. I seek safety in the shadow of His wings.

But sometimes I wonder if my troubles will ever go away. In fact, some days they seem to increase—and I wonder if, this time, God is going to keep His promise.

Still, I stand with the psalmist and cry, "Let me not be put to shame in my hope!" Hope is the mainspring of my life. Hope lets me look ahead with confidence. Hope takes fear out of the darkest night and enables me to survive yet another day of uncertainty. And hope I can, for God, who gave His only Son to save me, will not turn from me. As

Jesus pointed out when He healed the paralytic, healing a body is not any harder than forgiving sins (Mark 2:1–12).

I do not know what tomorrow may bring, but of one thing I am sure: Jesus will be with me even as He is today. Lord, "let me not be put to shame in my hope!"

### Prayer

Merciful Jesus, I do not know what is in store for today, much less tomorrow, but I am sure that You are with me. No matter what happens, I know that Your strong arms are around me.

Give me hope even in the darkest of nights—hope in Your Son who has rescued me from all my enemies. Forgive my sin and cleanse me from all my shame through the merits of Your Son, Jesus Christ, my Lord, who gave His life for me and continues to live in me now and forever. Amen.

$\sim$

# Looking beyond the Hills

I lift up my eyes to the hills.
From where does my help come?
My help comes from the LORD,
who made heaven and earth.

The LORD is your keeper;
the LORD is your shade on
your right hand.
The sun shall not strike you by day,
nor the moon by night.

The LORD will keep you from all evil;
He will keep your life.
The LORD will keep
your going out and your coming in
from this time forth and
forevermore. (Psalm 121:1–2, 5–8)

Many feel deep satisfaction and peace when looking at the mountains. Everything else seems so insignificant and transitory in comparison. In that sense, the mountains remind us of God. In their strength and permanence, we are pointed to the greater strength and the ultimate permanence of God, who made the mountains.

Looking at the mountains, we feel serene, unworried, unruffled. After all, who can move the mountains and overthrow God? He who made all the mountains and the worlds on which they stand "will not let your foot be moved; He who keeps you will not slumber" (verse 3). The sparrow knows that to be true.

This everlasting God who made the mountains, made *me*. The Lord is *my* refuge and strength. The burning sun shall not come over the hills and scorch me, and the subtle moon shall not spy on me and condemn me (verses 5–6). Although the ghost of past sins wants to haunt me, and though the worries of life try to crush me, the Lord promises to keep me from all harm, to watch over my whole life (verses 7–8).

Frail and full of sin, we look to the mountains—particularly to the one mountain on which God poured out His mercy for us through His Son's death: Calvary.

## Prayer

Gracious and divine Father through Jesus, in Your family I find health and in Your grace, forgiveness. By Your love and mercies, I am sure of my salvation.

Lift me out of the worries and anxieties of the present moment. Remove all sin from my imperfect heart. Fill my soul with hymns of thanksgiving as I remember Your goodness each day.

Grace me with contentment and patience so I may trustingly live one day at a time as I lean on You, my Father in Christ Jesus. Amen.

# From the Deep to God

Out of the depths I cry to You, O LORD!
> O Lord, hear my voice!
Let Your ears be attentive
> to the voice of my pleas for mercy!

If You, O LORD, should mark iniquities,
> O Lord, who could stand?
But with You there is forgiveness,
> that You may be feared. (Psalm 130:1–4)

If in the midst of such gloomy depths we look to our individual sins, we might think that our sinful acts put us there. That is why we need to hold before our eyes the promise of this psalm: "If You, O LORD, should mark iniquities, O Lord, who could stand? But with You there is forgiveness."

What joy! I am in Christ Jesus, and He is in me, so the Father does not look at my sins but on His Son's holiness that is now mine, graciously given to me in my Baptism. Therefore, when I knock at His door of mercy, it is opened to me. I will never find His heart loveless or unsympathetic. No one who comes to Him will be cast out.

Still, I have to thank God for using this depth from which I cry. Were it not for this depth, I might think I was self-sufficient, that I had no need for God. That awareness prods me to once again find refuge in the wounded side of Jesus and help from the throne of the Father's grace.

Therefore, "I wait for the LORD, my soul waits, and in His word I hope" (verse 5).

## Prayer

O Lord, heavenly Father, Your loving-kindness is new every day and Your mercies as countless as the stars. Continue to bless me with an unshaken faith in You and Your promises. Bring healing to my weary body and fill my soul with hope for tomorrow.

Forgive me whenever I have doubted You and have offended You with my sins. Remove from my heart all anxieties and worries, which arise every hour to vex me. Draw me closer to You, through the Savior I adore: Jesus Christ. Amen.

~

# God Watches over Me

O LORD, You have searched me and known me!

Where shall I go from Your Spirit?
Or where shall I flee from Your presence?
If I ascend to heaven, You are there!
If I make my bed in Sheol, You are there!
If I take the wings of the morning
and dwell in the uttermost parts of the sea,
even there Your hand shall lead me,
and Your right hand shall hold me.
If I say, "Surely the darkness shall cover me,
and the light about me be night,"
even the darkness is not dark to You;
the night is bright as the day,
for darkness is as light
with You. (Psalm 139:1, 7–12)

The psalmist saw many dark days, yet he was certain that no darkness could prevent God from seeing him. At the throne of God, everything is as clear as day. To know that truth is important when lying on a sickbed, in pain and worry. God knows all the sickbeds in this world, and He sees the needs and wants of each one.

When we are sick, life seems to make no sense. When we are confused, perplexed, and disturbed, even little noises irritate us. Nothing seems to explain why we are in this plight. Instead, everything seems to intensify it.

We wallow in a dark gloom until we remember that around the throne of God no darkness can hide us from His sight. He has an answer for every question; no mystery perplexes Him.

Seeing us, He promises, "Be still, and know that I am

God" (Psalm 46:10). Although His help does not always come according to our plan or accomplish everything we had hoped it would, God urges us to "be still," to listen and accept the way He works. His ways are always better than ours.

"Even the darkness is not dark to You"—nor is the future dim to Him. God sees it so clearly that we can live our lives today, unafraid and calm about tomorrow. And even when I am afraid and anxious, I can still take my tears and terror to Him and be assured that He will never cast me out of His presence.

*Prayer*

Eternal Lord, under whose eyes we pass our fleeting days, may Your Holy Spirit help me to see Your love. Create in me a clean heart, filled with faith in Christ Jesus, whose undying love took my sins to the cross.

By Your grace, help me to soar above the temporary hurts of this world and to find comfort with the promises of Your Son, my Redeemer.

Help me to conquer my fears, to overcome my gloomy moods, and to sing praises to You, now and always, because of Jesus, my Savior. Amen.

~

# The Faithfulness of God

Hear my prayer, O LORD;
    give ear to my pleas for mercy!
    In Your faithfulness answer me,
        in Your righteousness!

Answer me quickly, O LORD!
    My spirit fails!
Hide not Your face from me,
    lest I be like those who go down
        to the pit.
Let me hear in the morning of
        Your steadfast love,

> for in You I trust.
> Make me know the way I should go,
> for to You I lift up my soul. (Psalm 143:1, 7–8)

God always answers prayers—just as He promised through His Son, who said, "Ask, and it will be given to you" (Matthew 7:7). Such promises from God see us through the long nights.

God always answers prayer. Yes, always. However, wiser than we are, His answers are not always in the way we might expect. Our view of life is sometimes too narrow, and we see things only from the depths; God sees all things perfectly from above. He knows all the pieces and how they move— and uses them to answer our prayers.

God always answers prayer, but His timing may be different from ours. Again, in the depths of a pit, time seems to pass ever so slowly. We forget that from God's perspective, a thousand years are but a day, a twinkling of an eye.

Why, then, pray for physical healing today if His answer might be spiritual health in eternity starting tomorrow? We pray because we know that God's answer will always be for our good; we pray because we need consciously to put ourselves into His hands, by the power of the Spirit; we pray because prayer focuses on the Word of God and its promises, through which He strengthens our faith and trust in Him.

Jesus knows our every weakness—take it to the Lord in prayer.

### Prayer

O God, my help through all stages of life, I need You every hour. In my present infirmities, I do not know where to turn; the way seems dark and hopeless. Therefore, I come to You. Guide me as I pass through these troublesome days.

Cleanse my soul of sin, strengthen my faith, and give me a fuller measure of Your grace for the coming hours. I boldly pray because of Your Son, Jesus the Christ, the same today, tomorrow, and forever. Amen.

# Visitation Devotions

# ANGER, BITTERNESS, SELF-PITY, TURMOIL

*For additional resources, see Section III, p. 135*
*For additional prayers, see Section IV, p. 219*

## Sinned Against

God is a righteous judge, and a God who feels indignation every day. (Psalm 7:11)

The feeling of anger is our cry for justice. Wrath and fury against injustice burns in the human soul like an unquenchable fire. However, this is but a small taste of the wrath that God has against the sin that has hurt you.

Righteous, healthy anger can drive us to defend what is right. However, it is difficult to follow St. Paul's advice: "Be angry and do not sin" (Ephesians 4:26a). Anger is a ravenous fire that may spread and destroy, especially in the one in whom it burns. Our innate desire for justice is so strong that our anger may cause us to become like those who have sinned against us. To suppress anger is also not good. This only drives the bitter poison deeper and stifles the faith that alone can save. You are a sinful human being who has been sinned against. This should not have happened to you, but it has.

Sometimes you may feel as if there is no escape from the dark, cruel, ugly, diabolical blackness of sin. It is sorely felt; its consequences for you are great. You deserve God's wrath and judgment, for you are a beggar. You owe the Master a great debt; you are in need of His grace.

Cry out to God in your anger and bitterness. Cry out to the God of justice. Your salvation, even in this, can only be found outside yourself. The greatest injustice occurred on the cross where Jesus, who knew no sin, became sin for you (2 Corinthians 5:21). On the cross, Jesus was sinned against by bearing your sin. The righteous wrath of the Father against sin killed Jesus for you. You are His child, whom He has created, whom He loves. Trust Him to avenge you, for He has on the cross. "Vengeance is Mine, I will repay, says the Lord" (Romans 12:19). "For the anger of man does not produce the righteousness that God requires" (James 1:20).

The oasis of relief for the bitterness of your soul, the only place where justice meets grace and neither is compromised, is the cross of Jesus Christ. God's wrath is poured out for the grave wrong committed against you, poured out upon His Christ. He has spent it upon His Son for the forgiveness of the whole world. Your sin is washed away in His blood. It is no more. He has paid the price. This is the best possible news for you.

Dwell at the foot of the cross awhile. Know the forgiveness of your sin, the forgiveness of the one who hurt you, the washing away of all sin's effects upon you. Jesus' blood makes you clean and whole. It is at the altar, waiting for you in the cup of salvation. Rest in His wounds; by them you are healed.

### Prayer

Lord Jesus Christ, in bearing our sins You experienced the full shame of being sinned against. Have mercy on us, as we suffer from the anger and bitterness of the injustices that have been inflicted upon us. Help us to dwell in forgiveness at the foot of Your cross so we might be released from everything that enslaves us, for You live and reign with the Father and the Holy Spirit, one God, now and forever. Amen.

## ANXIETY, APPREHENSION, FEAR

*For additional resources, see Section III, p. 138*
*For additional prayers, see Section IV, p. 219*

### Walking through Fire

But now thus says the LORD, He who created you, O Jacob, He who formed you, O Israel: "Fear not, for I have redeemed you; I have called you by name, you are Mine. When you pass through the waters, I will be with you; and through the rivers, they shall not overwhelm you; when you walk through fire you shall not be burned, and the flame shall not consume you. For I am the LORD your God, the Holy One of Israel, your Savior." (Isaiah 43:1–3a)

"Fear not." This seems like an unreasonable request from God. To stand in the presence of our Creator and Judge as a broken and sinful creature should invoke the greatest of fear and shame. His holiness is an unquenchable fire, and we are afraid to be burned and consumed.

Yet the Lord God does speak to us, and His first words are not of judgment but of absolution and comfort: "Fear not." Jesus spoke these words to Peter when he was terrified, as a sinful man, to be in Jesus' presence. We cannot stand before God because of our own merits and deeds. Although we are sinful and unclean, we can stand without fear before God because He has redeemed us through Christ. He calls us to Himself by name, and our name is "You are Mine."

We are first called by name in the waters of Holy Baptism. This washing of regeneration and renewal of the Holy Spirit offers forgiveness of sins, life, and salvation. For where there is forgiveness of sins, there is also life and salvation. God does not forget the promise He made to us in our Baptism. He remains ever faithful to it. "When you pass through the waters, I will be with you."

We were buried into Christ's death in our Baptism, but we were also raised to a new life in Him. This new life is not without hurt, trial, or temptation. In fact, our new life is beset with them, and the old fear creeps in on us. But the promise of God is not for only one day. He guides us waking and guards us sleeping every day. Even when we are most vulnerable and unable to act, He does not leave us or forsake us. We walk through fire, but we are not burned. Anxious thoughts and the troubles of the world threaten to over-whelm us, but they cannot! It is not our own strength that quenches the fiery arrows of the devil. It is the promise and presence of God, who on the cross defeated the devil. Our own strength will fail, but He never will. God is with us. Amen.

*Prayer*

Our Father in heaven, You have redeemed us with the holy, precious blood of Your Son. You have reconciled us to

You in the waters of Holy Baptism. Guide and keep us in our lives as we meet trial and temptation. Strengthen our faith, that we may ever be mindful that You have called us by name and that we are Yours, through Your Son, Jesus Christ, our Lord. Amen.

## Guilt

*For additional resources, see Section III, p. 142*
*For additional prayers, see Section IV, p. 220*

### The Way of the Lord

Remember Your mercy, O Lord, and Your steadfast love, for they have been from of old. Remember not the sins of my youth or my transgressions; according to Your steadfast love remember me, for the sake of Your goodness, O Lord! Good and upright is the Lord; therefore He instructs sinners in the way.

(Psalm 25:6–8)

The Lord is good. He sees your need, your pain, and all your troubles. He provides for you even when you sin and turn away from Him. He remains constant in His mercy and goodness.

The Lord's way is clear, but because of your rebellious ways, you are always bearing the fruit of brokenness, shame, and death. You know you have sinned against God; your conscience tells you that you are guilty before Him.

Even when the way of rebellion enters creation, the Lord still reigns in His kingdom. He has not changed. His great love and mercy remain from the beginning. You may never forget your sins and your guilt, but God remembers not the sins of your youth or your rebellious ways. Scripture says, "God will not take away life, and He devises means so that the banished one will not remain an outcast " (2 Samuel 14:14b).

The way of the Lord is through His Son, Jesus Christ, who went the way of the cross to forgive your sin and remove your guilt. Jesus entered our world to free you from sin's slavery. Instead of your sin and shame, God remembers the sacrifice of His Son on the cross as in Baptism He clothes you with His righteousness. When you feel guilt over sin, it is the Holy Spirit convicting you of sin. When you hunger and thirst for forgiveness, it is the Holy Spirit pointing you to Christ. The Holy Spirit cuts through your guilt and shame to give you trust in Christ alone.

The Lord's goodness can overcome any amount of evil. No sin is small enough to escape His attention, and no sin will ever be too large to be forgiven. God incarnate already bore every punishment; Jesus on the cross is always bigger than your sin.

The Lord's ways are not humankind's ways; therefore, the Lord instructs sinners in the love and mercy of Christ. His ways are the means of grace—Baptism, Absolution, and the Lord's Supper. The Lord works through His Word and Sacraments to breathe His own life into us. The Lord even shares His own glory with us! He binds the wounds of the wounded with His attentive care and His constant Word. He frees us from sin to give us new life and freedom in His Son!

### Prayer

Almighty and everlasting God, You do not desire the death of sinners, but rather that we turn from our evil ways and live. Although we deserve only Your wrath, we flee to Your mercy in Christ Jesus, who gave His body and His blood for our redemption. Grant that we may ever thus believe and never waver. Grant that in such faith we stand worthy before Your altar and Your throne. Strengthen us through Your means, in Jesus' name. Amen.

## IMPATIENCE, BOREDOM, RESTLESSNESS

*For additional resources, see Section III, p. 147*
*For additional prayers, see Section IV, p. 221*

### Forgetting Boredom and Remembering Life

Let my cry come before You, O LORD; give me understanding according to Your word! Let my plea come

before You; deliver me according to Your word. . . . Let
my soul live and praise You, and let Your rules help
me. (Psalm 119:169–170, 175)

Every day is the same. We wake, eat, and sleep. Sometimes it
seems that the only disturbance is the constant dripping of
the bathroom faucet. "God, how long will this take? God, do
You expect me to sit here forever?" We are impatient; we
want to get on with our life. Our boredom and restlessness
get the best of us.

Many times God calls upon us to do the impossible:
Deny yourself. Take up your cross. Pray continually. Ask this
mountain to fall into the sea and it will. But sit here and
wait? This seems impossible. Perhaps we do not see things
according to the way God sees them. Trust God even in the
face of deathly boredom? In our sin, we may have forgotten
how to be interested in life and to be satisfied with so little.
We forget the world was created as a gift for us to enjoy. Our
lives of waking and sleeping are so consumed by the constant drip of boredom we forget the gift of life.

Our culture encourages boredom and restlessness, and we
fail to see life as rich and wide. Everything appears to be out
of reach. You may feel that you have wasted your life and
missed opportunities. And you can't go back. All you are
given is the present, so you must let go of those memories and
see that God promised you more than you could possibly
imagine. He promised you joy, even in the midst of suffering,
even in the midst of boredom, impatience, and restlessness.

It is ironic that we often get restless when we have the
least control. We think if we can get out of a certain situation, we will take back control over our lives and know
peace. It is a scary thing to let go and just be—to have
nowhere to go, no one to see, no purpose in life. Opening
yourself to the truth in these moments is frightening. But
letting go of the illusion of control reveals the mysterious
promises of God.

In letting go, the silence may be deafening. But then,
through the voice of Jesus in His Gospel, the Holy Spirit

whispers in your ear words that give you understanding. Only in His quiet voice does the world make sense. Only now are you able to see the cosmos in the midst of the chaos and know that God's presence orders all things according to His will. His Word delivers you, transforming your impatience into patience, your boredom into joy, your restlessness into satisfaction. Now your soul patiently waits to hear from God, joyfully praising His name and remembering what you once forgot—that all things work for the good of those who are called according to His purpose.

### Prayer

O Son of God, You patiently endured the pain and suffering of the crucifixion. Give to us Your patience so we may praise You even in our trials and travails, and raise us up on the Last Day. In Your name we pray. Amen.

## ADDICTION

*For additional resources, see Section III, p. 150*
*For additional prayers, see Section IV, p. 222*

## Incorruptibility

I have been crucified with Christ. It is no longer I who live, but Christ who lives in me. And the life I now live in the flesh I live by faith in the Son of God, who loved me and gave Himself for me. (Galatians 2:20)

At the present time, all that appears to be living in you is that which you are addicted to. It has dominion over you, body and mind. It has broken you, corrupted your whole being, and you want freedom from this terrible burden. You may think that the only thing living in you is the substance of your addiction, but Paul tells you otherwise and speaks what appears to be foolish words: "It is no longer I who live, but Christ who lives in me."

Although this life of addiction overwhelms you, Christ is still living in you. Even in the midst of this addiction, you are the Lord's. You belong to Him. You are baptized. When your body was drenched with the water of the font, Jesus laid claim to you, and nothing, not even this addiction, will steal you away from Him.

No matter how much you crave what you are addicted to, Jesus loves you more. He loves you so very much that He has not only laid claim to you, but He has defined you anew, made you anew, and continues to define and make you anew when He joins you to His holy body and precious blood. You cannot overcome your addiction by your own efforts. Only in Christ are you able to do this. His body and blood do not merely wage war against your addiction, but His body and blood are the means by which your addiction may be overcome, even if the craving never goes away. When He enters your mouth in the Holy Supper, He enters you to rule and care for your whole being.

When Jesus died on the cross, He who knew no sin became sin for us. He took on even our most hideous addictions. In His victorious resurrection, Jesus demonstrated that He is utterly incorruptible. Sin, death, and, yes, even addiction, did not have their hold on Him. When you eat and drink His body and blood, you become one with His incorruptible flesh. The crucified and resurrected Lord is joined to you in this tangible and substantial way. He now gives to you everything that belongs to Him in this sacred meal, including His incorruptibility.

Although your addiction may harm you and even may appear to be destroying you, you need not fear. Rather, focus on what Jesus did as He was suffering, and put your trust in the God of all comfort and consolation. You are joined to Him—body, blood, soul, and divinity—and in Him you are incorruptible, just as He is incorruptible.

You may not feel that way now—perhaps you never will. But your feelings of despair over your addiction will not change this reality. The final outcome of your broken life will be the same as that of the crucified Christ Jesus—a life of joy, freedom, forgiveness, hope, and incorruptibility is yours in Him unto life everlasting.

*Prayer*

O almighty God, merciful Father, who in love has joined us to the precious body of Your Son, Jesus Christ, in the water of Holy Baptism, grant that we find peace and comfort in being incorruptible, even as He is incorruptible; through the same, Jesus Christ, our Lord, who lives and reigns with you and the Holy Spirit, one God now and forever. Amen.

## LONELINESS

*For additional resources, see Section III, p. 153*
*For additional prayers, see Section IV, p. 223*

### The Groaning of the Spirit

Likewise the Spirit helps us in our weakness. For we do not know what to pray for as we ought, but the Spirit Himself intercedes for us with groanings too deep for words. (Romans 8:26)

Your body is in bondage to decay. This is declared to you each day, sometimes softly in a bruise, sometimes loudly in terminal illness. Even with your best efforts, the marks of imperfection that your body bears cannot be ignored, and you are weak. Not only your body, but your whole self is also caught in decay. Relationships falter and are broken by sin. You feel abandoned by friends and family, and your spirit groans within you.

But you are not alone. Jesus cried out in a loud voice from the cross, "My God, My God, why have You forsaken Me?" (Matthew 27:46). He was forsaken by the Father that you may be reconciled to Him. In Jesus' forsakenness is your forgiveness. Never again do you walk through life alone. In Baptism, the Holy Spirit was given to you. When you feel alone, even when you are so overwhelmed with loneliness that you cannot pray, the Spirit intercedes for you with groanings too deep for words. Not only does the Spirit groan for you, but all of creation also groans with you! "For we know that the whole creation groans and labors with birth pangs together until now" (Romans 8:22). We do not bear the sufferings of this present time alone. All of creation helps to bear up our suffering, and God continually abides with us through His Son. In Him we wait for the glory that is to be revealed to you.

### Prayer

Almighty God, grant that those who live alone may not be lonely but find fulfillment in loving You and their neighbors as they follow in the footsteps of Jesus Christ, our Lord. Amen. (*LW Agenda*, p. 370)

~

## Tears in His Bottle

You have kept count of my tossings; put my tears in Your bottle. Are they not in Your book? (Psalm 56:8)

How long, O Lord? Why do You leave me here alone? For what purpose? When will someone come?

Our Lord created you to long for, and to be for, someone else. Most of all, He created you for a relationship with Himself. That is why He made a way to come close to you in Christ.

It cost the Lord dearly to come for you. He left the Father and felt that separation so sharply that He often withdrew "to desolate places" and prayed (Luke 5:16). There was no place more lonely than the cross. Others hurling insults, His friends scattered and gone, Jesus bore all sin and its ugly consequences. Even the Father was pouring out the bitter cup of wrath on Him: "My God, My God, why have You forsaken Me?" (Matthew 27:46).

Do you feel as if Christ has forsaken you? You taste a drop of His loneliness now. In this, draw close to Him. Take heart: the separation is not forever, but His kingdom is eternal. God's kingdom is now, in the person of Jesus. By His wounds you are healed.

It is your purpose to be loved by Him and to love in

return. No situation of life can prevent your communion with Him. In Jesus' body and blood, even your thinking and feeling do not inhibit it, but He comes to you in the simplest and most significant of ways—eating and drinking—into your very person.

You are not forgotten. He keeps all your tears. Blessed be the name of the Lord.

### Prayer

Almighty God, merciful Father, by Word and Sacrament You have created Your Church in this world to be a godly communion and family. Grant Your blessing to those who dwell in loneliness that they may find a place of solace and pleasant fellowship among people faithful to You; through Jesus Christ, our Lord. Amen. (*LW Agenda*, pp. 369–70)

## Old Age

*For additional resources, see Section III, p. 156*
*For additional prayers, see Section IV, p. 223*

### Growing Old in Christ

O Lord, make me know my end and what is the measure of my days; let me know how fleeting I am! . . . And now, O Lord, for what do I wait? My hope is in You. . . . Hear my prayer, O Lord, and give ear to my cry; hold not Your peace at my tears! For I am a sojourner with You, a guest, like all my fathers.
(Psalm 39:4, 7, 12)

Someone once said, "We are all terminal." That is true. We are born to die. That is our end, our destiny. None of us know when that will be or how it will happen. All we can do is pray: "O Lord, make me know my end and what is the measure of my days; let me know how fleeting I am!" The elderly understand this, for in our old age we are aware of the frailty of life.

People who grow old understand David's prayer in

Psalm 39. As bodies grow weak and minds become feeble, we become obsessed with ourselves, our aging. It is hard for us to think of anything else, for our bodily aches and pains, our growing old, becomes our main focus. As a result, we have no peace, for we are at war with ourselves, with our growing old.

Only the Lord is able to help you turn away from yourself to Him and to your neighbor. Only Christ is your hope. So you wait on Him and pray with David: "Hear my prayer, O LORD, and give ear to my cry; hold not Your peace at my tears!" You need the peace that only Jesus can give, especially when you give way to tears. For the way is treacherous, even as you grow old, especially as you grow old. And He has gone that way for you, all the way to a cross where He conquered death by His death and showed you in His resurrected body what you shall one day be and what you already are now.

Like the Lord, you are a stranger in this world as you make your pilgrimage from life to death. Just as He did not travel alone to Jerusalem but was accompanied by the Spirit of the Father, so you also do not journey alone but with Him, by His Spirit, and with all the saints who have gone before you in the faith. To grow old in Christ is to grow old in His Church, fed by Him along the way by His life-giving words and His salutary body and blood in the Supper He has prepared for you.

Growing old is not for the faint of heart. It is a form of suffering, for you see how this frail body is broken down by the wear and tear of the years. But if your journey is in Christ, if you are growing old in Christ, those marks of age are marks of His honor and His wisdom. As you make your way to the heavenly Jerusalem, your advancing age reminds you that the life you now lead in Christ will continue in Christ forever and ever.

### Prayer

Almighty God and gracious Father, in Your mercy look on all whose increasing years bring them weakness, anxiety, distress, or loneliness. Provide them with homes where love and respect, concern and understanding are shown. Grant them willing hearts to accept help and, as their strength wanes, increase their faith and assurance of Your love through Jesus Christ, their Savior. Amen. (*LW Agenda*, p. 369)

## POOR AND NEEDY

*For additional resources, see Section III, p. 160*
*For additional prayers, see Section IV, p. 225*

### God Stoops and Makes You Princes

Who is like the LORD our God, who is seated on high, who looks far down on the heavens and the earth? He raises the poor from the dust and lifts the needy from the ash heap, to make them sit with princes, with the princes of His people. (Psalm 113:5–8)

God "looks far down." Some translations say that God "stoops." He does not look without responding to the need He sees there.

God stoops. He lifts out of the dust and the ashes. But He does not do this from above. He does not reach down from His glory and pluck you out. No, He came to be poor, the mighty King born in a stable, to feel the brunt of the full weight of all your need. It brought Him lower than the dust, into the very depths of the grave. From there He raises you up for all time. He raises you up today on His shoulders like a faithful shepherd.

"God stoops" means that He has mercy. At the beginning of each Divine Service, we cry, "Lord, have mercy." We mean: Lord, we are in need. We are suffering under the yoke of a fallen world. Our sin keeps us from You. Lord, stoop! You are the only one who can help us. Fill our every need with Your presence. Come, Lord Jesus.

And the Lord does come to us in His miraculous, but always human, ways. He speaks a living and active Word into our ears, creating faith, giving hope like a spring of water out of dry ground, giving love that fills us and spills over to others. The Word comes, too, in body and blood, so faithfully beyond all our defenses of reason and feeling. These means are sure because Christ gave them. And may He also send from among His people hands to help, feet to serve Him by meeting felt need, to bring salve and balm, nourishment and provision, kindness and love.

As the psalmist proclaims: Although you are poor and needy, you sit with princes for eternity. Your Prince of Peace took your place of need and paid your way—not with gold or silver. You sit in His place, with the riches of His precious blood, today and for eternity.

### Prayer

O God of all mercy, You heal those who are broken in heart and turn the sadness of the sorrowful to joy. We commend to Your care those who suffer want and anxiety because they are in need. Remember those who are destitute, homeless, or neglected in any way. Forgive us when we have failed to care for the poor and needy, and help us to bear one another's burdens as Your Son bore ours on the cross. Hear us, O Lord, for the love of Him who for our sakes became poor, Your Son, our Savior, Jesus Christ. Amen.

## SPIRITUAL OPPRESSION

*For additional resources, see Section III, p. 164*
*For additional prayers, see Section IV, p. 225*

### Protection from the Devil

Now war arose in heaven, Michael and his angels fighting against the dragon. And the dragon and his angels fought back. (Revelation 12:7)

I saw Satan fall like lightning from heaven. Behold, I have given you authority to tread on serpents and scorpions, and over all the power of the enemy, and nothing shall hurt you. Nevertheless, do not rejoice in this, that the spirits are subject to you, but rejoice that your names are written in heaven. (Luke 10:18–20)

In the angelic war in heaven, Satan stands as our adversary in the heavenly court, prosecuting humanity. The defeat of Satan is in the courtroom where Michael is the defense attorney, pleading Christ's sacrifice for the sin of the whole world against the deceiver of the whole world. The victory is Christ's, the slaughtered Lamb of God, who in His death is also the conquering Lion of Judah.

Michael the archangel leads God's angelic armies in battle against the armies of Satan and his angels who threaten to destroy God's chosen child, the Messiah. The conflict is over the fate of man. But the assault of Satan and his angels is doomed to failure, for St. John announces simply and completely that they were "defeated and there was no longer any place for them in heaven" (Revelation 12:8).

Jesus says, "I saw Satan fall like lightning from heaven." The reason for Satan's defeat is the slaughter of the Lamb. The accuser can no longer accuse us, for Christ, by His perfect life and His atoning death, took away the guilt and shame of the world, removing all grounds for accusation against humankind. The floodgates of mercy are now open, and God's grace and forgiveness pour forth in abundance because the Lamb has been slain and His blood has been shed for all. The voice of the accuser is forever silenced.

This war is still won through the word of our testimony about the blood of the Lamb. As Jesus watches Satan fall like lightening from heaven, He sums up the effects of the mission of the disciples He sent into the harvest. In proclaiming Christ and His Gospel, in their healing, there was victory over Satan and his angelic armies. Even they recognized that "the demons are subject to us in Your name!" (Luke 10:17).

How can sinners be declared innocent by another's death? Only if His death, the death of the Son of God, somehow becomes your death, for as St. Paul says: "there is now no condemnation for those who are in Christ Jesus"

(Romans 8:1). His death is now your death, for you are baptized into Christ, plunging into His death and rising in His resurrection to newness of life. As His child, conformed to His image, born in the Church, you have conquered the accuser by His blood—the blood of the Lamb who suffered the horror of the cross on our behalf.

### Prayer

Through Baptism, your name is written in heaven, preserved in that status through the testimony of His Word and through His feast of eternity. Here is the joy of all who hear and believe that the angelic war in heaven has been won. Therefore, with angels and archangels and all the company of heaven we declare with St. John: "Rejoice, O heavens and you who dwell in them" (Revelation 12:12). Amen.

~

## Christ's Baptismal Armor

> For as many of you as were baptized into Christ have put on Christ. (Galatians 3:27)

The devil is subtle. His portrayal in horror movies, that of horns and a spiked tail, is not true. Like a snake, the devil slithers his way into your life, takes you over, has you rationalizing your sins, and, even worse, believing you deserve God's good favor because of your works, believing there is no spiritual battle to be fought.

The devil is real; evil is everywhere; demons are wrapped around you, slowly squeezing you to death. It is hopeless if you depend on yourself. You cannot fight the devil alone. You need Christ to fight for you.

Christ began His ministry defeating Satan in the wilderness; Christ ended His ministry defeating Satan on a cross. Weak, naked, suffering, dying, Jesus conquered all the principalities and powers through His blood. Dying, Jesus triumphed over Satan; rising, He declared the victory. It is over. Jesus defeated Satan for you once and for all.

Jesus cloaks you with His victory. Baptized into Christ

you put on Christ as if He were your clothing. That clothing is armor—Christ's baptismal armor—the belt of truth, the breastplate of righteousness, the shoes of peace, the shield of faith, the helmet of salvation, and the sword of the Spirit (Ephesians 6:10–20). You are ready for battle. Go, fight, and win—clothed in Christ.

## Prayer

Lord Jesus Christ, You came in humility and weakness to defeat the powers of sin, death, and the devil. Cloth our weakness with Your righteousness by Your baptismal grace that we might withstand the power of every adversary; for You live and reign with the Father and the Holy Spirit, one God, now and forever. Amen.

## GOD'S PURPOSE IN SUFFERING

*For additional resources, see Section III, p. 172*
*For additional prayers, see Section IV, p. 227*

### Jesus Scars

You know it was because of a bodily ailment that I preached the gospel to you at first, and though my condition was a trial to you, you did not scorn or despise me, but received me as an angel of God, as Christ Jesus. (Galatians 4:13–14)

From now on let no one cause me trouble, for I bear on my body the marks of Jesus. (Galatians 6:17)

Jesus scars—that is what we bear on our bodies as the baptized. You can't see them in most people, but they are there. We call those scars sufferings. Every Christian has them, but not every Christian knows they are Jesus scars.

Jesus scars do not make sense to the world. For the world, Jesus scars are a sign of weakness and failure. They come from Jesus, who died the humiliating and shameful death of crucifixion. What could be weaker than that?

The Galatians were mercenaries—tough, worldly people. They found Paul half-dead by the side of the road, beaten for preaching the Gospel, a weak, pathetic mess. All over his body were Jesus scars—bleeding, putrid scars. In this weakness, Paul preached the Gospel to the Galatians. Through his body, his scars, and his suffering, the Galatians received Paul as an angel of God, as Christ Jesus Himself. For the same powers that crucified Jesus persecuted Paul. He bore on his body the marks of Jesus for preaching Christ crucified.

Suffering for Jesus is what the baptized do. It forms you into His image and makes you what you are. It helps you say that no matter what suffering you endure, it is all gift, it is all good. You cannot escape suffering, but you can understand it through Christ—that suffering is the greatest mystery and the greatest blessing of life.

Most people flee suffering. They either ignore it or drug themselves so they do not have to feel its depth. Suffering does two things: it either alienates us from God or throws us on His mercy. That is why it is necessary to make meaning out of suffering—to see Christ in your suffering. Christ suffered for you on the cross and gives you, in your sufferings, the privilege of participating in His suffering. That is why in your Baptism you suffered, died, were buried, and rose with Christ to a life that never ends. Christ dwells in you and you dwell in Him. That is why you eat His body, broken in death, and drink His blood, poured out in suffering for the forgiveness of your sins. Without His suffering, and your incorporation into Him, you have no way to understand what your suffering means.

Paul knew the end of the story—Christ rose and ascended and took us with Him into heaven, even now, right now, in body and blood. So Paul shouted into the darkness of suffering about the triumph already now, already here, already present in Christ's ongoing bodily presence among us. Paul bore that suffering on his own body as he received that suffering in, with, and under bread and wine.

With Paul, we rejoice in suffering—for we bear on our bodies the marks of Jesus.

*Prayer*

O God, by the patient suffering of Your only-begotten Son You have beaten down the pride of the old enemy. Now help us, we humbly pray, rightly to treasure in our hearts all that our Lord has of His goodness borne for our sake that after His example we may bear with patience all that is adverse to us; through Jesus Christ, our Lord. Amen. (*LW Altar Book*, p. 138)

~

## Why, God?

Then Job answered the LORD and said: "I know that You can do all things, and that no purpose of Yours can be thwarted. 'Who is this that hides counsel without knowledge?' Therefore I have uttered what I did not understand, things too wonderful for me, which I did not know." (Job 42:1–3)

Job's suffering was intense. Having lost health, family, and all possessions, he cursed the day of his birth. But his most intense suffering arose from his seemingly ruptured relationship with God. The cry of his soul was, "Why, God?"

His friends deepened his suffering by attempting to answer that question. Surely, they said, there must be some secret sin for Job to confess, for which God was punishing him. But Job was a righteous man, and this was not about his sin. We have the inside scoop on Job's suffering: Satan, not God, was bringing these things upon him because of his righteousness.

We offer many possible answers to the reason for our suffering: Perhaps God sent it to make us stronger. Or perhaps He is trying to teach us a lesson of life so we can help others. It is all part of His plan for our lives. He is trying to get us to draw closer to Him because we have strayed. Maybe we did do something to deserve it after all.

All of these answers must be evaluated against God's clear word: "Do not be deceived, my beloved brothers. Every good gift and every perfect gift is from above, coming down from the Father of lights with whom there is no variation or shadow" (James 1:16–17).

Many times our suffering is the result of a world fallen into sin, sickness, and death. Sometimes it arises from our own sinful nature, or from someone who has hurt us. We may not know the source of our suffering, whether the devil, the world, or our flesh. But why does God allow your suffering? Why did He allow Job's? Is He really in control? Does He really care that you are in pain?

Job longed for an intercessor, a friend, someone to reconcile him to God and "lay his hand on us both" (Job 9:33). In answer to Job's cry, God showed up. But He never answered Job's "Why?" God simply said, "I AM," and Job responded, "I lay my hand on my mouth" (Job 40:4). He stopped guessing at things "too wonderful" for him to know and was made still because God is God—present, powerful, and in control.

For us, too, God has shown up—on the cross. Jesus, true God and true man, saves you as well as Job from the sting of sin on the cross. He chose the place of ultimate suffering to reveal Himself to you. What do you see? He is present in your place of suffering. His greatest love for you is known in His cross, where He loved you in the midst of suffering. In His goodness and innocence, He felt the full brunt of the suffering you now feel. He is here, He is in control, and your suffering is only temporary. He knows.

In your suffering, instead of "Why?" ask, "Where? Where are You, God?" See Him sharing your suffering at the hands of the world, the devil, the flesh. He has won for you your final deliverance. Find comfort in His wounds. Find comfort in His promise: "I will never leave you nor forsake you" (Hebrews 13:5).

### Prayer

Gracious Father, You have given Your only Son to endure the punishment and shame of our sin, and He has suffered in our behalf. Grant us strength to endure the weight of our cross in this life. May our eyes ever be turned to the cross of Christ where Your glory is revealed through Your Son, Jesus Christ, our Lord. Amen.

∽

## Suffering at His Side, Bearing Our Cross

Then Jesus told His disciples, "If anyone would come after Me, let him deny himself and take up his cross and follow Me. For whoever would save his life will lose it, but whoever loses his life for My sake will find it." (Matthew 16:24–25)

The Lord came to earth and joined us in our suffering. He took our sufferings onto Himself. Jesus hung on the cross with the full weight of sin and death upon Him. Jesus, the Son of the living God, suffered in His humanity for our sake.

Suffering is not a punishment. Suffering is not a sign of personal weakness. Suffering does not separate us from God. Jesus used suffering to show the extent of His love for us. Throughout His life, Jesus suffered the attacks of the devil, the world, and human flesh for us. His final act of suffering was the humiliating and shameful death of crucifixion as He gave up His life for us.

The devil and the world think they triumph in suffering, but Jesus proved them wrong. In bearing His cross, Jesus gave life to the world. Christ triumphs over suffering.

We follow where our Master leads. His cross is forgiveness and salvation. Our cross is love toward a world that rejects us. Our cross points to His cross, and our heavenly Father witnesses and reacts with compassion to all who suffer in His name.

The Lord promises to help us and be with us. Our lives are dependent on God's care, and He is strong, faithful, and steadfast. As our High Priest, Jesus took each of our specific burdens onto Himself. He bore them as only the Son of God could. Now Jesus promises to live in us through His Word and Sacraments, carrying us through this life and into eternity.

We do not suffer without hope. Christ is our hope. In

Baptism we are joined to Him—to His life, death, and resurrection. His death is now our death; His life is now our life. We are buried with Him in His grave, dug into stone. And as He rose up from the grave, so also do we rise from our baptismal waters to a life that never ends. Just as surely as water was applied to us in our Baptism, so also as surely does our Lord forgive our sins in Absolution. We may suffer now, but our suffering will stop, for we trust God's Word, which says our suffering cannot compare with the glories we will inherit.

The ways of the Lord are not our ways, but Jesus is our comfort. Jesus shows us that God never abandons His creation but always works for good and salvation, even when His works are hidden from our eyes. "We share abundantly in Christ's sufferings, so through Christ we share abundantly in comfort too" (2 Corinthians 1:5).

### Prayer

Heavenly Father, You are strong and You made us Your people. Defend us for the sake of Your Son, who goes before us. Carry us as we carry our crosses. As Your Son, Christ Jesus, lay down His life so that we may live, so now live in us through Your Word that we are not overcome but ultimately triumph. Sustain us by Your Spirit as we walk through the valley of the shadow of death. In Jesus' name. Amen.

∼

## Mere Breath

When You discipline a man with rebukes for sin, You consume like a moth what is dear to him; surely all mankind is a mere breath! Here my prayer, O LORD, and give ear to my cry; hold not Your peace at my tears! For I am a sojourner with You, a guest, like all my fathers. (Psalm 39:11–12)

All that Jesus does, He does for us. For us He prays the Psalms. The Psalms are the prayer book of Jesus, and one way to read them is from the voice of Christ. From the cross

He cried out the words of Psalm 22: "My God, My God, why have You forsaken Me?" Christ is the Suffering Servant, and in Psalm 39 He cries out once again in His suffering. He stood silent before His accusers, guilty of all the sin of the world, with the wrath of God upon Him. His life was nothing more than a breath, a brief sojourn upon the earth. He was consumed, and He was struck by the hostility of the hand of God. This suffering He bore on our behalf, such punishment as our sin deserved, and it killed Him. The world does not understand this mystery of the cross. In the shameful and humiliating death of Christ is also His glory. On the cross, sin, sickness, devil, and death are defeated. Their defeat is secure and eternal, and Christ displays their defeat when He rises on the third day.

All that Jesus does, He does for us. The Christian is baptized into the death of Jesus and raised to a new life in Him. The life of the Christian is not without suffering—indeed, it is permeated with it. But the pain and shame each Christian bears is not empty and without purpose. When Christians put on Christ, they put on His suffering. They, like Him, become suffering servants. Like Him, it is in the pain of the personal cross that the glory of God is revealed. St. Paul writes: "My grace is sufficient for you, for my power is made perfect in weakness. . . . For the sake of Christ, then, I am content with weaknesses, insults, hardships, persecutions, and calamities. For when I am weak, then I am strong" (2 Corinthians 12:9–10). This is the theology of the cross. In weakness, the glory of God is revealed through Christ.

Our suffering, though real and painful, has lost its eternal sting. It has been defeated and destroyed on the cross. Yet, as in Psalm 39, surely all humankind is a mere breath. Our lives appear short. We are sojourners here, and the discipline we receive in suffering can appear fruitless and meaningless. Humankind is mere breath, but on account of Jesus Christ and His death on the cross, this breath is not our own. Our life has been taken up through Baptism into the new life of Christ. We are a new creation made in the image of God. Into our nostrils, He has breathed His own breath. We no longer operate by our own strength. We are no longer alone to trudge through life. In our weakness, the strength of God is revealed. And the strength of God is the cross of Jesus Christ.

### Prayer

Gracious Father, You have given Your only Son to endure the punishment and shame of our sin, and He has suffered on our behalf. Grant us strength to endure the weight of our cross in this life. May our eyes ever be turned to the cross of Christ where Your glory is revealed through Your Son, Jesus Christ, our Lord. Amen.

## AFTER ATTEMPTED SUICIDE OR SELF-INFLICTED INJURY

### God Is Greater Than Our Hearts

For whenever our heart condemns us, God is greater than our heart, and He knows everything. Beloved, if our heart does not condemn us, we have confidence before God. (1 John 3:20–21)

The nature of our heart is to give us trouble—it is the nature of this world and the prince of this world. The devil is the one who condemns, not God. He troubles our heart into thinking that our life is not important before God.

But such condemnation is a lie. God loves us so much that He exhausted His condemnation on Jesus, so there is no longer any opportunity for you to be condemned. God spent His condemnation on His only Son. The crucifixion of Jesus may seem disconnected from you—far away, unrelated, and unsympathetic to your plight. But all of God's condemnation and disfavor was poured out on Jesus, not on you. Whenever you question your worth before God, look at the Man on the cross.

Whether our heart condemns us or not, God never condemns us, for He condemned Jesus on the cross instead of us. If our heart condemns us, God is greater than our heart and points us to the cross. If our heart does not condemn us, then our heart agrees with God. We have confidence before Him as we rest in the peace and reconciliation of Christ's death and resurrection.

God suffered that death for you. God died so that the sorrow and emptiness of death are overcome by Christ's resurrection. All of His displeasure was expended on a hill outside Jerusalem two thousand years ago, in the God-man Jesus Christ. He is God so that He could endure everything for you. He is man so that He could sympathize completely with you.

God's anger against sin has been levied against Jesus, His Son. In Christ, there is now for us only sympathy and nearness and love. God is here for you not as one who condemns, but as one who knows your heart, knows your sorrow, knows your struggle, and knows the pain, hatred, and condemnation you may receive from others. But God is greater than your heart, and He is greater than all others, even those who condemn you.

You may feel as if everyone close to you is against you. But there is one who is here for you: the God-man Jesus Christ. Now risen from the grave, He binds you up and says, "I love you. I know what you are feeling. I felt it too. I will not leave you. I will never let you fall. Trust in Me."

From the day you were baptized, Jesus has been with you. As you continue to hear His Word, He is with you. He submits to your deepest needs as you eat His body and blood. He takes what you have and makes it His own. He takes what is His and gives it to you. All of this is to say that, whether your heart condemns you or not, God does not condemn you. He is with you, and He calls you to have confidence before Him in His Son, Jesus Christ, our Lord.

### *Prayer*

O Lord Jesus, You came into this world not to condemn the world but to redeem it by Your blood. When our heart condemns us, You forgive us; when we see no hope, You come with Your gifts to give us life that never ends. Help us in this dark hour to know the consolation of Your saving Gospel that You never leave us but hold us in Your tender mercies; for You live and reign with the Father and the Holy Spirit, one God, now and forever. Amen.

## BAPTISMAL IDENTITY—CALL TO REPENTANCE

*For additional resources, see Section III, p.176*
*For additional prayers, see Section IV, p. 229*

### Everyone Whom the Lord Calls

And Peter said to them, "Repent and be baptized every one of you in the name of Jesus Christ for the forgiveness of your sins, and you will receive the gift of the Holy Spirit. For the promise is for you and for your children and for all who are far off, everyone whom the Lord our God calls to Himself."

(Acts 2:38–39)

Peter stood before the crowds of Jews on the day of Pentecost and preached to them Christ crucified, the fulfillment of God's promise that He gave through the Old Testament prophets. Peter's words cut the people to the heart, and they asked, "Brothers, what shall we do?" (Acts 2:37).

We often ask ourselves the same question. The Word of God spoken through the mouth of the pastor rends our hearts, and we ask, "What shall we do? What shall we do to be saved?" The answer Peter gave to the crowds is the same for us today. We can do nothing of ourselves. The promise of salvation and the forgiveness of sins is not found in our actions but in the call of the Lord our God who saves us as we receive His grace. It is God who calls us to Himself through the preaching of the Word, and this Word is written on our heads and on our hearts in Holy Baptism. Here Peter is the mouth of the Lord, calling the people to receive the promise of salvation in faith in Christ Jesus, crucified and risen.

Faith grasps the promise first attached to us and to our children in Holy Baptism. This, too, is a gift and not attained by our action. The Word works faith, and faith works contrition in the heart and sorrow over past sins. It is not despair, but a godly sorrow that desires to repent and receive forgiveness. Repentance is a gift worked out by the call of God. Thus, through the work of God first begun in Baptism, forgiveness of sins, life, and salvation are received in faith with joy. Amen.

## Prayer

Soul of Christ, sanctify me; body of Christ, save me; blood of Christ, refresh me; water from the side of Christ, wash me; passion of Christ, strengthen me; O good Jesus, hear me; within Your wounds hide me; never let me be separated from You; from the malicious enemy defend me; in the hour of my death call me, and bid me come to You that with Your saints I may praise You for all eternity. Amen. (*Daily Office*, p. 703)

~

## Forever Today

Take care, brothers, lest there be in any of you an evil, unbelieving heart, leading you to fall away from the living God. But exhort one another every day, as long as it is called "today," that none of you may be hardened by the deceitfulness of sin. For we share in Christ, if indeed we hold our original confidence firm to the end. As it is said, "Today, if you hear His voice, do not harden your hearts as in the rebellion."

(Hebrews 3:12–15)

Originally, there were seven days in a week, each day taking its turn in the cycle. However, when Jesus rose victorious from the dead on Sunday, it was not only the first day of the week, and the third day after the crucifixion, but also the eighth day, the first day of the new creation. Jesus rose from the dead on the eighth day, one greater than the former seven days. In His death and resurrection, our Lord took the old, sin-ridden creation, once completed in seven days, and made it new. From the resurrection on, there has never been another day, but always and everyday the eighth day, the day of the new creation.

Since it is "today," or the ongoing eighth day, hearts hardened by the deceitfulness of sin are called to repentance and faith. So "today" is the day of the new creation. "Today" is the day that Christ makes you new. New life, new start, and new direction, as Jesus lovingly turns you around and forgives you of all your sin.

Christ has made all things new—including you!

### Prayer

Lord God, heavenly Father, You created the world in six days, rested on the seventh, and restored all things to Yourself on the eighth day when Your Son rose from the dead. May His new resurrected life fill us with hope that no matter how great our sins, He is greater in His forgiveness and His mercy; through Jesus Christ, our Lord. Amen.

## BAPTISMAL IDENTITY—FORGIVENESS AND RECONCILIATION

*For additional resources, see Section III, p. 179*
*For additional prayers, see Section IV, p. 229*

### Overwhelmed by Grace

And he arose and came to his father. But while he was still a long way off, his father saw him and felt compassion, and ran and embraced him and kissed him.

(Luke 15:20)

Hitting rock bottom is the easy part. "Sinner" is what we are. It comes naturally. Like everyone around us, we are by nature rebellious, disobedient, unfaithful prodigals.

That is why we identify with the prodigal, not the elder brother. "You're right, Jesus, we are by nature sinful and unclean." It is easy being a sinner. Thank God for grace. We think that if we get this sin thing right, then all is right with God.

When the prodigal son hit rock bottom and started to eat pig food, he had to act quickly or he was going to die. So he returned home to his merciful father, sorry for his sins: "Father, I have sinned against heaven and before you. I am no longer worthy to be called your son" (Luke 15:21). But he would work off the debt he owed: "Treat me as one of your hired servants" (Luke 15:19).

Perhaps the prodigal thought he had it wired. Fess up that you are sinner, make a plan how to get back into the father's employ, and all will be right. "I can save my life and save face at the same time. I'll work my way back, on my own terms. I'll show them I am worthy to be back."

There is no confession here. Better to be a sinner, a prodigal, than a self-righteous younger brother whose repentance is an attempt to save himself by his own works. In this confession the prodigal hits rock bottom. He joins the elder brother and every Pharisee Jesus ever condemned by getting it all wrong, for not seeing the gift, the grace.

Each day the son was gone the father would look down the road leading to his house, hoping he would see his son coming home. Then one day, while he was still far off, the father saw him. The father's mercy overflowed—he ran, fell on his son's neck, and showered him with kisses. Overwhelmed by grace, the son truly repents: "Father, I have sinned against heaven and before you. I am no longer worthy to be called your son."

There was no need to work off his debt, for it is all by grace—costly grace—the grace of the life of the Son of God in exchange for the life of the world. The prodigal turned self-righteous son now sees pure grace in the father, grace that only comes from a tree outside Jerusalem where the gift of life to the world was given by the shedding of the blood of Jesus, the very Son of God. At the cross, there is nothing for us to do. Jesus died for sinners, for you—there is nothing you can do about it. That is grace. Jesus loves the prodigal so much that He is willing to give up His life for him.

"While you are still far off" your merciful Father sees you, runs to you, falls on your neck, showers you with kisses, and kills the fatted calf, showing you mercy and forgiveness at a feast that knows no end—even though you are His prodigal.

## Prayer

Lord God, our heavenly Father, You stood afar, waiting to see Your prodigals appear at the gate. Then, running to us, You overwhelmed us with grace and invited us to sit at Your table to rejoice at our homecoming. Help us to repent of our sins, and strip us of every thought that we might merit Your salvation. Then bring us home to be with You at the marriage feast of the Lamb in His kingdom, which has no end; through Your Son, Jesus Christ, our Lord. Amen.

~

## Cry Out to the Lord

I waited patiently for the LORD; He inclined to me and heard my cry. He drew me up from the pit of destruction, out of the miry bog, and set my feet upon a rock, making my steps secure. He put a new song in my mouth, a song of praise to our God. Many will see and fear, and put their trust in the LORD. (Psalm 40:1–3)

You drowned in your Baptism, kicking, dying. You did not know what was going on around you. You could not know, but the Lord looked at you, turned His ear toward you, and cared for you.

He drew you up out of the dark waters, out of your sin, and into Himself. He gives you His Word and Himself as a song. He gives you Himself, hurting, vulnerable, and exposed on the cross; He died for you. He also gives you Himself glorified and transfigured; He has risen from the dead and now gives you life!

All your sins were washed away in your Baptism—you were fully reconciled to God. In Baptism the Lord made you His own dear child. He watches over you and manages what you cannot. He will never leave you.

This baptismal promise is for us, for those before us, and for those after us. It is built on the rock of our salvation—Jesus Christ. He is our anchor and our strength. He secures our path. The Lord heard your cry even when you cried out against Him. Now He fills your mouth with a different cry. Jesus is the content of our song. He is the power and the breath of your voice.

We sing of who He is. We sing what He has done. We sing His message of grace and salvation. We can even sing the psalms He sang with His disciples and, earlier, with His parents. We sing with the angels and with all the saints who have gone before us. The Lord has restored the song of creation!

Jesus is your rock. He cannot be shaken. He cannot be broken. He has paved the path of righteousness with His very self, so that the Word, the light for your path, illuminates Him! Jesus is your present reality and your future destination.

Many will see and fear and put their trust in the Lord. The Lord inspires our awe and respect. He gives us certainty in our relationship with Him. His mercy will never change.

### Prayer

Heavenly Father, You sent Your only-begotten Son out of the heights of heaven, down to the depths of earth. Christ took all the destruction and punishment of sin away from us and paid it Himself. In Him You inclined Your ears to hear us, so now Jesus hears our every need. Hear our confession and forgive us our sins. Fully restore us to Yourself. Keep us secure in Your Son, grounded in Your Word. Teach us to sing Your praises and tell of Your deeds. Send out Your Word and Your servants so that all will be baptized into Your name, through Jesus Christ, our Lord. Amen.

$\sim$

## Approach His Grace

For we do not have a high priest who is unable to sympathize with our weaknesses, but one who in every respect has been tempted as we are, yet without sin. Let us then with confidence draw near to the throne of grace, that we may receive mercy and find grace to help in time of need. (Hebrews 4:15–16)

At times, it is hard to imagine that Jesus, the sinless one, is on your side. Yet have no fear. Jesus knows exactly what you are going through. He was tempted as you are, and though He was not a sinner, He became sin for you. On the cross, He bore the sins of the whole world, even yours. Christ is the greatest sinner, not because of His own sin but because He bears in His body the sin of the whole world.

In His sin-bearing death, Jesus has destroyed your sins forever. They can harm you no more. All Jesus has for you now is forgiveness, life, and salvation. The very body and blood of Jesus on the cross you now receive when you eat His body and drink His blood at the Lord's Supper. He now dwells in your body and soul forever.

At times, your sins may seem to get the best of you, but they will never defeat you, because Christ has defeated them. So "with confidence draw near to the throne of grace." Go to the holy altar and receive the very body and blood of Jesus Christ. This is where true mercy and grace are to be found—in Jesus Himself.

### Prayer

Lord Jesus Christ, by Your blood You entered the heavenly places to make a sacrifice for our sins. Give us confidence to enter the most holy place of Your Supper where the very same body and blood are given us to eat and drink for the forgiveness of sins and the entrance into heaven, where You live and reign with the Father and the Holy Spirit, one God, now and forever. Amen.

∼

## A Love that Lives for Us

I waited patiently for the LORD; He inclined to me and heard my cry. He drew me up from the pit of destruction, out of the miry bog, and set my feet upon a rock, making my steps secure. He put a new song in my mouth, a song of praise to our God. Many will see and fear, and put their trust in the Lord.

(Psalm 40:1–3)

Fractured and isolated, the sinful man looks inward, unable to live outside himself. The pit of destruction he lives in is his own self-love. He needs a different kind of love, one that is able to do what it promises, one that will put a song of salvation in his mouth. He needs a love that reconciles and gathers. God in Jesus Christ manifests this love. Jesus' love is that rock upon which you stand, what makes your steps secure. He brings you back to your Creator and gathers you together with the rest of the saints. Jesus Christ on the cross, the propitiation for our sins, forgives your sins and reunites you with God. It is through the Son, in His love, that we have the life we were meant to live.

God made the first move by loving us regardless of our sinful response to His love. This is simply His way of dealing with us; God works by grace and mercy rather than by merit and cruelty. It is His joy to love us even though we cannot understand being loved unconditionally. God knew that the world needed His Son because only His Son knows what true love is. Where we need time and effort to learn what love is, God simply is love. In this act of sending His Son to be the satisfaction for our sins we are loved. By His act of coming close to us in Jesus Christ we now cling to Him and know that our world is restored to where it was meant to be: God and man living together in Jesus Christ.

### Prayer

Gracious heavenly Father, You sent Your Son to be the propitiation for our sins. Reconcile us to Yourself and grant us Christ's life so that we may be caught up in Your continual work of restoring the world to Yourself; through Jesus Christ, Your Son, our Lord. Amen.

## Baptismal Identity—Gratitude

*For additional prayers, see Section IV, p. 231*

### An Open Gate

Make a joyful noise to the LORD, all the earth! Serve the LORD with gladness! Come into His presence with singing! Know that the LORD, He is God! It is He who made us, and we are His; we are His people, and the sheep of His pasture. Enter His gates with thanksgiving, and His courts with praise! Give thanks to Him; bless His name! For the LORD is good; His steadfast love endures forever, and His faithfulness to all generations. (Psalm 100)

Through the waters of Holy Baptism, Christ has made us worthy to enter into the presence of the Lord, praising Him with the angels, thanking Him for all He has done! We marvel and adore Him, for Jesus opened the gate to heaven by becoming man and taking our sin and sorrow onto Himself. His love and power extends over all. All nations will bow before His throne.

We thank our tender Shepherd because He sought us when we had gone astray. He opened the gate to heaven for us when He washed us by water, Spirit, and Word. He calls us by name. He feeds and cares for us, rejoicing over us. He multiplies His flock, leading us out of danger and into paradise.

We are His. He frees us to live in Christ with thanksgiving and love as He does, eternally. On earth and in heaven, we will live under Him in His kingdom, in everlasting innocence, righteousness, and blessedness forever! Thanks be to God! Amen.

### Prayer

Lord Jesus Christ, shepherd of our bodies and our souls, lead us with joy to our everlasting home as You nurture us now on our pilgrimage by Your life-giving presence, for You live and reign with the Father and the Holy Spirit, one God, now and forever. Amen.

## Rejoice with Joy Inexpressible

Though you have not seen Him, you love Him.
Though you do not now see Him, you believe in Him
and rejoice with joy that is inexpressible and filled
with glory, obtaining the outcome of your faith, the
salvation of your souls. (1 Peter 1:8–9)

We have an inheritance through the resurrection of Jesus
Christ that is imperishable, undefiled, and unfading. Christ
bore the wrath of God for our sins as our substitute and
gave us His honor as the firstborn son. Inheritance is not an
earthly wealth, which is subject to the destruction of age and
rust. It is eternal and imperishable.

Our adoption as sons occurs when we are baptized,
buried into Christ's death and raised to new life in Him. In
Him we become a new creation. The robe of death, our
inheritance from Adam, is cast aside in the waters of Holy
Baptism. In Baptism we receive what we have not deserved,
the robe of Christ's righteousness. Out of God's great love
for us, He bestows on us mercy and forgiveness. We are
prodigals whom the Father, seeing a long way off, has run
out to receive with joy. We are born again to a living hope, to
an inheritance that is imperishable.

Just as the Father now receives us with joy as sons, we
shout with joy for the undeserved gift that we have received.
"In this you rejoice, though now for a little while, if necessary, you have been grieved by various trials" (1 Peter 1:6).
Although we have received a great inheritance, while we
remain in the world, we are beset with various trials. These
trials are a result of sin. We struggle against the devil, the
world, and our own flesh daily. At times, the trials make
the living hope in Christ seem distant and dim. But the trials do not diminish the gift. In suffering we are joined to
the suffering of Jesus Christ, and the strength of God is
displayed. He has had mercy on us in our weakness and
continues to have mercy on us as we weakly struggle. Baptism is a life that is lived every day, and every day we are
reminded of our own inability to save ourselves. But the

promise made to us in Baptism is sure. It is imperishable, and it brings us joy.

Sorrow presses us at times in our lives, and the joy of our Baptism may not clearly be felt. We may not feel God near us. We may feel abandoned or alone. Sadness and emptiness may lead us to question our faith. If we really believed, would we not always feel happiness in our salvation? But we cannot forget what Paul calls an inexpressible joy. The joy of our salvation is greater than can be expressed in feelings, though sometimes our feelings do offer us a happy foretaste. The assurance of our salvation is not found in the expression of our feelings, but in the promise of God applied to us in Holy Baptism. The promise of God is irrevocable.

### Prayer

Thank the Lord and sing His praise; tell everyone what He has done. Let all who seek the Lord rejoice and proudly bear His name. He recalls His promises and leads His people forth in joy with shouts of thanksgiving. Alleluia. Alleluia. Amen. (*LSB*, p. 164)

~

## Thankfully Serving

When He had washed their feet and put on His outer garments and resumed His place, He said to them, "Do you understand what I have done to you? You call Me Teacher and Lord, and you are right, for so I am. If I then, your Lord and Teacher, have washed your feet, you also ought to wash one another's feet. For I have given you an example, that you also should do just as I have done to you." (John 13:12–15)

When our Savior joins Himself to us, our world is never the same again. Everything is changed. Jesus invades our personal space in the deluge of water as the Holy Spirit re-creates us from a sinner into a saint. When we rise out of the waters of Baptism, the Word Incarnate is now a lamp to our feet and a light to our path. We are not left scrambling to find the way to walk, but Jesus guides us by His words and works that reveal the truth that He came to serve us by washing dirty feet on the night on which He was betrayed. On that same night, He gave thanks over bread that is now His body broken in death and the cup of His blood. In remembrance of Him, we follow in Jesus' way as we give thanks by our works, serving one another on bended knee, demonstrating Christ's humbleness in our acts of mercy and charity.

Jesus enlivened us by His obedience unto death, even death on a cross, and His resurrection from the grave. In gratitude we joyfully follow Him. Jesus' obedient word and works become our thankful word and works as we retell the stories of His service to a world broken by sin and death. Our gracious Lord now gives us His work to do and His Word to say. Gratefully, we join Jesus in His service to the world, washing one another's feet as we embark together on the way in His Life.

### Prayer

We give You thanks, O God, that through the waters of Holy Baptism You re-created us to be Your children, bringing us out of darkness into light. Continue to nurture us with the body and blood of Your Son, Jesus Christ, our Lord, in whose name we pray. Amen.

## BAPTISMAL IDENTITY—PEACE

*For additional resources, see Section III, p. 182*
*For additional prayers, see Section IV, p. 232*

### Peace on Earth as It Is in Heaven

Glory to God in the highest, and on earth peace.
(Luke 2:14)

Peace in heaven and glory in the highest! (Luke 19:38)

At Jesus' birth, there is peace on earth. When He enters Jerusalem on Palm Sunday, there is peace in heaven. At

Jesus' birth and death, earth and heaven are joined together in peace. Jesus also said, "Do not think that I have come to bring peace to the earth. I have not come to bring peace, but a sword" (Matthew 10:34).

Which is it? Peace or a sword? From our human perspective, it looks more like a sword as we see families broken by divorce, nations divided over religious matters, people at odds with each other over how to govern our nation.

How about you? Are you at peace? Or do you feel divided in your family, in your marriage, at work, about your vocation, about your health, about your relationship with God?

In this life, peace on earth is fleeting. We have moments of peace, but sin has so infected our lives that we feel its effects more acutely than we experience the peace of the angels at Jesus' birth.

The peace Jesus brings to earth is the peace of heaven—a peace accomplished through a death more violent than any sword. Jesus' death brings a peace for you with God, though you may not feel it. Where Jesus is present, there is His heavenly peace where sin is forgiven, your enemies hold no claim on you, and your life is defined by His unending life of love. Christ is in you, and so is His peace that passes all understanding.

### Prayer

Lord God, heavenly Father, as we struggle here below with divisions among us, searching for peace among men, remind us daily of the peace of heaven purchased through the bloody death of Your Son, Jesus Christ, our Lord, who with You and the Holy Spirit, one God, now and forever. Amen.

~

## Peace in the Midst of Storms

You keep him in perfect peace whose mind is stayed on You, because he trusts in You. Trust in the LORD forever, for the LORD GOD is an everlasting rock.

(Isaiah 26:3–4)

Those who seek peace are in the middle of a storm. Strong winds pitch against us mightily, until we do not know which way to turn. Dashing waves threaten to wash over us—what if we are lost? Our chosen ways of escape may be blocked or impossible. More often, it is hard to tell what is the right thing to do or to think, the thick cloud of uncertainty hangs about us long beyond what we thought we could bear.

Our God is a God of miracles. The storm is not too great for Him. "And He awoke and rebuked the wind and said to the sea, 'Peace! Be still!' And the wind ceased, and there was a great calm" (Mark 4:39).

Often the real storm is one that ravages us within. Real peace comes not from calming the storm outside, but from calming the storm within. Only Jesus is able to give this peace. Otherwise, it would be peace only as the world gives.

Why are you restless and afraid? Do you not know that your Lord is in control? He has things well in hand. Be still. Do not try to make your own peace. Listen to the booming voice of His holiness: "Then the LORD answered Job out of the whirlwind and said: . . . 'Have you an arm like God, and can you thunder with a voice like His? . . . Then will I also acknowledge to you that your own right hand can save you'" (Job 40:6, 9, 14).

If you cannot save yourself or control the storm, what can you do? Stay your mind on Jesus. Seek Him where He may certainly be found: in His Word, in the baptismal water through which you were saved, and in His body and His blood. Hold fast to Jesus and to nothing else. This same Jesus, whose right hand saved you, has a promise for you more sure than the foundations of the world: He will keep you in perfect peace.

In this world, do you have trouble? Take heart. Jesus has already overcome the world. Fight the battle, knowing your Captain has secured the outcome. Let the waves wash over you as you joyfully stand on the everlasting, immovable

Rock. Nothing will wash you away. Put your head down and lean into the wind with courage; peace be with you. And when you grow weary, climb into His strong tower and have sweet rest. Fall asleep in the boat, leaning against your Lord.

*Prayer*

Lord Jesus, the stiller of storms, the voice in the whirlwind, speak to us Your words of peace and focus our minds on You. Give us strength, courage, and wisdom to endure the storms of life and to see in You the peace that passes all understanding; for You live and reign with the Father and the Holy Spirit, one God, now and forever. Amen.

# BAPTISMAL IDENTITY—THANKSGIVING

*For additional resources, see Section III, p. 185*
*For additional prayers, see Section IV, p. 233*

## Christ, the Greater Gift

All Your works shall give thanks to You, O LORD, and all Your saints shall bless You!" (Psalm 145:10)

What has Jesus really done for me? For what shall I give Him thanks?

It is no good to be polite to God. He knows us too well. We do not always feel like giving thanks, yet God calls us to give thanks in all things, especially when our needs are great and our pain acute. Then our thanksgiving is even sweeter, especially when the gift is just what we needed.

In the beginning, Jesus was the Word that spoke all things into existence. The joy we have when a new life enters the world is a dim reflection of the rejoicing all creation sang on its first day. You are His work! Your very existence sings Him praise. If you were silent, "the very stones would cry out" (Luke 19:40).

And there is yet a greater gift. He is the one who comes to you. Jesus takes what is ruined, rotten through and through, and He bleeds for you. His blood covers you; it flows from His cross, cleansing, healing, and redeeming you. It comes into your very body, creating a mystical union with Him. You are His saint! New and perfect, nothing keeps Him from you. You are His dearly beloved; He speaks tender words to you and holds you close.

Rejoice, O Saint! Breathe in the gift, and breathe out His thanksgiving. Declare that the only thing you need for all eternity, you already have. "I will run in the way of Your commandments when You enlarge my heart!" (Psalm 119:32).

## Prayer

Lord Jesus Christ, the giver of all good gifts, our thanksgiving overflows for the life You created in us and the new life we now have in You through Holy Baptism. Continue to shower us with Your gifts as we offer thanksgiving for our ongoing communion with You in Your body and blood; for You live and reign with the Father and the Holy Spirit, one God, now and forever. Amen.

~

# The Gift of Baptism

Having been buried with Him in baptism, in which you were also raised with Him through faith in the powerful working of God, who raised Him from the dead. (Colossians 2:12)

For most of us, Baptism is a distant memory. What we do now is hear the preaching of the Gospel, commune at the Lord's Table, and pray for Church and world. These things seem more immediate to our spiritual life. But we are also told to "remember our Baptism." What benefit does Baptism have for us today?

The gift of Baptism continues forever. Baptism buries you and raises you from the dead. Baptism is resurrection. Because you are baptized, you will never die again. You have already died, and you are already living eternally before God.

To be sure, your body will fall asleep. But God atoned

for your sins through the blood of Jesus Christ. The future time of cleansing is now—in your Baptism—where your sins are forgiven and you are joined with Christ forever. Our catechism tells us confidently that a new man daily rises "to live before God in righteousness and purity forever." Your new life continues each day, thanks to Jesus Christ, who was raised from the dead, and now has raised you from the death of your sins. So you live free from guilt, free in forgiveness, life, blessedness, and salvation.

### Prayer

Lord God, every day our bodies are wasting away. Death is our final destiny. Yet Your Son, Jesus Christ, conquered death by His death, and in His resurrection, He shows us what we are now in Baptism and what we will one day be in the resurrection of all flesh. We give You thanks for this new life and pray that You help us daily to die and rise with Jesus Christ, our Lord, in whose name we pray. Amen.

~

## The House of the Lord

O You who hear prayer, to You shall all flesh come. When iniquities prevail against me, You atone for our transgressions. Blessed is the one You choose and bring near, to dwell in Your courts! We shall be satisfied with the goodness of Your house, the holiness of Your temple! (Psalm 65:2–4)

Our Lord came in the flesh to atone for our transgressions, to cover and forgive our sins. In His flesh He paid our debts and in His flesh He offers new life. He speaks His Word and it is so. He washes us clean in the waters of Baptism and gives us new life and fresh starts! He listens to our prayers. We are blessed indeed!

We are welcomed into His house when dangers come and temptations claim us. His pastors restore us by Holy Absolution, on His authority, by His command. Washed in His water, we listen and are fed at His Table.

We are welcomed to rejoice and give thanks! He opens His home to everyone. He freely offers clothes of righteousness and entrance into His family. His abundant goodness satisfies.

Jesus is the door to the Father's house. He strengthens us through His Word. He prepares a place for us and will welcome us into the New Jerusalem forever. Blessed are those who dwell in His courts. All flesh will come to Him and behold His holiness. No one is like our Lord!

### Prayer

Lord Jesus Christ, Your house of worship is where You dwell with Your gifts of forgiveness, life, and salvation. Lead us by Your voice to the heavenly Jerusalem where, with bodies washed clean by Your blood, we might inherit the life You promised us in the waters of Holy Baptism; for You live and reign with the Father and the Holy Spirit, one God, now and forever. Amen.

## Baptismal Identity—Trust in God

*For additional resources, see Section III, p. 188*
*For additional prayers, see Section IV, p. 233*

### Steadfast Love

Behold, the eye of the LORD is on those who fear Him,
on those who hope in His steadfast love.

(Psalm 33:18)

Rely on the Lord, for He provides! He is constant and caring. His steadfast love is as bound to us as His flesh was bound to the cross. His love is active and conquering, giving us life, hope, and healing. His mercy, applied by Word and water, flows to blot out each transgression. Baptized into Him, His death fights the very death and darkness of our own flesh.

What is our "fear of the Lord?" We are awed by Him, by His stature, and by His mercy! We praise and respect Him for being beyond our control and comprehension!

What is our hope? Our hope is Jesus Christ, who restores us to the heavenly Father, whose eyes are now turned to us! His Word works wonders, and He creates good out of every situation. He prevents our labors from being in vain.

The Lord's goodness endures forever; His mercies never end. He is "majestic in holiness, awesome in glorious deeds, doing wonders" (Exodus 15:11). The Lord rides "victoriously for the cause of truth and meekness and righteousness" (Psalm 45:4). He prepares a crown of life for each of us and gives us perfect hope in His perfect Son. We are secure in His hand, and our needs are always before Him.

### Prayer

Lord Jesus, You are our only Hope. Give us faith to trust You in all things; grant us a healthy fear to worship You in holiness, and shower us with Your mercy in all our sufferings. For with the Father and the Holy Spirit, Your goodness continues to grace our lives. Amen.

～

## Suffering with Jesus

But the one who endures to the end will be saved.
(Matthew 24:13)

Jesus spoke these words to His disciples during Holy Week. It would not be long after that He would make His way to Gethsemane, then on to the cross. Although His disciples were looking for signs of the end of the world, Jesus was actually describing the true end of time, when the cosmos would be shaken and creation would be made new through His bitter suffering and death and glorious resurrection on the eighth day. Therefore, having set His face to the cross (Luke 9:51), and seeing the suffering and persecution that would come His way, Jesus assured His disciples that He would endure, and they would as well.

Although you are not facing Roman soldiers ready to take your life, you know all too well that the life of a baptized Christian is not always easy or enjoyable. There is suffering and persecution to be sure. However, joy comes in knowing that you do not have to endure alone but that when you suffer, you are joined to the suffering of Jesus. This is the same Jesus who endured to the end of His life and has promised to endure with us to the end of the age.

You are a baptized child of God. You have been incorporated into the body of Jesus. What Christ does, you now do in Him. He endured to the end and was raised to immortality. In Christ, you will most certainly do the same.

### Prayer

O Lord, by Your bountiful goodness release us from the bonds of our sins, which by reason of our weakness we have brought upon ourselves, that we may stand firm until the day of our Lord Jesus Christ, who lives and reigns with You and the Holy Spirit, one God, now and forever. (*LSB Altar Book*, p. 741)

~

## Then and Now

And He who was seated on the throne said, "Behold, I am making all things new." Also He said, "Write this down, for these words are trustworthy and true." And He said to me, "It is done! I am the Alpha and the Omega, the beginning and the end."

(Revelation 21:5–6)

We work hard in high school to earn good grades so we can get into the right college, then we buckle down for another four years to land the right job. Next, we pound the pavement, properly positioning ourselves to meet the right people to help us move up the company ladder. Finally, we marry the right man or woman and plan a life together that perpetuates the same life for our children. If life were that simple, allowing us to sit down and plot out our course, we might never place our life in God's hands. We might actually believe the false idea that if we do what is right and plan accordingly, we can trust in a life created in our image.

However, today Jesus Christ says this to us, "Behold, I am making all things new." The small verb "I am" puts all creative efforts for life not in our hands but in the hands of Jesus. Notice Jesus "is" making, not "was" making. He is in the thick of things, making all things new right now. When we see ourselves falling apart, Christ is putting us back together. Jesus is taking our old ways of trusting ourselves and making new ways of ever trusting in Him. Jesus is not only transforming our old self into a new self, but He is also bringing to us in the present what lies in the future. Jesus is encompassing our entire life in order for us to see that the end can be seen now.

Just in case we are not sure what Jesus means, He has John write it down. In a sense He is making sure that we understand this is trustworthy and true. It is not simply a truth, it is how we comprehend and interpret reality, and so it is the Truth. This is the way it is for us, and because this is the way things are, we can wholeheartedly trust in Jesus Christ. When Jesus says, "I am the Alpha and Omega, the beginning and the end," He is wrapping Himself around the world to assure us that He is making all things new for us.

Jesus is working in very personal terms here. He is making you new. He is redeeming you. He is calling you and enlightening you with His gifts. There is no room for Jesus to be out of your life. He is creating and sustaining you through the falling apart times. His hands are on you, washing you with water from the spring of life. There is no worry with Jesus, because His gift is without payment. He had His eye on you before cost was ever involved. Jesus paid that debt already; from His perspective it is finished, and the completion of our life is in Him.

### Prayer

Lord Jesus, through Your death You have made all things new, and through the waters of Holy Baptism You joined us to Yourself in the new creation. Continue to make us new by the truth of Your Word and the power of Your Spirit, that we may be enabled to serve You and our neighbor; for You live and reign with the Father and the Holy Spirit, one God, now and forever. Amen.

## Childbirth—During Pregnancy

### Days Prepared for You

You formed my inward parts; You knitted me together in my mother's womb. I praise You, for I am fearfully and wonderfully made. Wonderful are Your works; my soul knows it very well. My frame was not hidden from You, when I was being made in secret, intricately woven in the depths of the earth. Your eyes saw my unformed substance; in Your book were written, every one of them, the days that were formed for me, when as yet there were none of them.

(Psalm 139:13–16)

The Lord formed you even as He forms your child. He knit you even as your child is knit within you, given fingers and toes, eyes and ears—every precious member and sense.

Praise the Lord, for you are fearfully and wonderfully made. He takes care of you and richly and daily provides you with all that you need to support this body and life. He speaks to you through His Word, listens to you, feeds and nourishes you.

Jesus is the source of your life. He triumphed over sin and conquered death for you. He gives hope, compassion, and life. The devil, doubts, and even trouble and disaster may come, but be patient and wait for the Lord. Even when the devil and the world plague you, your needs are never hidden from your heavenly Father. His eyes saw you before your substance was formed, and He sees you now. Each of the days prepared for you has been recorded in God's book of life. And the Lord guards the day and keeps you in His care.

Your child grows ears to hear the Lord. Your child grows fingers, hands, and arms to reach for Jesus, who takes little infants into His arms. You and your child together hear the Word of the Lord, which speaks life and faith into each of you. His message comes to the ears of mother and child to make a child leap within the womb in recognition of Jesus, our Savior. Trust in the promise of your Baptism, which seals you with the Father forever.

The Lord's works are wonderful! He creates life through His servants and prepares eternity for all who believe. His message penetrates the womb and works its own hearing.

### Prayer

Heavenly Father, You created the world and re-created Your children through Holy Baptism. Guard and preserve the work of Your hand. Lord Jesus Christ, You invited infants to come to You and held children in Your arms. Grant this child health and long life to grow in Your Church and in Your service. Holy Spirit, You are the Lord and Giver of life. Speak through Your prophets and send Your Word to strengthen mother and child. Even as You have already redeemed the world, establish in this child certain faith and salvation in Jesus Christ to the praise and glory of Your holy name. Amen.

## CHILDBIRTH—BEFORE CHILDBIRTH

*For additional prayers, see Section IV, p. 235*

### Blessed Be the Fruit of Your Womb

In those days Mary arose and went with haste into the hill country, to a town in Judah, and she entered the house of Zechariah and greeted Elizabeth. And when Elizabeth heard the greeting of Mary, the baby leaped in her womb. And Elizabeth was filled with the Holy Spirit, and she exclaimed with a loud cry, "Blessed are you among women, and blessed is the fruit of your womb! And why is this granted to me that the mother of my Lord should come to me? For behold, when the sound of your greeting came to my ears, the baby in my womb leaped for joy. And blessed is she who believed that there would be a fulfillment of what was spoken to her from the Lord." (Luke 1:39–45)

When God created man and woman, He blessed them and gave them the command to be fruitful and multiply. Thus humans were to fill the world, have dominion over every living thing, and lovingly tend the earth and its creatures. But everything went awry when Adam and Eve sinned. Creation turned against human beings and fought their efforts to subdue and tend it. Pain, illness, and death accompanied the multiplication of the human race. Yet despite the curse of sin, the first blessing of God to man stood firm. The Lord continued to bless humanity through the fruit of the woman's womb.

From creation, God has been intimately connected to the unborn child. "For You formed my inward parts; You knitted me together in my mother's womb. I praise You, for I am fearfully and wonderfully made. Wonderful are Your works; my soul knows it very well" (Psalm 139:13–14). Creation is a wonderful work of God, and it continues to be expressed in the formation of a child.

The fullness of creation is found in God's only Son. God knit together Jesus in the womb of a lowly handmaiden, and by this act of creating again out of nothing, He reconciled to Himself a world dead in sin. God made Himself present in a world that had rejected Him. His presence produced faith, even in those yet to be born. John the Baptist leapt for joy in his mother's womb at the voice of Mary, the mother of his Savior. Elizabeth responds with a blessing to Mary and to the fruit of her womb. The blessing of God to Adam and Eve became a curse by the corruption of sin. Jesus Christ is a blessing specifically because He became a curse for the destruction of sin. His life, death, and resurrection are a restoration of the first blessing of God on the day of man's creation.

On the day of our Baptism, we are knit anew in the womb of our mother, the Church, and the fruit of this womb is blessed. Expectant mothers are a picture of the new creation, a sign of God's promise to continue to multiply His people. This promise is for us and for our children. God abides with the unborn child in the womb, even as Jesus Christ once dwelt in His mother's womb. And just as John the Baptist, the child leaps for joy at the sound of the Savior's voice.

### Prayer

Gracious Father in heaven, You have reconciled the world to Yourself through the birth of a little Child. We ask that You keep this mother and child safely in Your care. Blessed be this woman and blessed be the fruit of her womb through Your Son, Jesus Christ, our Lord. Amen.

## CHILDBIRTH—FOLLOWING CHILDBIRTH

*For additional prayers, see Section IV, p. 235*

### Caring for the Little Children

He will tend His flock like a shepherd; He will gather the lambs in His arms; He will carry them in His bosom, and gently lead those that are with young.

(Isaiah 40:11)

Behold this tiny, precious new life. "Make a joyful noise to the LORD, all the earth! . . . It is He who made us, and we are His" (Psalm 100:1, 3).

As parents you are blessed to care for this tiny person who has come to be through you. Over the next days and weeks, you will experience a small taste of the tenderness your Lord has toward you; how He is moved to action by your dependence on Him and to what lengths He goes for you; how deep His passion runs. At the thought of losing you for all eternity, Jesus came into your suffering to bear all sin on the cross and into the grave. Through Him your life is spared. This is the manner of love you have received, that you "should be called children of God" (1 John 3:1).

The vulnerability and need of this infant is a fitting picture of how our heavenly Father sees us. Active and capable in the world, we may forget that we are unable to provide for ourselves, to feed and nourish our faith, to be cleansed of our sins, even to survive eternally apart from the One who saves us every day and does all these things on our behalf.

The Baptism of a child is the Lord Himself placing His name upon the child through the means of water and the Word. "Truly, I say to you, unless you turn and become like children, you will never enter the kingdom of heaven" (Matthew 18:3). A child receives what is given in love. It is not the lambs who choose the Lord, but the Lord who gathers the lambs in His arms and carries them in His bosom. We are saved by His works, not ours.

The Father also gathered the infant Lamb of God in His arms through the arms of Jesus' earthly parents. To Joseph, God gave counsel, guidance, and strength to provide for and protect the baby. To Mary, God gave the hope of what the child would be and accomplish. She believed in her Lord with a faith that is an enduring example to the Church.

As Mary treasured Jesus in her heart, as Joseph took courageous action to protect Him, so has your child been placed into your loving care. God has ordained your vocations as mother and father, and He will equip you to carry them out.

So, then, give this little one all good things, just as your heavenly Father has done for you. Gather this child as a mother hen gathers her chicks, just as Jesus gathers you. Pray for this child, that (*he or she*) might not turn from the Holy Spirit given in Baptism, the same Spirit who is faithful to strengthen and nourish faith. And as parents, receive your heavenly Father's promise: He will gently lead those who are with young.

*Prayer*

Heavenly Father, grant to those whom You have blessed with the joy and care of children calm strength and patient wisdom to bring them up in Your faith, teaching them to love what is just and true and good, after the example of Your Son, our Savior, Jesus Christ. Amen.

## CHILDBIRTH—AT A PREMATURE BIRTH

### Jesus Loves Children

Now they were bringing even infants to Him that He might touch them. And when the disciples saw it, they rebuked them. But Jesus called them to Him, saying, "Let the children come to Me, and do not hinder them, for to such belongs the kingdom of God. Truly, I say to you, whoever does not receive the kingdom of God like a child shall not enter it." (Luke 18:15–17)

Jesus loves children. He loves them so much that even when the disciples tried to hold them back, Jesus called for their release that they might come to Him to receive His hallowed touch. Yet we often think of these "children" as toddlers or adolescents who, like their parents, have been caught up in the excitement of Jesus' earthly ministry, and seeing their parents flocking to Jesus, these children naturally join in. However, the word that St. Luke uses to describe those being brought to Jesus is the word for "infants" and can even be used for those yet unborn. Thus people were bringing newborn babes, or those still in the womb, to receive the touch of Christ.

Jesus longs to touch your own dear child, no matter how young and helpless. As the psalmist said, so says your child, "On You was I cast from my birth, and from my mother's womb You have been my God" (Psalm 22:10). Your child belongs to God, having been called and nourished through Word, touch, body, and blood.

Everything that went into your ears, your mouth, and your skin also went into your child. What you heard, (*he or she*) heard. What you ate, (*he or she*) ate. What you felt, (*he or she*) felt. Moreover, while carrying your child in the womb, you were in church, receiving the good gifts of Christ. Thankfully, your child received what you received. Christ's good gifts were not for you alone. As Christ spoke the Word of absolution, of life, of new creation to you through your pastor, He also spoke to your child. As Christ placed His hands on your head through your pastor praying for you and blessing you, He also touched your child. And as Christ delivered to you by the hands of your pastor His holy body and precious blood, the medicine of immortality, He also delivered this sacred meal to your child. Why? Because as Jesus said, the kingdom of God belongs to your child, and those in the kingdom are blessed to receive the gifts of Christ.

No matter what the future may bring, you can be confident that Christ has spoken to your child, touched your child, and fed your child with the food of heaven, even in the womb. Although you have given birth sooner than expected, Jesus is faithful. He continues to care for both you and your child. He loves your child. And as we know from St. Paul, nothing in all of creation, not even a premature birth, will ever be able to "separate us from the love of God in Christ Jesus our Lord" (Romans 8:39).

## Prayer

Lord Jesus, You touched the little children as a sign of Your love for them. Touch this child with Your nurturing presence that during these uncertain days, (*he or she*) may grow into Your likeness and receive the gifts You have promised to all those who love You; for You live and reign with the Father and the Holy Spirit, one God, now and forever. Amen.

## CHILDBIRTH—FOR STILLBORN, DEATH SHORTLY AFTER BIRTH, OR MISCARRIAGE

*For additional prayers, see Section IV, p. 236*

### Your Child Is with the Lord

[David] said, "While the child was still alive, I fasted and wept, for I said, 'Who knows whether the LORD will be gracious to me, that the child may live?' But now he is dead. Why should I fast? Can I bring him back again? I shall go to him, but he will not return to me." (2 Samuel 12:22–23)

It seems the most terrible of injustices that a baby, barely knit together in the womb, should die. For those who have lived to 70 or more, we say, "At least she lived to a good old age." Even when young people die, we have memories of the games they played or the work they did. We knew them as individuals. Why does God take the helpless and leave those who are practiced in their sin? Why does He let parents outlive children?

We should know that your baby is not in pain or suffering. We may share David's hope that his uncircumcised newborn infant is with the Lord (2 Samuel 12:23). We, like David, know that God is a God of mercy and loving-kindness. He binds us to Baptism as the means of grace appropriate for bringing faith and forgiveness to infants, but God may have a method that He does not reveal to us whereby He works faith in infants of the faithful who for some reason could not be baptized. Because we do not know, we should not neglect baptizing infants. God's will is always for the best, and we do know that it is the will of our Savior, Jesus, to receive even infants (Luke 18:15).

Indeed, your baby is not suffering. Could there be anything better for your child than to be knit together according to the Lord's handiwork and then to be received into His eternal kingdom? We on this earth have months or years of toil and hardship yet to endure, and we see Jesus only by faith. We may hope your child sees Him now, face-to-face, that your child is comforted now, even if we are not fully.

Our Lord Jesus Christ does remain with us to comfort us in our sorrow. He was conceived and knit together in Mary's womb, born as an infant to redeem even infants, and suffered on the cross to receive into Himself the suffering of all people. He receives your sorrow now and unites you to Himself—and, we may presume, to your baby—when you gather with all the company of heaven in the worship of the Church and sing "Holy, Holy, Holy" and eat and drink His body and blood. Our Lord is with you even as He prepares a place for you and promises you, "Let the little children come to Me and do not hinder them, for to such belongs the kingdom of heaven" (Matthew 19:14).

## Prayer

Almighty God, by the death of Your Son Jesus Christ You destroyed death and redeemed and saved Your little ones. By His bodily resurrection You brought life and immortality to light so that all who die in Him abide in peace and hope. Receive our thanks for the victory over death and the grave that He won for us. Keep us in everlasting communion with all who wait for Him on earth and with all in heaven who are with Him, for He is the resurrection and the life, even Jesus Christ, our Lord. Amen. (*LSB Agenda*, p. 139)

## BEFORE SURGERY

*For additional prayers, see Section IV, p. 236*

### Medicinal Side

Since it was the day of Preparation, and so that the bodies would not remain on the cross on the Sabbath (for that Sabbath was a high day), the Jews asked Pilate that their legs might be broken and that they might be taken away. So the soldiers came and broke the legs of the first, and of the other who had been crucified with Him. But when they came to Jesus and saw that He was already dead, they did not break His legs. But one of the soldiers pierced His side with a spear, and at once there came out blood and water.

(John 19:31–34)

As Jesus hung lifeless on the cross, He was preparing for His Sabbath rest in the tomb and His victorious resurrection from the grave on the eighth day. His battle was done. You are preparing as well, and before surgery it is natural to have anxiety, even fear. Put your trust in someone else's hands. Your doctors will work to bring you health and healing. However, remember that you have already received better care than any earthly doctor could give.

Jesus Christ is the great physician of body and soul who will work through your doctors and nurses and medicines to bring physical healing. This same Jesus allowed the soldier to pierce His side that He might pour out the fountains of life for you. His holy water washes you in Baptism, and His holy blood feeds you at His altar. Even amid your trial and tribulation, look to Christ. See His pierced side and behold the medicine of immortality. You are healed, both now and forever.

### Prayer

Lord God, heavenly Father, may the water and the blood flowing from Jesus' side on the cross that healed the whole creation now heal this, Your loved one, in both body and soul; through Jesus Christ, our Lord. Amen.

$\sim$

## Now Is the Time for Living

Now He is not God of the dead, but of the living, for all live to Him. (Luke 20:38)

Our Lord showed us that He is with us in our suffering and our brokenness. As you are about to enter surgery, know that the Lord is with you even in a dark moment such as this. Now is the time of living for Jesus, for you and all believers, because Jesus has transformed you by His resurrection. You were re-created in the womb of Baptism where you were resurrected from the death of the old Adam. You are already part of the resurrection community, so you do not need to fear what is before you. The Lord is your light and salvation. Whom shall you fear (Psalm 27:1)?

In the death of Jesus Christ you conquered by His loss, but the Lord goes one better, for His victory is now yours too. As you enter the operating room, know that the heavenly community is with you as it is when you sing the Sanctus during the Divine Service—"Holy, Holy, Holy Lord, God of power and might." You are part of that community, for you have communion with Jesus, who is not a God of the dead but of the living. As His child, you are born again to live to Him. There is no fear for you because Jesus Christ, who is the same then as now, has already rescued you out of every darkness, and He goes with you now. Blessed be the name of the Lord!

### Prayer

Living God, Your almighty power is made known chiefly in showing mercy and pity. Grant us the fullness of Your grace to lay hold of Your promises and live forever in Your presence; through Jesus Christ, Your Son, our Lord. Amen. (*LSB Altar Book*, p. 835)

## AFTER SURGERY

### The Revealing Presence of God

But for me it is good to be near God; I have made the Lord GOD my refuge, that I may tell of all Your works.
(Psalm 73:28)

In God's sanctuary, His promises ring true for us. He is present for us with His gifts of forgiveness, salvation, and eternal life. In the presence of God, our eyes and minds are transformed to see that to be near God is to be in good health, and this healing always serves a greater purpose.

Your body is no longer yours, for it has been bought with a price; it now belongs to Jesus Christ. You are part of Christ's body and have a refuge there with Him where everything serves the purpose of communion with Him and all the company of heaven. This fellowship with Him is better than health or wealth, for Jesus Christ guided you through surgery so that you will proclaim His good works, and His good work is you!

Jesus Christ is the source of all healing because whether your flesh fades or your heart hurts, God is your refuge. He is strong and His portion never fails. You are always near God, and His goodness will continue to flow to you, and pure joy will burst forth in songs and stories of His wonderful works. Although you may be suffering now and your recovery may be long, God will never leave you nor forsake you in life or death, sickness or health, because to be near the Lord is to be full of His good health. Blessed be the name of Jesus.

### Prayer

Lord Jesus, in this time of recovery from surgery, visit Your servant with Your nurturing and healing presence, that (*his or her*) time of recovery may be quick and complete, and (*he or she*) may return to (*his or her*) life whole and healed; for You live and reign with the Father and the Holy Spirit, now and forever. Amen.

$\sim$

## The Lord Renews Your Strength

> Even youths shall faint and be weary, and young men shall fall exhausted; but they who wait for the LORD shall renew their strength. (Isaiah 40:30–31).

In this surgery, you have received the healing of God through the doctor. Yet this surgery, as much of a blessing as it is, is not permanent. One day again you will faint and be weary and fall exhausted. As our text states, even the young man wears out. So it is not our physical strength in which we hope, or the doctors who restored this strength, but in the Lord Himself. Our Lord Jesus Christ calls us to wait for Him, whether healthy or sick.

Jesus has overcome our problems by giving in to the physical suffering of this world. As a young man He became faint and weary; He finally fell exhausted under the scourge of the Romans and the weight of the cross that He bore to Calvary. His Father did not answer His prayers by healing His body but left Him to die. Jesus suffered the breaking of His own body so that our broken bodies would be restored and resurrected.

Jesus had done nothing to deserve His death, so God raised Him from the dead and restored His body. Although you may feel tired and nauseated and in pain, you now wait on your resurrected Lord and pray that He will renew your strength. We give thanks that He has delivered you through this surgery and praise Him that He has joined you to Himself. Your own body, the one that struggled through surgery, will be raised from the dead to be with Christ forever, never to undergo surgery again, never to die again.

*Prayer*

Lord Jesus Christ, in Your life among us You felt faint and weary, and in the Garden of Gethsemane You prayed for strength. As we wait for healing in this time after surgery, we also pray for renewed strength, that You might restore health and wholeness in this time; for You live and reign with the Father and the Holy Spirit, one God, now and forever. Amen.

## Recovery from Sickness

*For additional resources, see Section III, p. 191*
*For additional prayers, see Section IV, p. 237*

### The Healing Touch of Jesus

And [Jesus] said to her, "Daughter, your faith has made you well; go in peace, and be healed of your disease." (Mark 5:34)

Many people ask why God does not heal everyone, especially when we pray for healing. But Jesus shows us true healing.

On His way to lay hands on Jairus's daughter and heal her, a woman with a flow of blood, who had spent all her money on doctors to be healed, touched the tassel of Jesus' cloak and was healed. Jesus perceived the power coming out of Him and asked, "Who touched Me?"

The power of Jesus, the Creator, brings healing and wholeness to a creation broken by sickness and sin. Jairus's daughter, age 12, was about to reach the fullness of what it meant to be a woman when she died. By raising her from the dead, Jesus gave her the life God intended for her. The woman with the flow of blood had been an outcast for twelve years. By healing her, Jesus restored her to life by cleansing her and making her whole and acceptable to the community of Israel. Jesus acted, the woman believed, and she had peace with God and man.

Jesus acted on the cross where He took upon Himself your diseases and made you and all creation well. Then in Baptism, He did for you what He did for Jairus's daughter and the woman—He healed you eternally by joining you to Himself and giving you the life God intended for you. Go in peace, and be healed of your disease.

### Prayer

Heavenly Father, during His earthly ministry Your Son Jesus healed the sick and raised the dead. By the healing medicine of the Word and Sacraments pour into our hearts such love toward You that we may live eternally; through Jesus Christ, our Lord. Amen. (*LSB Altar Book*, p. 718)

~

## Jesus Is the Cure for All Our Diseases

Bless the LORD, O my soul, and forget not all His benefits, who forgives all your iniquity, who heals all your diseases, who redeems your life from the pit, who crowns you with steadfast love and mercy, who satisfies you with good so that your youth is renewed like the eagle's. (Psalm 103:2–5)

Praise the Lord! It was His will and good pleasure to answer prayer, as He always does, and to make you well. Praise Him for the hands of others who cared for you in your distress. Praise Him for the healing and renewal He has graciously brought.

This healing of the earthly body gives a sense of the joy we have in our recovery from the sickness of sin. Apart from Christ, all is uncertain regarding our condition. We long for the hope and the assurance of eternal wellness. We feel the weight and the pain of the disease, the original sin that infects us, and long for relief. We hang on to every word of Jesus, the great Physician of body and soul.

And there is good news! Jesus is the cure. He became sick in your place, bore your burdens to the grave, and left them there. It happened in you when you were baptized into His death, the water washing sin away, the darkness fleeing at the name of the Father, Son, and Holy Spirit. And just as Christ was raised, you came out of the water with a new life in which sin has no place.

In this life, we still suffer the effects of sin, until sickness is banished forever. At the same time, you are the saint, set free as you are now, clean and well, sitting up in bed and rejoicing in the new day He has won for you.

## Prayer

Lord God, You sent Your Son to heal the creation of its sickness and its sin. We give You thanks that through His blood You have healed us of the eternal consequences of our sins, and we rejoice in the physical healing of this, Your servant, for whom we now pray; through Jesus Christ, our Lord. Amen.

## MINISTRY TO A SICK PERSON

*For additional resources, see Section III, p. 195*
*For additional prayers, see Section IV, p. 238*

### The Good News of Jesus' Healing Blood

Now when the sun was setting, all those who had any who were sick with various diseases brought them to Him, and He laid His hands on every one of them and healed them. . . . He said to them, "I must preach the good news of the kingdom of God to the other towns as well; for I was sent for this purpose."

(Luke 4:40, 43)

Jesus is the king of the kingdom of God. His coronation was on a cross with a crown of thorns, where His blood cleansed all creation from its sin and its sickness. This is the good news Jesus came to preach—that in Him all creation is set free from the virus of sin and the sickness it brings.

You have been set free from all sin and sickness in the waters of your Baptism. The blood of Jesus cleansed you as you were joined to Him and received from Him a life that never ends. In your sickness, He is coming to you with the medicine of immortality—His holy, healing Word that is nothing but good news about His cross and resurrection that sets you free.

He is with you now, laying His hands on you through His words, healing you of the eternal consequences of sin and sickness. We pray for your healing, if it is the Lord's will, even as we know now that you are healed and whole through the refreshing waters of the font.

### Prayer

Almighty God, You know we live in the midst of so many dangers that in our frailty we cannot stand upright. Grant strength and protection to support us in all dangers and carry us through all temptations; through Jesus Christ, Your Son, our Lord. Amen. (*LSB Altar Book*, p. 761)

## In the Midst

Yet You, O LORD, are in the midst of us, and we are called by Your name; do not leave us.

(Jeremiah 14:9b)

The Lord breathed life into Adam. The Lord walked in the Garden of Eden and spoke with Adam. Now the Lord is especially present in His house. He walks with us and speaks to us by His Word. He fulfills all His promises. He touches us through the water of Baptism and through the bread and wine of Communion. He gives us His Spirit and He gives us Himself.

He gave us His name in our Baptism and calls us His own. He washes us clean and tends to our needs, sending us His servants into all areas of our life.

The Lord does not leave His people. Jesus visited the feverish, the bleeding, the broken, the leprous. He comes for the suffering, the poor, and the conflicted. He took on flesh to face all that we face. He took on flesh to give us a new, safe world and a life with Him without sickness, fear, or sadness.

The Lord is with us, in our midst. We are His and He is ours. He gave us His name, and we can cry to Him at any sign of trouble. He hears us and does not leave us. He comes to us in His resurrected life, by His Spirit, through His Word and Holy Supper.

### Prayer

Lord Jesus, You promised Your disciples that You would never leave them or forsake them, that You would be with them always, even to the end of the age. Dwell in our midst by Your grace, that in our sufferings You would continue to uphold us by Your presence; for You live and reign with the Father and the Holy Spirit, one God, now and forever. Amen.

~

## On the Palms of My Hands

Can a woman forget her nursing child, that she should have no compassion on the son of her womb?

> Even these may forget, yet I will not forget you. Behold, I have engraved you on the palms of My hands. (Isaiah 49:15–16a)

Throughout our life, people may disappoint us, even our own fathers, even our own mothers. This is the nature of our humanity—we are sinners who sometimes hurt or neglect even those closest to us, those whom we love. Isaiah acknowledges that this neglect is present in a sinful world.

God our Father never forgets His children. In illness, we are weak and broken. Our families and friends may seem far from helping. We may even feel as though our own bodies have forsaken us. Those closest to us may forget, yet God will not forget His compassion. Jesus Christ came into a fallen creation to restore it to wholeness. He took sin, illness, and death upon Himself and defeated it on the cross. He does not forget His compassion for us. We are as close to Him as His own hands. Although we still experience illness and bodily death, we can rest in the promise that Christ does not forget us. Behold, with nails He has engraved us on the palms of His hands.

Jesus has given us a community of saints who are His hands and His feet. Through them, He embraces us. Through the prayers of the Church our needs and wants are never forgotten. And through our communion with Christ in His Church, in His very body and blood, we are joined to the company of saints who have all been engraved on the palms of His hands.

### Prayer

Lord God, heavenly Father, You hold the whole world in Your hands, bloodied by His act of restoring creation. Remember this, Your servant, broken by sickness and in need of Your healing. In Your compassion, carry (*him or her*) in these same hands to health and restoration; through Jesus Christ, our Lord. Amen.

## Help from the Lord

I lift up my eyes to the hills. From where does my help come? My help comes from the LORD, who made heaven and earth. . . . The LORD will keep you from all evil; He will keep your life. The LORD will keep your going out and your coming in from this time forth and forevermore. (Psalm 121:1–2, 7–8)

Israel looked to the hills, the place of strength, for deliverance. In times of battle they watched for strong horses and mighty men to ride down from the hills to rescue them.

In sickness, you are in need of deliverance. From where does your help come?

We are thankful for doctors and nurses and for the help of the medicines they bring. We pray for them and know that the Lord works through them as instruments of His healing. We rest on the support of family and friends. The Lord has given them to us to point us to the One who loves us perfectly, our Deliverer and our confidence.

In these long moments of waiting, spend time with the One who keeps you. Know the Lord through His Word. Receive Him in His body and blood. Tell Him your troubles. Know that the source of your help is an eternal wellspring, steady and unfailing. Also speak to a trusted friend, or your pastor or deaconess, to help give you clarity and hope and to pray for you during this difficult time.

It was Jesus who came down from the hills, riding on the lowly foal of a donkey, who came to rescue, to heal, and to save you. He has secured your safety, now and for eternity. He will keep your life. He does all things well.

### Prayer

Lord Jesus, You came down from heaven to redeem a lost and fallen world. Come down to us now and give us help in this time of need; for You live and reign with the Father and the Holy Spirit, now and forever. Amen.

## Never Alone

My God, my God, why have You forsaken me? Why are You so far from saving me, from the words of my groaning? O my God, I cry by day, but You do not answer, and by night, but I find no rest.

(Psalm 22:1–2)

Tradition says that as Jesus hung on the cross He prayed all the Psalms. The one that is most often associated with Jesus' crucifixion is Psalm 22. Jesus prayed these words because He exemplified what it meant to suffer. Not only was He tortured and crucified, but He was suffering physically while bearing the sin of the whole world. However, suffering did not have the final say; it is not the end result. As Jesus Himself declared to those downtrodden Emmaus disciples, "Was it not necessary that the Christ should suffer these things and enter into His glory?" (Luke 24:26). Suffering must come before glory, both for Christ and for you.

Being a part of the Body of Christ through Holy Baptism, you are not your own. You belong to Christ. You reside in His body. Now, in your own suffering, you are joined to the suffering of Christ. Like Him, your end will not be your suffering, but the glory of eternal life. Moreover, since Christ has done His part, God will not forsake you. He is not far from saving you. He does indeed answer you. In Christ, you are accompanied now as you suffer, and at the appointed time, you will be delivered into everlasting glory.

### Prayer

Lord Jesus, in Your suffering You showed us the way to everlasting life. In our suffering, show us Your mercy and Your healing, and point us to that final healing where we will join You and the Father with the Holy Spirit, now and forever. Amen.

# In Christ Is Refuge

He will cover you with His pinions . . . . (Psalm 91:4a)

Stone, concrete, and steel are the materials of most strong shelters, but the Christian's shelter is made of wood, water, and wings. Building your fortress out of the wood of the cross, hiding yourself in Christ with the waters of Holy Baptism, and living in the shadow of the wings of Him who stretched out His arms for you, God made it so there is no place for the enemy to attack you. The vile viper may assault you with trials and temptations, but with Jesus Christ as your refuge and strength, ten thousand demons may fall at your side.

Right now, sickness may assail you, and sickness is what you are fighting against. Our Lord is with you in this fight. And He is with you in the great battle against the source of all sickness: "For we do not wrestle against flesh and blood, but against the rulers, against the authorities, against the cosmic powers over this present darkness, against the spiritual forces of evil in the heavenly places" (Ephesians 6:12).

Resting in the shadows of the crucifixion, Jesus will protect you from the noonday devil lurking in the scorching heat of the desert life of temptations. For it is in the desert where Jesus is battling for you against Satan. The demons will try to attack you whether there be terror by night or arrows or evil or plague or lions or even deadly disease. They are sent by Satan to cause you to doubt God's continuing care. Satan tried to use this psalm against Jesus to tempt Him to deny God's closeness in the midst of suffering. Now you use it as a means to hold fast to the promises of God—that the Father will deliver, protect, answer, rescue, honor, and resurrect you for Christ's sake as a loving Father does His child.

The desert would not be the last time Jesus would battle the slithering serpent, for His blood began spilling in the Garden of Gethsemane and continued to spill on the cross in His battle against the evil one. The garden, not the desert, was the right time for the angels to come and beat back the demons. For Jesus' foot was reserved to strike the serpent's head, not the temple stones.

Jesus Christ turns His sufferings, trials, and death into our shield, buckler, and fortress. He uses them as means to save us, for through His death by crucifixion, Jesus took death, the great enemy of life, and turned it into the entrance into eternal life. By His blood and agony in the garden, Jesus shows us that in His sufferings as God and man He is now close to us in our sufferings. In your sufferings, you are united to Jesus Christ, who shows you His salvation. In Christ, you are surrounded by the fortress of His body, with His angels and all the saints who have died and risen in Him ready to do battle for you. So call upon His name and He will answer you. He will be with you in this trouble. With long life He will satisfy you and show you His salvation.

### Prayer

Lord God, heavenly Father, You sent angels to tend to Jesus as He struggled against the devil in the wilderness and in the Garden of Gethsemane. Send Your holy angels to minister to us in our sickness and in our brokenness. Unite us to Your Son, and give us His strength to fight all our foes; in His name we ask for Your protection and Your help. Amen.

～

## Where Is Your God?

As a deer pants for flowing streams, so pants my soul for You, O God. My soul thirsts for God, for the living God. When shall I come and appear before God? My tears have been my food day and night, while they say to me continually, "Where is your God?"

(Psalm 42:1–3)

In our very faithful moments, we yearn and pant for God, desiring to be with Him. So why does God sometimes seem to make Himself distant? Why does God let our sickness last so long and allow us to wear out? The devil taunts us, "Where is your God?"

Yet God has promised that He will heal us and restore us. It is not wrong, in response to this promise, to ask Him where He is! Instead of the cry of unbelief that the devil would have us make, we cry out in faith because God has promised to heal and forgive.

Jesus called out to His Father even more desperately: "My God, My God, why have You forsaken Me?" Jesus' pain reached the very depths of hell. And because this suffering was greater than ours—because this suffering included ours—when God raised Jesus, He also raised us. So our Baptism reminds us and includes us in this resurrection. Jesus' body and blood are ours, so that our suffering is taken up into His. Where is your God? He is here, bearing your illness with you, fulfilling His promise to remain with you as the living God.

### Prayer

Almighty God and Father, our souls are downcast, yet we constantly thirst for You. Give us continuing hope and confidence in You because of the life, death, and resurrection of Jesus Christ, Your Son, our Lord, who lives and reigns with You and the Holy Spirit, one God, now and forever. (*LSB Agenda*, p. 141)

## MINISTRY TO A SICK CHILD/THE PARENTS

*For additional prayers, see Section IV, p. 240*

### The Believing Unbelief

And Jesus said to him, ". . . All things are possible for one who believes." Immediately the father of the child cried out and said, "I believe; help my unbelief."

(Mark 9:23–24)

"Why, Lord, is this happening?" It is a question we all ask ourselves when our loved one is sick. Our faith may be shaken by seeing someone we love suffer, but then along comes a father's confession: "I believe; help my unbelief"! The father is responding to Jesus' terse words about the possibility of the impossible, which He spoke of to His disciples. They failed in casting out the demon because they did not believe, but for the father, he believed, though his faith was as a mustard seed.

Perfect faith belongs to Jesus Christ, whose faithfulness is perfect. It is by His faith that our prayers are answered. Although it may appear as if our prayers for healing are unanswered, know in the end that they are fulfilled. Our prayers for healing and life are fulfilled in the resurrection where our Lord heals your child. For your child has received the endless, resurrected life through the waters of Baptism. For now, though, we lean upon Jesus Christ. Jesus does not leave your child broken in sickness, but He holds tightly to (*his or her*) hand and lifts (*him or her*) up to be with Him. We cry to Jesus, "I believe," and we know that He will deliver on His promise of eternal life together with Him and the saints. We also cry, "Help my unbelief," trusting that He will give the faith of Jesus Christ to us until that time when we shall all see our Lord face-to-face in God's heavenly kingdom.

### Prayer

Lord Jesus Christ, our support and defense in every need, continue to preserve Your Church in safety, govern her by Your goodness, and bless her with Your peace; for You live and reign with the Father and the Holy Spirit, one God, now and forever. Amen. (*LSB Altar Book*, p. 730)

∽

## Guardian Angels

See that you do not despise one of these little ones. For I tell you that in heaven their angels always see the face of My Father who is in heaven. (Matthew 18:10)

The guardian angel is not merely a story, but a truth taught in the Scriptures. An angel is watching over your child in (*his or her*) joy and distress. Like the angels themselves, our Father's protection is not always seen, understood, or even believed, especially in a time of illness such as this.

Yet we have Jesus' own promise that His Father cares for the little ones. The angels not only guard the children, they also see our Father's face; they see His mercy, His care—His love for those in need. This care and love is as close as the Word, for Jesus' word is active and true. His word of Baptism assures us that your child is in the care of the Father, Son, and Holy Spirit. His promise of forgiveness means that no matter the extent and suffering of this illness, your child will indeed be healed, whether now or in the resurrection. And just as the Father looked with sorrow on the suffering of His Son, Jesus, and so restored Him to life, so He looks with sorrow on the suffering of your own child. Because of His Son, your child will rise again, free from this illness. The angel obeys the command of the Father, but you receive His promise.

### Prayer

O God, from whom all good proceeds, grant to us, Your humble servants, Your holy inspiration, that we may set our minds on the things that are right and, by Your merciful guiding, accomplish them; through Jesus Christ, Your Son, our Lord. Amen. (*LSB Altar Book*, p. 634)

## AFTER INJURY IN AN ACCIDENT

### An Ongoing Reality

Be merciful to me, O God, be merciful to me, for in You my soul takes refuge; in the shadow of Your wings I will take refuge, till the storms of destruction pass by. I cry out to God Most High, to God who fulfills His purpose for me. He will send from heaven and save me; He will put to shame him who tramples on me. (Psalm 57:1-3)

Throughout this psalm, there are two forces constantly at odds: the enemy and the Lord. The enemy brings suffering, while the Lord brings deliverance. Although suffering is a polar opposite of deliverance, both are characteristic of the Christian life.

Throughout the Scriptures, deliverance by water usually means more trouble is on the way. As the children of God passed through the Red Sea, they were destined for forty years of trouble and hardship in the desert. Even Jesus, having stood among sinners and passed through the water of the Jordan River, was destined for forty days of temptation by the devil. The same can be said of any baptized Christian. The baptismal life, your life, is often more difficult and troublesome after Baptism than before. The devil is attacking harder than ever, and it may appear as if you are all alone in your battle. Even now, in the midst of injury, it appears the devil and his "storms of destruction" have won the day.

But never forget the ongoing reality of Holy Baptism. It is not the beginning of a hellish life, but it is an intimate union with Jesus Himself, who suffers with you, rejoices with you, helps you understand all suffering through His good and gracious will, and will bring you eternal deliverance at the appointed time. Your body and your soul may be "in the midst of lions," as the psalmist says, but the Lord "will send from heaven" to save you. Jesus will visit you, even as He does right now. He will come to your hospital room, your house, or wherever you may be, bringing to you His good gifts of Word, absolution, body, and blood.

Take heart today. Jesus is here. His steadfast love will never fail. The "storms of destruction" will soon pass you by. Deliverance and glory are yours in Jesus Christ.

### Prayer

Lord God, heavenly Father, You delivered us from the enemy through the death of Your Son, Jesus Christ, our Lord, with whom we are united in Holy Baptism. Continue to deliver us, we pray, from our diseases and afflictions by Your merciful gift of healing as You feed us holy food and give us to drink of the cup of everlasting life; through Jesus Christ, our Lord. Amen.

## COMFORT AND CONSOLATION

*For additional resources, see Section III, p. 199*
*For additional prayers, see Section IV, p. 241*

### Assuring Promise

All that the Father gives Me will come to Me, and whoever comes to Me I will never cast out.... For this is the will of My Father, that everyone who looks on the Son and believes in Him should have eternal life, and I will raise him up on the last day. (John 6:37, 40)

The Father promised Jesus, His only-begotten Son, that anyone who looks on the Son and believes in Him will have eternal life and be raised up bodily on the Last Day. Jesus came into the world for that purpose—to restore our eternal relationship with God. Because Jesus came, everyone who believes in Him will be raised and live in a place prepared for each of us by Jesus Himself.

Jesus faced many trials and struggles in His life. He saw the sickness, death, and decay of the world. He saw hatred and deception, the hated and the deceived. He watched children and loved ones die. He Himself died—betrayed, abandoned, and alone.

The Father's promise is true: believers will be raised to life just as the Father raised His Son. The Father wants us with Him for all eternity. Jesus sends His Holy Spirit to create and sustain such saving faith in us through His Word and Sacrament.

Despite our earthly suffering and pain, we are reconciled to the Father; we are heirs of His kingdom. The Father and Son work together for our welfare and our good.

*Prayer*

Gracious Father, Your blessed Son came down from heaven to be the true bread that gives life to the world.

Grant that Christ, the bread of life, may live in us and we in Him, who lives and reigns with You and the Holy Spirit, one God, now and forever. Amen.

~

## Quietly Waiting

> The steadfast love of the LORD never ceases; His mercies never come to an end; they are new every morning; great is Your faithfulness. . . . It is good that one should wait quietly for the salvation of the LORD.
>
> (Lamentations 3:22–23, 26)

During illness, we do much waiting. We wait at the doctor's office. We wait for the prognosis of our health. We wait in line at the pharmacy. We wait for visits from family and friends. Often this waiting is filled with anxiety, discomfort, and even anger. Sometimes we are waiting for a cure that does not seem to come.

Here, in Lamentations, the prophet describes a different kind of waiting. It is quiet and full of comfort. It is the wait for a cure that comes in Jesus Christ. This cure provides health eternal. It is the salvation of the Lord, and the cure resides where He is. You hear it in the voice of your pastor when he preaches the Gospel to you and pronounces forgiveness in Absolution. You see it in Holy Baptism and feel it as the water is poured onto your head. You hold it in your hand and taste it in your mouth in Holy Communion. Here is the salvation of the Lord for which you wait quietly. Here is your eternal cure from sin, sickness, and death.

The salvation of the Lord does not depend upon your good deeds or even your own faithful waiting. It is God who is faithful through His Son. His love never ceases. His mercies never end. Great is His faithfulness that comes to you new every morning. Amen.

### Prayer

Faithful God, whose mercies are new to us every morning, we humbly pray that You would look upon us in mercy and renew us by Your Holy Spirit. Keep safe our going out and our coming in, and let Your blessing remain with us throughout this day. Preserve us in Your righteousness, and grant us a portion in that eternal life which is in Christ Jesus, our Lord. Amen. (*LSB*, p. 309)

## Prolonged Recovery/Lingering Illness

*For additional resources, see Section III, p. 202*
*For additional prayers, see Section IV, p. 242*

### Swallowed Up by Life

> For while we are still in this tent, we groan, being burdened—not that we would be unclothed, but that we would be further clothed, so that what is mortal may be swallowed up by life. He who has prepared us for this very thing is God, who has given us the Spirit as a guarantee. (2 Corinthians 5:4–5)

A tent was no insignificant thing to a Jew at the time of Paul's second letter to the Corinthians. Paul knew tents well; he was a tentmaker by trade. Tents provided shelter for the poor and the rich. It was even a tent that, for a time, housed the ark of the covenant, a means by which God resided with His people. God resided with His people a second time, when He took on the tent of human flesh and dwelt among us.

Tents do provide shelter, but it is temporary shelter, intended for a people who wander. And even the best of tents do not completely shield from the blistering desert heat or icy winter winds. Our bodies are such tents—imperfect, temporary shelters. In long-lasting illness, our tents are constantly beaten, as by a torrential rain, and we begin to wonder if they will collapse under such an enduring storm. We groan, being burdened.

But God has provided for us a better shelter, the promise of which was first sealed with the Holy Spirit in our Baptism and will be fully restored in the resurrection of the body when our Lord comes in judgment. For this flesh is a good gift from God, though now it is burdened and hurting. Although great tempests come and beat upon us, they will not prevail. In the righteousness of Christ, we are further clothed, and the mortal is swallowed up by life eternal. Amen.

*Prayer*

Lord God, shelter us in Jesus, Your Son, by the baptismal grace that joined us to Him forever. Protect us from all that threatens our life by His strength and care, for His presence dwells in us by His Spirit. Amen.

~

## The Strength to Be Weak

> But [Jesus] said to me, "My grace is sufficient for you, for My power is made perfect in weakness." Therefore I will boast all the more gladly of my weaknesses, so that the power of Christ may rest upon me.
>
> (2 Corinthians 12:9)

A paradox. Weakness is the opposite of power. As the world defines it, weakness cannot mean power. Yet the words of Jesus are so sure that we have Paul's amazing statement that he boasts gladly in his weaknesses. Boasting is not the first thing we think of when weak. We want to be freed of our weaknesses, our pain, our worn out bodies. Even when we endure our troubles quietly and patiently, we look in hope to the time that we will be relieved. Yet the Scriptures speak of the boasting of weakness!

As weak as you are, Christ was weaker. He did not simply come in His power and eliminate sin and its effects by His mighty arm, like a warrior in battle. He came in weakness to bear weakness, to feel it, to sympathize with us. In weakness He showed power over sin by dying for it, power over Satan by defeating him while hanging naked on a cross. Christ's power is shown in His mercy, His forgiveness, His love. Now He is everyone's king by His power made perfect in weakness, everyone's friend by suffering what we suffer.

So embrace your Friend. You are baptized into Christ. Hear His promises that His power is greater than your weakness. Eat His body broken for you, His blood shed for the forgiveness of your sins. Know that He is closer to you than any other person—that His power does rest upon you. You are weak, but you are not alone. You are weak, so Christ is strong.

## Prayer

Lord Jesus, in our weakness, be our strength. In our suffering, join us to Your suffering. In our despair, show us the hope of Your resurrection. In our Baptism, show us Yourself, so we may not boast in ourselves but in the salvation we have in You. For You live and reign with the Father and the Holy Spirit, one God, now and forever. Amen.

# MINISTRY TO A DYING PERSON

*For additional resources, see Section III, p. 205*
*For additional prayers, see Section IV, p. 242*

## Depart in Peace

Lord, now You are letting Your servant depart in peace, according to Your word; for my eyes have seen Your salvation that You have prepared in the presence of all peoples, a light for revelation to the Gentiles, and for glory to Your people Israel. (Luke 2:29–32)

Most people pray for a peaceful death, that is, a death where there is no pain or suffering. Simeon tells of a different kind of peaceful death.

Imagine waiting in the temple year after year for the Savior to appear. Then, there He is—a 40-day-old infant in the arms of His mother, Mary. What joy and peace—peace that reigns between heaven and earth because God has become flesh to take away the sins of the world.

Simeon may now depart in peace; he has seen the Lord's salvation; he has held the Lord in his arms. So have you. You have taken the Lord's body in your hands and placed it in your mouth; you have taken the cup and tipped His life-giving blood to your lips. You have touched the Lord and tasted that He is good. He has given you the peace of heaven in His body and blood. "Depart in peace," says the pastor, as you leave the table of the Lord, and you do.

Your death is the entrance into a life that never ends. When you close your eyes in death, you will be with Christ and His angels and archangels and all the company of heaven.

Lord, now let this, Your servant, depart in peace.

### Prayer

Almighty and ever-living God, as Your only-begotten Son was this day presented in the temple in the substance of our flesh, grant that we may be presented to You with pure and clean hearts; through Jesus Christ, our Lord. Amen. (*LSB Altar Book*, p. 957)

∼

## The Cup of Salvation

I am already being poured out as a drink offering, and the time of my departure has come. I have fought the good fight, I have finished the race, I have kept the faith. Henceforth there is laid up for me the crown of righteousness, which the Lord, the righteous judge, will award to me on that Day, and not only to me but also to all who have loved His appearing.

(2 Timothy 4:6–8)

The Lord chose you and made you His own in Baptism. He gave you faith and sustains your life in Christ. His eyes saw you before you were born, and He sees you now. The Lord guards this day for you, keeping you in His care.

You have a crown of righteousness earned by the life, death, and resurrection of our Savior, Jesus Christ. The righteous Judge, God Himself, finds no wrong in you, for you are His child, washed clean and fully restored to Him. All fears will pass and all your tears will be wiped away.

Before Christ poured out His soul to death, He was transfigured, giving us a glimpse of our own future. You, too, will be glorified in your body. Christ rose in triumph to prepare a special place for you and for all who love Him. You, too, will be raised to live in a place without pain, loss, or fear, where you will live with all the saints in His paradise forever.

### Prayer

Merciful Father, You promise to forgive our transgressions and not hold our sins against us. We ask You to keep in safety our *brother/sister*, who is Your own dear child both now and forevermore; through Jesus Christ, Your Son, our Lord. Amen. (*LSB Agenda*, p. 140)

## The Earth Melts

The nations rage, the kingdoms totter; He utters His voice, the earth melts.... "Be still and know that I am God. I will be exalted among the nations, I will be exalted in the earth!" The LORD of hosts is with us; the God of Jacob is our fortress. (Psalm 46:6, 10–11)

In the face of death, the earth melts away before us. Our bodies are tired and broken. Like the nations, we may rage and totter at death's approach. We are angry at this enemy, and we wonder where God is. The earth, all that we have ever seen or known, begins to melt away. Amid the rage, the Lord speaks: "Be still and know that I am God."

When the Israelites fled slavery in Egypt, they stood before the Red Sea in a panic. How were they to cross such a large body of water without even one boat? They cried out to Moses, "Is it because there are no graves in Egypt that you have taken us away to die in the wilderness?" Moses answered the people in the same manner as the psalm: "The LORD will fight for you, and you have only to be silent" (Exodus 14:10, 14).

Where is God when death draws near? The Lord of hosts

is with us, and He is fighting death on our behalf. Indeed, His battle against death took Him to the cross, and He was victorious. This victory is for us. The Red Sea has parted, and God leads His people across on dry land. The enemy has been drowned in the water, and by the strength of the Lord, the people come safely to the promised land.

"There is a river whose streams make glad the city of God, the holy habitation of the Most High. God is in the midst of her; she shall not be moved; God will help her when morning dawns" (Psalm 46:4–5).

### Prayer

O God, our refuge and strength, You have cleansed Your children in the waters of Holy Baptism. Renew our hearts in the true faith that knows Your forgiveness and daily accepts Your good and gracious will; through Jesus Christ, Your Son, our Lord. Amen. (*LSB Agenda*, p. 141)

~

## The Lord Is Waiting for You

He will swallow up death forever; and the Lord God will wipe away tears from all faces, and the reproach of His people He will take away from all the earth, for the Lord has spoken. It will be said on that day, "Behold, this is our God; we have waited for Him, that He might save us. This is the Lord; we have waited for Him; let us be glad and rejoice in His salvation." (Isaiah 25:8–9)

You have waited for the Lord. You have endured the weight of sin in this life, and have persevered in faith in your Lord Jesus Christ. The fulfillment of His promise to wipe away all your tears is nearer now than it once was.

What lies ahead is unknown to you. You do not know the way. Even now, look to your Good Shepherd to lead you from this wilderness, across the deep river Jordan, into the promised land.

I tell you, Christian, you will walk through on dry

ground. Having already died with Christ in your Baptism, you will not taste death, but will pass through death to life. Death is swallowed up forever. His blood has already paid the wages of your sin.

As you journey this last stretch, through the valley of death, He is attentive to you and tender. Like a lamb you are borne on His shoulders. Soon you will see Him face-to-face. This is the Lord. You have waited for Him; He is now waiting for you.

### Prayer

Lord God our Father, keep safe Your servant on the path of eternal life, for You alone are *his/her* refuge. May *he/she* rest secure in the promise of our Lord's resurrection; through Jesus Christ, Your Son, our Lord. Amen. (*LSB Agenda*, p. 140)

~

## Being Remembered

He said, "Jesus, remember me when You come into Your kingdom." (Luke 23:42)

These are the words of the dying thief who was crucified next to Jesus. The thief speaks as a believer. He does not ask that Jesus allow him a second chance to make up for all that he had done wrong. Rather, the thief simply asks Jesus to remember him.

When it comes to sins forgiven, the Lord has a terrible memory. The psalmist declares, "As far as the east is from the west, so far does He remove our transgressions from us" (Psalm 103:12). But when it comes to His mercy, His memory is unmatched.

It is for the purpose of being gracious and merciful that the Lord remembers someone. In Mary's song (the Magnificat), she speaks of the Lord helping Israel "in remembrance of His mercy" (Luke 1:54). The Lord always remembers in light of His promise of deliverance through Jesus Christ. Why is He gracious to Israel? Because He remembered her in light of Christ. Why is He gracious to the thief on the cross, even promising him paradise? Because He remembered him in light of His own sacrificial death. The Lord remembers those He loves.

Here you are now. The days of your earthly life are beginning to wane, yet you need not despair. Simply look back on the mercy the Lord has showered on all those whom He has remembered. Just as He has remembered them and delivered them, He has remembered you. Rejoice! Like the thief on the cross, paradise is yours.

### Prayer

Lord Jesus Christ, You reign among us by the preaching of Your cross. Forgive Your people their offenses that we, being governed by Your bountiful goodness, may enter at last into Your eternal paradise; for You live and reign with the Father and the Holy Spirit, one God, now and forever. Amen. (*LSB Altar Book*, p. 837)

~

## With the Lord There Is No Fear

> The LORD is my light and my salvation; whom shall I fear? The LORD is the stronghold of my life; of whom shall I be afraid? (Psalm 27:1)

There is no fear where there is love because love casts out fear (Romans 8:15). In the midst of fighting off death, we perhaps fear the unknown, but thanks to Christ's crucifixion we know where death leads. Death is now a refuge for us, providing the respite from our suffering. The pain and suffering in life cannot hurt us anymore. Even in the midst of death, we are not afraid, because God first loved us (1 John 4:9). The love of God is perfected in the death of His saints because our death is the portal to the immortality of Jesus Christ's resurrection. Jesus is waiting for you to welcome you home to your heavenly Father. He is your light and your salvation. In Him there is no fear.

The stark reality for you, however, is that your body is dying. The whole truth does not end here, for you know that Christ died your death on the cross. You did all the dying that needs to be done in Baptism, when you received Christ's death as your own and His resurrection as well (Romans 6:4). From that moment, Jesus took your hand to lead you through all trials and travails. Fear not, Jesus still has your hand. He will not let go, even as you travel into death, for your death is swallowed up in the victory of Christ's cross (Isaiah 25:6–9). Death is a stop, not a destination, on your way to the room Christ prepared for you in your heavenly house (John 14:3).

You are now part of the land of the living, the kingdom of God, in Christ Jesus. He is the door to eternal life in the heavenly promised land. In His kingdom there is no death, no pain, no suffering, for Jesus Christ will wipe away all tears and calm all fears so that you may gaze upon the beauty of our God (Revelation 21:4). Wait for the Lord; be strong, and let your heart take courage; wait for the Lord!

## Prayer

O Lord, we recall Your right judgment against our sin as the time of death comes upon us, yet we know that You graciously hear our cries for mercy. Accept our prayer for our *brother/sister* in *his/her* time of need, and finally bring *him/her* to praise You with all Your saints in heaven; through Jesus Christ, our Lord. Amen. (*LSB Agenda*, p. 140)

∼

## God's Precious Saints

Precious in the sight of the LORD is the death of His saints. O LORD, I am your servant; I am your servant, the son of your maidservant. You have loosed my bonds. (Psalm 116:15–16)

How is death precious to the Lord? God is the God of life. He breathed His own Spirit into man so that we live as the unique bearers of His image. God did not create this world with death. Death is a result of sin, and sin is in opposition to this God of life. Does God really look at death as precious?

But the verse says, "the death of His saints." It is not death that is precious to God, but His saints. Death is an enemy of God. It is the result of sin. Sin leads to death, but death swallows up sin. After a man has died, he no longer sins. The unfaithfulness of his heart, the harshness of his words, and the selfishness of his actions are all dead. Sin has no more power. The old man that began to drown in Baptism is now swallowed up forever, and there is only the new life that we have in Christ. This is why Baptism is compared to dying: in Baptism, sin and the devil's hold over us dies. At our earthly death, sins can no longer be committed.

In our Lord's death, He took on the true death of hell that should have been ours. On the cross, the enemies of God were truly destroyed, the devil's plan backfired, and death and sin swallowed up themselves. Through His death, Jesus has loosed the bonds of your death. You are free from the death of hell, and your own passing is but a brief slumber that takes you to the arms of Jesus Christ. Because He endured your death—taking it upon Himself—you have true life and will never truly die.

Therefore, just as your death is His, so His life is yours. When God raised Jesus up, He raised you up and made this resurrection yours in your Baptism. And He has continued to assure you of this life. When you eat and drink Christ's body and blood, this living God unites Himself again to you, forgiving your sin, and rejuvenating you, even as your body appears to be failing. Your body, broken by death, will be restored by this body of God and will live forever, the culmination of the life of faith that you have in Christ. In these days and hours before death, look to Christ who died the full death of hell so that you will live a new life. His resurrected body and blood are yours. His promise is yours. He has loosed your bonds forever. Precious, indeed, in the sight of the Lord is the death of His saints.

*Prayer*

O Lord, precious in Your sight is the death of Your saints. According to Your gracious will, deliver [this Your servant] from the trouble and sorrow of this life that, having received the cup of salvation, *he/she* may rejoice in Your heavenly Jerusalem; through Jesus Christ, Your Son, our Lord. Amen. (*LSB Agenda*, p. 141)

## IMPENDING DEATH OR IRREVERSIBLE ILLNESS

### Drinking Jesus' Cup

Then Jesus went with them to a place called Gethsemane, and He said to His disciples, "Sit here, while I go over there and pray." And taking with Him Peter and the two sons of Zebedee, He began to be sorrowful and troubled. Then He said to them, "My soul is very sorrowful, even to death; remain here, and watch with Me." . . . "My Father, if this cannot pass unless I drink it, Your will be done." . . . Then He came to the disciples and said to them, "Sleep and take your rest later on. See, the hour is at hand, and the Son of Man is betrayed into the hands of sinners. Rise, let us be going; see, My betrayer is at hand."

(Matthew 26:36–38, 42, 45–46)

In the Garden of Gethsemane, Jesus prayed three times that the cup of suffering and death be taken from Him. Like you, He knew that His death was impending. The eternal plan of redemption was irreversible. There was no other way, but "the Son of Man must suffer many things . . . and be killed" (Luke 9:22). He saw the flogging, the crown, the cross, the nails, the spit, and the mockery He was about to face. Yet amid all that, He resolutely went to His death.

At this moment, your future may look just as bleak. What lies before you may not be easy to endure. Yet in Jesus

Christ you can cheerfully go forward and meet the days ahead. You can cheerfully go forward in the confidence that nothing that lies before you can ever harm you.

Jesus has drunk the fullness of the cup of suffering and death. He has consumed your suffering and your death. There is nothing left for you to drink. Now, as you suffer, you are brought into the suffering of Christ. As you go to your death, you are brought into the death of Christ. But never forget what comes after suffering and death: glory, life, and resurrection!

You have been incorporated into the precious body of Jesus Christ. You are baptized. You reside in Him and He in you. You are one in the same. What is yours is His and what is His is now yours. Your sins belong to Him. But His suffering is your suffering. His death will be your death. And His resurrection will be your resurrection as well. On the other side of your present struggles lies an empty tomb. Yes, "Jesus lives! The vict'ry's won!" (*LSB* 490).

So as you wait in your own Gethsemane, and as you prepare for your death, lift up your heart. Rise with Jesus and be on your way. For you do not go to your death alone, but Jesus goes with you. Life Incarnate is by your side. "Now no more can death appall, Now no more the grave enthrall" (*LSB* 633:6). But they have been conquered by Jesus Christ. You belong to Him. You will surely rise again. Fear not. Life eternal is yours.

### Prayer

Almighty and everlasting God, You sent Your Son, our Savior Jesus Christ, to take upon Himself our flesh and to suffer death upon the cross. Mercifully grant that we may follow the example of His great humility and patience and be made partakers of His resurrection; through Jesus Christ, our Lord. Amen. (*LSB Altar Book*, p. 586)

## ACCEPTANCE OF INEVITABLE DEATH

*For additional resources, see Section III, p. 209*
*For additional prayers, see Section IV, p. 243*

### Joy at the Break of Day

Weeping may tarry for the night, but joy comes with the morning. (Psalm 30:5b)

At the dedication of the temple, Israel sang of life and death because there was life in the death of the lamb. You, too, see life and death in the true temple of God, the body and blood of Jesus Christ, the Lamb whose death is your life.

The Father heard Jesus crying for help in Gethsemane, and the Father healed Him in the resurrection, but only after the crucifixion's sorrowful night. Now the Father hears you, too, because that same body and blood is in you, but like Jesus, the resurrection comes after tarrying in death for a moment.

In the midst of being knocked down, God promised that He would draw Israel up and restore them to life. God the Father brought Jesus up from the grave, and He does the same for you. As death takes you into the pit of the grave, Jesus grasps you by the hand and lifts you out, so you may join Him in the eternal feast of praise and thanksgiving.

For Jesus, the grueling night of His Passion gave way to the dazzling daybreak of Easter morning. You, too, will arise in the morning for joyful dancing and singing. For you are baptized, washed with the blood of the Lamb, and clothed with Christ's gladness, transforming your dying body into a heavenly body.

### *Prayer*

Lord Jesus, You know that our lives are but a breath. By Your incarnation You have shared our mortality and saved us from our transgressions. Hear our prayers, still our cries, and quiet our weeping, for You live and reign with the Father and the Holy Spirit, one God, now and forever. Amen. (*LSB Agenda*, p. 140)

# That Which Is Better Is Yet to Come

> Truly, truly, I say to you, whoever hears My word and believes Him who sent Me has eternal life. He does not come into judgment, but has passed from death to life. (John 5:24)

When we face death, our thoughts and emotions may pull in different directions. "I am a sinner; I am deserving of death." Or, "Has my life been 'worth it'? Have I made a difference in my life?" Or, "Why does God permit the physical or emotional pain of death? Why can't He just take us without the anxiety?" Or, "Does God really care? Is there a God who is really waiting to bring me to a place of bliss, to His Son, Jesus Christ?"

The Bible tries to get us to see things from God's perspective, yet we are bombarded by what we see and experience: a childhood that may or may not have been carefree, an adult life of toil and worry about money, a period of decline that brings even greater anxiety about what comes after death. Death is the end of a life that, viewed from a worldly perspective, may not have been very joyful or successful.

But this is not the view of death announced by the Bible and taught by our Lord Jesus. Death is, to be sure, the end of a life that has had its anxieties and troubles, but it is an end of these things that are destroyed and left behind. Death is the last enemy to be destroyed, and in our own deaths the last of our labors, worries, and weaknesses is over. Hardship is over. There is joy to be found after death. There is fellowship with our heavenly Father through our Lord Jesus. The glimpses of bliss that we felt on earth—friendship, camaraderie, and holiday meals—these are the staples of life in heaven. Death is the end not of life, but the end of trouble. Only joy follows!

"Whoever hears My word and believes Him who sent Me has eternal life. He does not come into judgment, but has passed from death to life." Death is a passing to life with Jesus.

Death also, then, reminds us of the futility of our own lives. Death is the end of this vale of tears—and this is all our lives would have been were it not for the death of Jesus. Our lives and deaths do not impress God, but the life and death of Jesus have given value to you—to your life, to your work, and even to your death. In Baptism you were united to this death of Christ, so that your sufferings have become His and His work has become yours, so your Father looks with joy on everything about you. He is pleased to call you His child. He is overjoyed to hold you in His arms. He is waiting to bring you to Himself in heaven.

Take yet again the body and blood of Christ, and look forward to this life that is yours. You have not come into judgment, but have passed over from death to life.

### Prayer

O Lord, do not hide Your face from Your servant in the day of *his/her* distress. Incline Your ear to us and answer us speedily when we call; through Jesus Christ, Your Son, our Lord. Amen. (*LSB Agenda*, p. 141)

## COMMENDATION OF THE DYING

*See also Section V: Commendation of the Dying, p. 260*
*For additional resources, see Section III, p. 213*
*For additional prayers, see Section IV, p. 243*

### Lord, Let at Last Thine Angels Come

After this I looked, and behold, a great multitude that no one could number, from every nation, from all tribes and peoples and languages, standing before the throne and before the Lamb, clothed in white robes, with palm branches in their hands, and crying out with a loud voice, "Salvation belongs to our God who sits on the throne, and to the Lamb!" And all the angels were standing around the throne and around the elders and the four living creatures, and they fell on their faces before the throne and worshiped God, saying, "Amen! Blessing and glory and wisdom and thanksgiving and honor and power and might be to our God forever and ever! Amen." (Revelation 7:9–12)

Every time that you received the body and blood of the Lord at the Lord's Supper you entered heaven. Jesus Christ, the crucified, risen, and ascended Lord, gave you in His body and blood a taste of heaven right now, even now, here on earth.

As you prepared to receive the Lord's Supper, you sang, "Therefore with angels and archangels and all the company of heaven, we laud and magnify Your holy name, evermore praising You and saying." In these words, you acknowledged that in this Holy Meal you joined with angels and archangels and all the saints, that is, with Christ and all who are with Him in heaven. Heaven came to earth in Jesus, and you are invited to enter heaven right now, even now, here on earth.

Throughout your life and even now, you worship the Lamb because He was slain and raised again. His sprinkled blood has made you and all creation clean. By His wounds you have been healed, and the food He gives you at this heavenly feast is His body broken in death, His blood poured out for the forgiveness of your sins.

Your Lord invites you to the Lord's Table, however burdened by sin and guilt and shame. You are battle-weary from fighting the good fight. With St. Paul, you long to be with Christ, for you know that there, before the throne and before the Lamb, you will join the great multitude that no one can number, clothed in white robes, with palm branches in their hands. You long to join them, without the noise of sin and death, so you can cry, "Salvation belongs to our God who sits on the throne, and to the Lamb!" You are ready to join the angels and saints before the throne of the Lamb and worship God, saying, "Amen! Blessing and glory and wisdom and thanksgiving and honor and power and might be to our God forever and ever! Amen."

You have suffered with Christ. You have borne the burden of the day. It is time to commend you to the Lamb:

*Prayer*

Lord, let at last Thine angels come,
To Abr'ham's bosom bear me home,
That I may die unfearing;
And in its narrow chamber keep
My body safe in peaceful sleep
Until Thy reappearing.
And then from death awaken me
That these mine eyes with joy may see,
O Son of God, Thy glorious face,
My Savior and my fount of grace.
Lord Jesus Christ, my prayer attend, my prayer attend,
And I will praise Thee without end. Amen. (*LSB* 708)

# DEATH OF A CHILD

*For additional prayers, see Section IV, p. 245*

## The Kingdom Belongs to Children, Now and Forever

Jesus said, "Let the little children come to Me and do not hinder them, for to such belongs the kingdom of heaven." (Matthew 19:14)

These words are spoken not only now, at the passing of your child, but they were spoken at the birth of your child. That is, they were spoken at your child's new birth by water and the Spirit. As part of the baptismal service, these words remind us that children, though they do not have the maturity of adults, are received by our Lord Jesus. In Baptism, your child received the kingdom of heaven. Jesus' words are a promise to you that even now your child is with Jesus in heaven.

In fact, Jesus' words tell us that not only are children received by Him but children also are those to whom heaven belongs. Just as the weak in Christ are strong and the poor are rich, so also the children are the faithful ones. In this account, Jesus teaches us not to keep children from His presence, from hearing His Word. Even as you brought your child to be baptized, to worship, and even to the altar with you, you brought your child to Jesus. Your child was a faithful one.

Your child now lives with Jesus, yet you remain here in sorrow. But Jesus is also with you here. Even as you long for fellowship with your child, Jesus, who binds us to each other on earth, also binds us to those with Him in heaven. Christians are not separated into those in heaven and those on earth. Rather, all who are baptized into Christ have received forgiveness of sins and are united as the Church, His saints, whether in heaven or on earth. Wherever Jesus is, there are His saints.

Even as Christ rules in heaven, He also lives as your friend here. Jesus takes on your burdens and gives you the blessings of heaven. He mourns with you as you mourn your child, and as you partake of His body and blood, He strengthens your fellowship with Himself and with your child. At the altar of God, you are as close to your child as ever, for your child worships at the heavenly altar even as you worship at the earthly one. Nothing can separate you from the love of Christ; nothing can separate you from this spiritual fellowship with your child. Even if for a little while you cannot hold your child in your arms, you are both held in the arms of your Savior. Your fellowship remains forever in the Lamb.

### Prayer

O Lord, heavenly Father, comfort these parents and their family who grieve the loss of their dear child. Enable them in steadfast faith and confident hope to look for the blessed day of the completion of our salvation, when all who trust in You shall meet again in heavenly joy and glory; through Jesus Christ, our Lord. Amen. (*LSB Agenda*, p. 114)

# SECTION III

## Visitation Resources

# ANGER, BITTERNESS, SELF-PITY, TURMOIL

*For devotions suitable for this topic, see Section II, p. 41*

Anger is neither to run rampant nor to be suppressed. Those who are angry should be encouraged to cry out to the God of justice and to leave vengeance in His hands. In the cross is found the satisfaction of justice in the wrath of God against sin poured out on Christ. In the cross is found the mercy and forgiveness of God who, in His Son, has atoned for the sins of the whole world.

## *Psalmody*

### PSALM 7:6–17

Arise, O LORD, in Your anger;
   lift Yourself up against the fury of my enemies;
   awake for me; You have appointed a judgment.
Let the assembly of the peoples be gathered about You;
   over it return on high.

The LORD judges the peoples;
   judge me, O LORD, according to my righteousness
   and according to the integrity that is in me.
Oh, let the evil of the wicked come to an end,
   and may You establish the righteous—
You who test the minds and hearts,
   O righteous God!
My shield is with God,
   who saves the upright in heart.
God is a righteous judge,
   and a God who feels indignation every day.

If a man does not repent, God will whet His sword;
   He has bent and readied His bow;
He has prepared for Him His deadly weapons,
   making His arrows fiery shafts.
Behold, the wicked man conceives evil
   and is pregnant with mischief
   and gives birth to lies.

He makes a pit, digging it out,
    and falls into the hole that he has made.
His mischief returns upon his own head,
    and on his own skull his violence descends.

I will give to the LORD the thanks
      due to His righteousness,
and I will sing praise to the
      name of the LORD, the Most High.

## Additional Psalms

30; 39; 73; 88; 94; 119:81–88; 139

## Readings

### ECCLESIASTES 7:9

Be not quick in your spirit to become angry, for anger lodges in the bosom of fools.

### MATTHEW 18:21–35

Then Peter came up and said to Him, "Lord, how often will my brother sin against me, and I forgive him? As many as seven times?" Jesus said to him, "I do not say to you seven times, but seventy times seven.

"Therefore the kingdom of heaven may be compared to a king who wished to settle accounts with his servants. When he began to settle, one was brought to him who owed him ten thousand talents. And since he could not pay, his master ordered him to be sold, with his wife and children and all that he had, and payment to be made. So the servant fell on his knees, imploring him, 'Have patience with me, and I will pay you everything.' And out of pity for him, the master of that servant released him and forgave him the debt. But when that same servant went out, he found one of his fellow servants who owed him a hundred denarii, and seizing him, he began to choke him, saying, 'Pay what you owe.' So his fellow servant fell down and pleaded with him, 'Have patience with me, and I will pay you.' He refused and went and put him in prison until he should pay the debt. When his fellow servants saw what had taken place, they were greatly distressed, and they went and reported to their master all that had taken place. Then his master summoned him and said to him, 'You wicked servant! I forgave you all that debt because you pleaded with me. And should not you have had mercy on your fellow servant, as I had mercy on you?' And in anger his master delivered him to the jailers, until he should pay all his debt. So also My heavenly Father will do to every one of you, if you do not forgive your brother from your heart."

**EPHESIANS 4:26–27**

Be angry and do not sin; do not let the sun go down on your anger, and give no opportunity to the devil.

### Additional Readings

Isaiah 53; Matthew 26:36–46; 2 Corinthians 1:3–7; Ephesians 6:10–17; Philippians 2:5–11; Hebrews 10:28–39; James 1:12–21; 1 Peter 5:6–11

### Prayers

O God, You see that of ourselves we have no strength. By Your mighty power defend us from all adversities that may happen to the body and from all evil thoughts that may assault and hurt the soul; through Jesus Christ, Your Son, our Lord, who lives and reigns with You and the Holy Spirit, one God, now and forever. Amen. (*LSB Altar Book*, p. 581)

Most merciful Father, with compassion You hear the cries of Your people in great distress. Be with all who now endure affliction and calamity, bless the work of those who bring rescue and relief, and enable us to aid and comfort those who are suffering that they may find renewed hope and purpose; through Jesus Christ, our Lord, who lives and reigns with You and the Holy Spirit, one God, now and forever. Amen. (*LSB Altar Book*, p. 993)

*For additional prayers, see Section IV, p. 219*

### Hymnody

Stricken, smitten, and afflicted,
See Him dying on the tree!
'Tis the Christ, by man rejected;

Yes, my soul, 'tis He, 'tis He!
'Tis the long-expected Prophet,
David's Son, yet David's Lord;
Proofs I see sufficient of it:
'Tis the true and faithful Word.

Tell me, ye who hear Him groaning,
Was there ever grief like His?
Friends through fear His cause disowning,
Foes insulting His distress;
Many hands were raised to wound Him,
None would intervene to save;
But the deepest stroke that pierced Him
Was the stroke that justice gave.

Ye who think of sin but lightly
Nor suppose the evil great
Here may view its nature rightly,
Here its guilt may estimate.
Mark the sacrifice appointed,
See who bears the awful load;
'Tis the Word, the Lord's anointed,
Son of Man and Son of God.

("Stricken, Smitten, and Afflicted," *LSB* 451:1–3)

### Additional Hymns

"I Am Trusting Thee, Lord Jesus" (*LSB* 729); "If God
Himself Be for Me" (*LSB* 724)

## Anxiety, Apprehension, Fear

*For devotions suitable for this topic, see Section II, p. 42*

When Jesus said to Peter, "Peace be with you," He
was pronouncing absolution upon him (John 20:19).
Jesus dwells within us, and we dwell within Him, so
there is no reason for anxiety, apprehension, or fear.
Yet sometimes the concerns of this world overwhelm
us, and we cannot help but become anxious. The

living words of Jesus in Holy Scripture continually proclaim to us: "Peace be with you."

## Psalmody

**PSALM 46**

God is our refuge and strength,
 a very present help in trouble.
Therefore we will not fear
  though the earth gives way,
 though the mountains be
  moved into the heart of the sea,
 though its waters roar and foam,
  though the mountains tremble at its swelling.

There is a river whose streams make glad the city of God,
 the holy habitation of the Most High.
God is in the midst of her; she shall not be moved;
 God will help her when morning dawns.
The nations rage, the kingdoms totter;
 He utters His voice, the earth melts.
The Lord of hosts is with us;
 the God of Jacob is our fortress.

Come, behold the works of the Lord,
 how He has brought desolations on the earth.
He makes wars cease to the end of the earth;
 He breaks the bow and shatters the spear;
 He burns the chariots with fire.
"Be still, and know that I am God.
 I will be exalted among the nations,
 I will be exalted in the earth!"
The Lord of hosts is with us;
 the God of Jacob is our fortress.

## Additional Psalms

4; 91; 121

## Readings

**JOHN 10:1–18**

"Truly, truly, I say to you, he who does not enter the

sheepfold by the door but climbs in by another way, that man is a thief and a robber. But he who enters by the door is the shepherd of the sheep. To him the gatekeeper opens. The sheep hear his voice, and he calls his own sheep by name and leads them out. When he has brought out all his own, he goes before them, and the sheep follow him, for they know his voice. A stranger they will not follow, but they will flee from him, for they do not know the voice of strangers." This figure of speech Jesus used with them, but they did not understand what He was saying to them.

So Jesus again said to them, "Truly, truly, I say to you, I am the door of the sheep. All who came before Me are thieves and robbers, but the sheep did not listen to them. I am the door. If anyone enters by Me, he will be saved and will go in and out and find pasture. The thief comes only to steal and kill and destroy. I came that they may have life and have it abundantly. I am the good shepherd. The good shepherd lays down His life for the sheep. He who is a hired hand and not a shepherd, who does not own the sheep, sees the wolf coming and leaves the sheep and flees, and the wolf snatches them and scatters them. He flees because he is a hired hand and cares nothing for the sheep. I am the good shepherd. I know My own and My own know Me, just as the Father knows Me and I know the Father; and I lay down My life for the sheep. And I have other sheep that are not of this fold. I must bring them also, and they will listen to My voice. So there will be one flock, one shepherd. For this reason the Father loves Me, because I lay down My life that I may take it up again. No one takes it from Me, but I lay it down of My own accord. I have authority to lay it down, and I have authority to take it up again. This charge I have received from My Father."

### ROMANS 8:31–35, 37–39

What then shall we say to these things? If God is for us, who can be against us? He who did not spare His own Son but gave Him up for us all, how will He not also with Him graciously give us all things? Who shall bring any charge against God's elect? It is God who justifies. Who is to condemn? Christ Jesus is the one who died—more than that, who was raised—who is at the right hand of God, who indeed is interceding for us. Who shall separate us from the love of Christ? Shall tribulation, or distress, or persecution, or famine, or nakedness, or danger, or sword? . . .

No, in all these things we are more than conquerors through Him who loved us. For I am sure that neither death nor life, nor angels nor rulers, nor things present nor things to come, nor powers, nor height nor depth, nor anything else in all creation, will be able to separate us from the love of God in Christ Jesus our Lord.

### Additional Readings

Isaiah 43:1–3a; Matthew 6:25–34; Philippians 4:4–7

### Prayers

Lord God, You have called Your servants to ventures of which we cannot see the ending, by paths as yet untrod, through perils unknown. Give us faith to go out with good courage, not knowing where we go but only that Your hand is leading us and Your love supporting us; through Jesus Christ, our Lord. Amen.

Almighty and everlasting God, You are always more ready to hear than we to pray and always ready to give more than we either desire or deserve. Pour down on us the abundance of Your mercy; forgive us those things of which our conscience is afraid; and give us those good things for which we are not worthy to ask except by the merits and mediation of Jesus Christ, Your Son, our Lord, who lives and reigns with You and the Holy Spirit, one God, now and forever. Amen. (*LSB Altar Book*, p. 832)

*For additional prayers, see Section IV, p. 219*

### Hymnody

Be of good cheer; your cause belongs
To Him who can avenge your wrongs;
Leave it to Him, our Lord.
Though hidden yet from mortal eyes,

His Gideon shall for you arise,
Uphold you and His Word.

As true as God's own Word is true,
Not earth nor hell's satanic crew
Against us shall prevail.
Their might? A joke, a mere facade!
God is with us and we with God—
Our vict'ry cannot fail.

Amen, Lord Jesus, grant our prayer;
Great Captain, now Thine arm make bare,
Fight for us once again!
So shall Thy saints and martyrs raise
A mighty chorus to Thy praise
Forevermore. Amen.

("O Little Flock, Fear Not the Foe," *LSB* 666:2–4)

### *Additional Hymn*

"Have No Fear, Little Flock" (*LSB* 735)

# Guilt

*For devotions suitable for this topic, see Section II, p. 44*

Guilt is a healthy response to our own sin and its consequences. But guilt can so consume us that we forget that in Christ and His atoning sacrifice we are innocent of all charges against us. We are forgiven and set free from the pangs of guilt through the blood of Jesus.

### *Psalmody*

**PSALM 51**

Have mercy on me, O God,
　　according to Your steadfast love;
according to Your abundant mercy
　　blot out my transgressions.
Wash me thoroughly from my iniquity,
　　and cleanse me from my sin!

For I know my transgressions,
and my sin is ever before me.
Against You, You only, have I sinned
and done what is evil in Your sight,
so that You may be justified in Your words
and blameless in Your judgment.
Behold, I was brought forth in iniquity,
and in sin did my mother conceive me.
Behold, You delight in truth in the inward being,
and You teach me wisdom in the secret heart.

Purge me with hyssop, and I shall be clean;
wash me, and I shall be whiter than snow.
Let me hear joy and gladness;
let the bones that You have broken rejoice.
Hide Your face from my sins,
and blot out all my iniquities.
Create in me a clean heart, O God,
and renew a right spirit within me.
Cast me not away from Your presence,
and take not Your Holy Spirit from me.
Restore to me the joy of Your salvation,
and uphold me with a willing spirit.

Then I will teach transgressors Your ways,
and sinners will return to You.
Deliver me from bloodguiltiness, O God,
O God of my salvation,
and my tongue will sing aloud
of Your righteousness.
O Lord, open my lips,
and my mouth will declare Your praise.
For You will not delight in sacrifice, or I would give it;
You will not be pleased with a burnt offering.
The sacrifices of God are a broken spirit;
a broken and contrite heart,
O God, You will not despise.

Do good to Zion in Your good pleasure;
build up the walls of Jerusalem;

then will You delight in right sacrifices,
in burnt offerings and whole burnt offerings;
then bulls will be offered on Your altar.

## Additional Psalms

32; 86; 139:1–17

## Readings

### ISAIAH 53

Who has believed what they heard from us? And to whom has the arm of the Lord been revealed? For He grew up before Him like a young plant, and like a root out of dry ground; He had no form or majesty that we should look at Him, and no beauty that we should desire Him. He was despised and rejected by men; a man of sorrows, and acquainted with grief; and as one from whom men hide their faces He was despised, and we esteemed Him not.

Surely He has borne our griefs and carried our sorrows; yet we esteemed Him stricken, smitten by God, and afflicted. But He was wounded for our transgressions; He was crushed for our iniquities; upon Him was the chastisement that brought us peace, and with His stripes we are healed. All we like sheep have gone astray; we have turned every one to his own way; and the Lord has laid on Him the iniquity of us all.

He was oppressed, and He was afflicted, yet He opened not His mouth; like a lamb that is led to the slaughter, and like a sheep that before its shearers is silent, so He opened not His mouth. By oppression and judgment He was taken away; and as for His generation, who considered that He was cut off out of the land of the living, stricken for the transgression of My people? And they made His grave with the wicked and with a rich man in His death, although He had done no violence, and there was no deceit in His mouth.

Yet it was the will of the Lord to crush Him; He has put Him to grief; when His soul makes an offering for sin, He shall see His offspring; He shall prolong His days; the will of the Lord shall prosper in His hand. Out of the anguish of His soul He shall see and be satisfied; by His knowledge shall the righteous one, My servant, make many to be accounted righteous, and He shall bear their iniquities. Therefore I will divide Him a portion with the many, and He shall divide the spoil with the strong, because He poured out His soul to death and was numbered with the transgressors; yet He bore the sin of many, and makes intercession for the transgressors.

**JOHN 3:16–21**

For God so loved the world, that He gave His only Son, that whoever believes in Him should not perish but have eternal life. For God did not send His Son into the world to condemn the world, but in order that the world might be saved through Him. Whoever believes in Him is not condemned, but whoever does not believe is condemned already, because he has not believed in the name of the only Son of God. And this is the judgment: the light has come into the world, and people loved the darkness rather than the light because their deeds were evil. For everyone who does wicked things hates the light and does not come to the light, lest his deeds should be exposed. But whoever does what is true comes to the light, so that it may be clearly seen that his deeds have been carried out in God.

## Additional Readings

Matthew 9:2–28; Ephesians 3:13–21; 1 John 4:19–21

## Prayers

Almighty God, whose Son Jesus Christ chose to suffer pain before going up to joy, and crucifixion before entering into glory, mercifully grant that we, walking in the way of the cross, may find this path to be the way of life and peace; through Jesus Christ, Your Son, our Lord, who lives and reigns with You and the Holy Spirit, one God, now and forever. Amen. (*LW*, p. 41)

O Lord, grant to Your faithful people pardon and peace that they may be cleansed from all their guilt and serve You with a quiet mind; through Jesus Christ, Your Son, our Lord, who lives and reigns with You and the Holy Spirit, one God, now and forever. Amen. (Adapted from *LSB Altar Book*, p. 932)

*For additional prayers, see Section IV, p. 220*

## Hymnody

> Lord, to You I make confession:
> I have sinned and gone astray,
> I have multiplied transgression,
> Chosen for myself my way.
> Led by You to see my errors,
> Lord, I tremble at Your terrors.
>
> Yet, though conscience' voice appall me,
> Father, I will seek Your face;
> Though Your child I dare not call me,
> Yet receive me in Your grace.
> Do not for my sins forsake me;
> Let Your wrath not overtake me.
>
> For Your Son has suffered for me,
> Giv'n Himself to rescue me,
> Died to save me and restore me,
> Reconciled and set me free.
> Jesus' cross alone can vanquish
> These dark fears and soothe this anguish.
>
> Lord, on You I cast my burden—
> Sink it in the deepest sea!
> Let me know Your gracious pardon,
> Cleanse me from iniquity.
> Let Your Spirit leave me never;
> Make me only Yours forever.
>
> ("Lord, to You I Make Confession," *LSB* 608)

### Additional Hymns

" 'As Surely as I Live,' God Said" (*LSB* 614); "By Grace I'm Saved" (*LSB* 566); "God Loved the World So That He

Gave" (*LSB* 571); "Jesus, Grant That Balm and Healing" (*LSB* 421); "Jesus Sinners Doth Receive" (*LSB* 609); "Oh, How Great Is Your Compassion" (*LSB* 559)

## IMPATIENCE, BOREDOM, RESTLESSNESS

*For devotions suitable for this topic, see Section II, p. 45*

Impatience, boredom, and restlessness are symptoms of a deeper problem: we are not at peace with God. Augustine once said that our souls are restless until they are at rest in Jesus. It is only through Christ's gifts—the gift of Himself and His presence in us—that will we be at rest with ourselves.

### *Psalmody*

**PSALM 92**

It is good to give thanks to the LORD,
　　to sing praises to Your name, O Most High;
to declare Your steadfast love in the morning,
　　and Your faithfulness by night,
to the music of the lute and the harp,
　　to the melody of the lyre.
For You, O LORD, have made me glad by Your work;
　　at the works of Your hands I sing for joy.

How great are Your works, O LORD!
　　Your thoughts are very deep!
The stupid man cannot know;
　　the fool cannot understand this:
that though the wicked sprout like grass
　　and all evildoers flourish,
they are doomed to destruction forever;
　　but You, O LORD, are on high forever.
For behold, Your enemies, O LORD,
　　for behold, Your enemies shall perish;
　　all evildoers shall be scattered.

But You have exalted my horn like that of the wild ox;
    You have poured over me fresh oil.
My eyes have seen the downfall of my enemies;
    my ears have heard the doom of my evil assailants.

The righteous flourish like the palm tree
    and grow like a cedar in Lebanon.
They are planted in the house of the LORD;
    they flourish in the courts of our God.
They still bear fruit in old age;
    they are ever full of sap and green,
to declare that the LORD is upright;
    He is my rock,
    and there is no unrighteousness in Him.

## Additional Psalms
93–100

## Reading

### 2 CORINTHIANS 4:7–18

But we have this treasure in jars of clay, to show that the surpassing power belongs to God and not to us. We are afflicted in every way, but not crushed; perplexed, but not driven to despair; persecuted, but not forsaken; struck down, but not destroyed; always carrying in the body the death of Jesus, so that the life of Jesus may also be manifested in our bodies. For we who live are always being given over to death for Jesus' sake, so that the life of Jesus also may be manifested in our mortal flesh. So death is at work in us, but life in you.

Since we have the same spirit of faith according to what has been written, "I believed, and so I spoke," we also believe, and so we also speak, knowing that He who raised the Lord Jesus will raise us also with Jesus and bring us with you into His presence. For it is all for your sake, so that as grace extends to more and more people it may increase thanksgiving, to the glory of God.

So we do not lose heart. Though our outer nature is wasting away, our inner nature is being renewed day by day.

For this slight momentary affliction is preparing for us an eternal weight of glory beyond all comparison, as we look not to the things that are seen but to the things that are unseen. For the things that are seen are transient, but the things that are unseen are eternal.

### Additional Readings

Genesis 1:1–2:4; Isaiah 55:6–10; John 1:1–14; Revelation 21:1–8

### Prayers

O Lord, merciful Father, who delivered us from sin and death, continue to rescue us from the snare of the devil and the world so that we live to tell the story of Jesus Christ, in whose name we pray. Amen.

Jesus Christ, light of life, who illuminates our world with Your truth, reveal to us Your saving will, and work in us to trust in Your purpose of eternal life, for Your mercy's sake. Amen.

O almighty Father and Creator, who created the world for Your pleasure and love, help us in this time of restlessness to remember Your purpose of life and grant us joy and knowledge of Your wonderful gift of creation, through Jesus Christ, Your Son, our Lord, who lives and reigns with You and the Holy Spirit, one God, now and forever. Amen.

O Son of God, You patiently endured the pain and suffering of the crucifixion. Give to us Your patience so that we may praise You even in our trials and travails, and raise us up on the Last Day. In Your name we pray. Amen.

*For additional prayers, see Section IV, p. 221*

### Hymnody

Awake, my heart, with gladness,
See what today is done;
Now, after gloom and sadness,
Comes forth the glorious sun.
My Savior there was laid

Where our bed must be made
When to the realms of light
Our spirit wings its flight.

The foe in triumph shouted
When Christ lay in the tomb;
But lo, he now is routed,
His boast is turned to gloom.
For Christ again is free;
In glorious victory
He who is strong to save
Has triumphed o'er the grave.

("Awake, My Heart, with Gladness," *LSB* 467:1–2)

### *Additional Hymns*

"I Will Sing My Maker's Praises" (*LSB* 977; available through *Lutheran Service Builder*); "In Peace and Joy I Now Depart" (*LSB* 938); "From Depths of Woe I Cry to Thee" (*LSB* 607); "Rejoice, My Heart, Be Glad and Sing" (*LSB* 737)

## ADDICTION

*For devotions suitable for this topic, see Section II, p. 47*

Although addiction can be overwhelming at times, those who suffer such an affliction need to be pointed to their incorruptibility in Jesus Christ. If the Son of God cannot be destroyed, neither can those who are in Him. The baptized Christian who is suffering from an addiction is still in Christ and needs the assurance that comes from residing in Christ's body.

### *Psalmody*

#### PSALM 121

I lift up my eyes to the hills.
From where does my help come?
My help comes from the LORD,
who made heaven and earth.

He will not let your foot be moved;
   He who keeps you will not slumber.
Behold, He who keeps Israel
   will neither slumber nor sleep.

The Lord is your keeper;
   the Lord is your shade on your right hand.
The sun shall not strike you by day,
   nor the moon by night.

The Lord will keep you from all evil;
   He will keep your life.
The Lord will keep
   your going out and your coming in
   from this time forth and forevermore.

## Additional Psalms

23; 46; 51; 91; 130

## Readings

### MATTHEW 15:21–28

And Jesus went away from there and withdrew to the district of Tyre and Sidon. And behold, a Canaanite woman from that region came out and was crying, "Have mercy on me, O Lord, Son of David; my daughter is severely oppressed by a demon." But He did not answer her a word. And His disciples came and begged Him, saying, "Send her away, for she is crying out after us." He answered, "I was sent only to the lost sheep of the house of Israel." But she came and knelt before Him, saying, "Lord, help me." And He answered, "It is not right to take the children's bread and throw it to the dogs." She said, "Yes, Lord, yet even the dogs eat the crumbs that fall from their masters' table." Then Jesus answered her, "O woman, great is your faith! Be it done for you as you desire." And her daughter was healed instantly.

### ROMANS 8:38–39

For I am sure that neither death nor life, nor angels nor rulers, nor things present nor things to come, nor powers, nor height nor depth, nor anything else in all creation, will be able to separate us from the love of God in Christ Jesus our Lord.

### Additional Readings

John 3:16; Romans 6:1–6; 2 Corinthians 4:6–9; Galatians 3:23–29; 6:15

### Prayers

O blessed Jesus, since You minister to all who are afflicted, look with compassion on those who through addiction have lost their health and freedom. Restore to them the assurance of Your unfailing mercy, remove the fears that attack them, strengthen them in the recovery of their self-possession and health, and give skill, patience, and understanding love to those who provide care for them; for Your own mercy's sake. Amen. (*LW Little Agenda*, p. 100)

Stir up Your power, O Lord, and come and help us by Your might, that the sins which weigh us down may be quickly lifted by Your grace and mercy; for You live and reign with the Father and the Holy Spirit, one God, now and forever. Amen. (*LSB Altar Book*, p. 557)

*For additional prayers, see Section IV, p. 222*

### Hymnody

> All depends on our possessing
> God's abundant grace and blessing,
> Though all earthly wealth depart.
> They who trust with faith unshaken
> By their God are not forsaken
> And will keep a dauntless heart.
>
> Many spend their lives in fretting
> Over trifles and in getting
> Things that have no solid ground.
> I shall strive to win a treasure
> That will bring me lasting pleasure
> And that now is seldom found.

When with sorrow I am stricken,
Hope anew my heart will quicken;
All my longing shall be stilled.
To His loving-kindness tender
Soul and body I surrender,
For on God alone I build.

("All Depends on Our Possessing," *LSB* 732:1, 3–4)

## Additional Hymns

"Children of the Heavenly Father" (*LSB* 725); "God's Own Child, I Gladly Say It" (*LSB* 594); "O Day Full of Grace" (*LSB* 503)

# LONELINESS

*For devotions suitable for this topic, see Section II, p. 49*

Loneliness plagues all of us, even those who live active lives, surrounded by many people. But for those who live alone or who have lost a spouse or have little contact with people, loneliness can feel overwhelming. Our Lord is always present in our loneliness, for we hear His voice in the living words of His Gospel and turn to Him in prayer. In our Baptism He binds Himself to us forever and promises never to leave or forsake us.

## Psalmody

**PSALM 6**

O LORD, rebuke me not in Your anger,
    nor discipline me in Your wrath.
Be gracious to me, O Lord, for I am languishing;
    heal me, O LORD, for my bones are troubled.
My soul also is greatly troubled.
    But You, O LORD—how long?

Turn, O LORD, deliver my life;
    save me for the sake of Your steadfast love.

For in death there is no remembrance of You;
in Sheol who will give You praise?

I am weary with my moaning;
every night I flood my bed with tears;
I drench my couch with my weeping.
My eye wastes away because of grief;
it grows weak because of all my foes.

Depart from me, all you workers of evil,
for the LORD has heard the sound of my weeping.
The LORD has heard my plea;
the LORD accepts my prayer.
All my enemies shall be ashamed and greatly troubled;
they shall turn back and be put to shame in a
moment.

## Additional Psalms

13; 27; 31; 42; 139:1–17

## Readings

### JOHN 14:1–6

"Let not your hearts be troubled. Believe in God; believe also in Me. In My Father's house are many rooms. If it were not so, would I have told you that I go to prepare a place for you? And if I go and prepare a place for you, I will come again and will take you to Myself, that where I am you may be also. And you know the way to where I am going." Thomas said to Him, "Lord, we do not know where You are going. How can we know the way?" Jesus said to Him, "I am the way, and the truth, and the life. No one comes to the Father except through Me."

### ROMANS 8:18–28

For I consider that the sufferings of this present time are not worth comparing with the glory that is to be revealed to us. For the creation waits with eager longing for the revealing of the sons of God. For the creation was subjected to futility, not willingly, but because of Him who subjected it, in hope that the creation itself will be set free from its bondage to decay and obtain the freedom of the glory of the children of God. For we know that the whole creation has been groaning together in the pains of childbirth until now. And not only the creation, but we ourselves, who have the firstfruits of the Spirit, groan inwardly as we wait eagerly for adoption as sons, the redemption of our bodies. For in this hope we were saved. Now hope that is seen is not hope. For who hopes for what he sees? But if we hope for what we do not see, we wait for it with patience.

Likewise the Spirit helps us in our weakness. For we do not know what to pray for as we ought, but the Spirit Himself intercedes for us with groanings too deep for words. And He who searches hearts knows what is the mind of the Spirit, because the Spirit intercedes for the saints according to the will of God. And we know that for those who love God all things work together for good, for those who are called according to His purpose.

### ROMANS 8:31B–39

If God is for us, who can be against us? He who did not spare His own Son but gave Him up for us all, how will He not also with Him graciously give us all things? Who shall bring any charge against God's elect? It is God who justifies. Who is to condemn? Christ Jesus is the one who died— more than that, who was raised—who is at the right hand of God, who indeed is interceding for us. Who shall separate us from the love of Christ? Shall tribulation, or distress, or persecution, or famine, or nakedness, or danger, or sword? As it is written, "For Your sake we are being killed all the day long; we are regarded as sheep to be slaughtered."

No, in all these things we are more than conquerors through Him who loved us. For I am sure that neither death nor life, nor angels nor rulers, nor things present nor things to come, nor powers, nor height nor depth, nor anything else in all creation, will be able to separate us from the love of God in Christ Jesus our Lord.

## Additional Readings

Isaiah 35:1–10; 43:1–3a; 49:13–15; Jeremiah 20:7–13;

John 15:7–11; Romans 5:1–5; 2 Corinthians 1:3–7; 4:13b–5:9; Philippians 4:4–7; Hebrews 12:1–2; 1 Peter 1:3–9; 4:12–14; 1 John 5:14–15

## Prayers

Lord God, Your gracious presence attends Your people wherever they go. Be with those whose lives are spent in solitude. Support them in times of challenge or loneliness, and surround them with caring Christian people so that they may find welcome, peace, and joy in Your ongoing kindness and love; through Jesus Christ, our Lord. Amen. (Adapted from *LSB*, p. 316)

Almighty God, merciful Father, by Word and Sacrament You have created Your Church in this world to be a godly communion and family. Grant Your blessing to those who dwell in loneliness that they may find a place of solace and pleasant fellowship among people faithful to You; through Jesus Christ, our Lord. Amen. (*LW Little Agenda*, p. 102)

*For additional prayers, see Section IV, p. 223*

## Hymnody

> O little flock, fear not the foe
> Who madly seeks your overthrow;
> Dread not his rage and pow'r.
> And though your courage sometimes faints,
> His seeming triumph o'er God's saints
> Lasts but a little hour.

("O Little Flock, Fear Not the Foe," *LSB* 666:1)

## Additional Hymns

"I Trust, O Christ, in You Alone" (*LSB* 972; available through *Lutheran Service Builder*); "In the Morning When I Rise" (*LSB* 976; available through *Lutheran Service Builder*); "Let Me Be Thine Forever" (*LSB* 689); "Now the Light Has Gone Away" (*LSB* 887); "O God, Our Help in Ages Past" (*LSB* 733)

# Old Age

*For devotions suitable for this topic, see Section II, p. 51*

Growing old brings us closer to our death and closer to God. But many who are elderly experience severe depression because of the loss of a spouse or loneliness from living alone or the fear of physical suffering and even of death itself. The elderly need the compassion of others who, by their presence, embody Christ for them.

## *Psalmody*

### PSALM 90

Lord, You have been our dwelling place
   in all generations.
Before the mountains were brought forth,
   or ever You had formed the earth and the world,
   from everlasting to everlasting You are God.

You return man to dust
   and say, "Return, O children of man!"
For a thousand years in Your sight
   are but as yesterday when it is past,
   or as a watch in the night.

You sweep them away as with a flood;
    they are like a dream,
   like grass that is renewed in the morning:
in the morning it flourishes and is renewed;
   in the evening it fades and withers.
For we are brought to an end by Your anger;
   by Your wrath we are dismayed.
You have set our iniquities before You,
   our secret sins in the light of Your presence.

For all our days pass away under Your wrath;
   we bring our years to an end like a sigh.
The years of our life are seventy,
   or even by reason of strength eighty;

yet their span is but toil and trouble;
> they are soon gone, and we fly away.
Who considers the power of Your anger,
> and Your wrath according to the fear of You?

So teach us to number our days
> that we may get a heart of wisdom.
Return, O LORD! How long?
> Have pity on Your servants!
Satisfy us in the morning with Your steadfast love,
> that we may rejoice and be glad all our days.
Make us glad for as many days as You have afflicted us,
> and for as many years as we have seen evil.
Let Your work be shown to Your servants,
> and Your glorious power to their children.
Let the favor of the Lord our God be upon us,
> and establish the work of our hands upon us;
> yes, establish the work of our hands!

## Additional Psalms

39; 71; 73:26

## Reading

### 2 CORINTHIANS 5:1–4

For we know that if the tent, which is our earthly home, is destroyed, we have a building from God, a house not made with hands, eternal in the heavens. For in this tent we groan, longing to put on our heavenly dwelling, if indeed by putting it on we may not be found naked. For while we are still in this tent, we groan, being burdened—not that we would be unclothed, but that we would be further clothed, so that what is mortal may be swallowed up by life.

## Additional Reading

Isaiah 46:4

## Prayers

Almighty God and gracious Father, in Your mercy look on all whose increasing years bring them weakness, anxiety, distress, or loneliness. Provide them with homes where love and respect, concern and understanding are shown. Grant them willing hearts to accept help and, as their strength wanes, increase their faith and the assurance of Your love through Jesus Christ, their Savior. Amen. (*LW Little Agenda*, p. 102)

Lord God, our continual refuge, our life in old age, in whose hands our time abides, look! The years that do not please me have come upon me. For my abilities in this advanced age are continually being taken from me, and all about me, difficulties and weaknesses have increased in number. You have so graciously and fatherly cared for me from the time that I was in the womb. Until now, from my youth, You have remained my hope. Therefore, I humbly ask You not to depart from me in my old age, in which I have grown gray and weak, but until my life's blessed end lift me up, bear me, and save me. Especially I pray to You, O gracious Father, that You would govern and lead me with Your Holy Spirit, that I may wholly dedicate the rest of my time on earth to be with You, so that, even in my sighing, I may remain faithful on this Christian pilgrimage. Strengthen me in this time of preparation for a blessed end. May I be ready, so that if today or tomorrow my life should reach its goal, I may, with old Simeon, in peace depart this world unto life eternal. Amen. (*LBP*, p. 160)

*For additional prayers, see Section IV, p. 223*

## Hymnody

Abide with me, fast falls the eventide.
The darkness deepens; Lord, with me abide.
When other helpers fail and comforts flee,
Help of the helpless, O abide with me.

I need Thy presence ev'ry passing hour;
What but Thy grace can foil the tempter's pow'r?
Who like Thyself my guide and stay can be?
Through cloud and sunshine, O abide with me.

Come not in terrors, as the King of kings,
But kind and good, with healing in Thy wings;

Tears for all woes, a heart for ev'ry plea.
Come, Friend of sinners, thus abide with me.

Swift to its close ebbs out life's little day;
Earth's joys grow dim, its glories pass away;
Change and decay in all around I see;
O Thou who changest not, abide with me.

Hold Thou Thy cross before my closing eyes;
Shine through the gloom, and point me to the
skies.
Heav'n's morning breaks, and earth's vain shad-
ows flee;
In life, in death, O Lord, abide with me.

("Abide with Me," *LSB* 878:1–4, 6)

### *Additional Hymns*

"O God, Our Help in Ages Past" (*LSB* 733); "The Lord's
My Shepherd, I'll Not Want" (*LSB* 710)

## POOR AND NEEDY

*For devotions suitable for this topic, see Section II, p. 53*

Those who are suffering from want are in need of
God's mercy, to know that He sees need and responds
to it. Although circumstances may cause it to appear
that those in need are abandoned and unloved, we see
with the eyes of faith. We see in the cross the ultimate
act of mercy—God entering into our need, carrying
our infirmity as a man, and redeeming us for life
everlasting. In possession of these great riches, we can
ask with an open heart that the One we trust meet all
our needs.

### *Psalmody*

**PSALM 86**

Incline Your ear, O LORD, and answer me,
for I am poor and needy.

Preserve my life, for I am godly;
  save Your servant, who trusts in You—
    You are my God.
Be gracious to me, O Lord,
  for to You do I cry all the day.
Gladden the soul of Your servant,
  for to You, O Lord, do I lift up my soul.
For You, O Lord, are good and forgiving,
  abounding in steadfast love to all who call upon You.
Give ear, O Lord, to my prayer;
  listen to my plea for grace.
In the day of my trouble I call upon You,
  for You answer me.

There is none like You among the gods, O Lord,
  nor are there any works like Yours.
All the nations You have made shall come
  and worship before You, O Lord,
and shall glorify Your name.
For You are great and do wondrous things;
  You alone are God.
Teach me Your way, O Lord,
  that I may walk in Your truth;
  unite my heart to fear Your name.
I give thanks to You, O Lord my
    God, with my whole heart,
  and I will glorify Your name forever.
For great is Your steadfast love toward me;
  You have delivered my soul from the depths of
    Sheol.

O God, insolent men have risen up against me;
  a band of ruthless men seek my life,
  and they do not set You before them.
But You, O Lord, are a God merciful and gracious,
  slow to anger and abounding in
    steadfast love and faithfulness.
Turn to me and be gracious to me;
  give Your strength to Your servant,

and save the son of Your maidservant.
Show me a sign of Your favor,

that those who hate me may see and be put to shame
because You, LORD, have helped me and comforted me.

## Additional Psalms

9:9–20; 41; 42; 49; 63; 72

## Readings

### LUKE 4:16–21

And He came to Nazareth, where He had been brought up. And as was His custom, He went to the synagogue on the Sabbath day, and He stood up to read. And the scroll of the prophet Isaiah was given to Him. He unrolled the scroll and found the place where it was written, "The Spirit of the Lord is upon Me, because He has anointed Me to proclaim good news to the poor. He has sent Me to proclaim liberty to the captives and recovering of sight to the blind, to set at liberty those who are oppressed, to proclaim the year of the Lord's favor."

And He rolled up the scroll and gave it back to the attendant and sat down. And the eyes of all in the synagogue were fixed on Him. And He began to say to them, "Today this Scripture has been fulfilled in your hearing."

### 2 CORINTHIANS 8:9

For you know the grace of our Lord Jesus Christ, that though He was rich, yet for your sake He became poor, so that you by His poverty might become rich.

## Additional Readings

1 Samuel 2:1–10; Isaiah 25; 41:8–20; Luke 1:46–55; 2 Corinthians 6:2–10

## Prayers

O blessed Jesus Christ, You are the manifestation of God's love, please give to us the same to exhibit Your work of mercy to the poor and the needy, the sick and dying, for Your name's sake. Amen.

Heavenly Father, though we do not deserve Your goodness, still You provide for all our needs of body and soul. Grant us Your Holy Spirit that we may acknowledge Your gifts, give thanks for all Your benefits, and serve You in willing obedience; through Jesus Christ, Your Son, our Lord, who lives and reigns with You and the Holy Spirit, one God, now and forever. Amen. (*LSB Altar Book*, p. 721)

*For additional prayers, see Section IV, p. 225*

## *Hymnody*

He came from His blest throne
Salvation to bestow;
But men made strange, and none
The longed-for Christ would know.
But, oh, my friend,
My friend indeed,
Who at my need
His life did spend!

In life no house, no home
My Lord on earth might have;
In death no friendly tomb
But what a stranger gave.
What may I say?
Heav'n was His home
But mine the tomb
Wherein He lay.

Here might I stay and sing,
No story so divine!
Never was love, dear King,
Never was grief like Thine.
This is my friend,
In whose sweet praise
I all my days
Could gladly spend!

("My Song Is Love Unknown," *LSB* 430:2, 6–7)

### *Additional Hymns*

"Come unto Me, Ye Weary" (*LSB* 684); "I Lie, O Lord, within Your Care" (*LSB* 885)

## SPIRITUAL OPPRESSION

*For devotions suitable for this topic, see Section II, p. 54*

The presence of evil is real, and we are protected from the devil only through the power that comes from the name of Jesus. When confronted by the darkness of the devil, we will be protected by the living voice of Jesus in His Word, the strong name of the Trinity into which we are baptized, the confession of the Apostles' Creed, and the Lord's Prayer.

### *Psalmody*

#### PSALM 53

The fool says in his heart, "There is no God."
  They are corrupt, doing abominable iniquity;
  there is none who does good.

God looks down from heaven
  on the children of man
to see if there are any who understand,
  who seek after God.

They have all fallen away;
  together they have become corrupt;
there is none who does good,
  not even one.

Have those who work evil no knowledge,
  who eat up My people as they eat bread,
  and do not call upon God?

There they are, in great terror,
  where there is no terror!
For God scatters the bones of him
    who encamps against You;

You put them to shame, for God has rejected them.

Oh, that salvation for Israel would come out of Zion!
When God restores the fortunes of His people,
Let Jacob rejoice, let Israel be glad.

## Additional Psalms

30; 34; 67; 91

## Readings

### LUKE 11:14–22

Now He was casting out a demon that was mute. When the demon had gone out, the mute man spoke, and the people marveled. But some of them said, "He casts out demons by Beelzebul, the prince of demons," while others, to test Him, kept seeking from Him a sign from heaven. But He, knowing their thoughts, said to them, "Every kingdom divided against itself is laid waste, and a divided household falls. And if Satan also is divided against himself, how will his kingdom stand? For you say that I cast out demons by Beelzebul. And if I cast out demons by Beelzebul, by whom do your sons cast them out? Therefore they will be your judges. But if it is by the finger of God that I cast out demons, then the kingdom of God has come upon you. When a strong man, fully armed, guards his own palace, his goods are safe; but when one stronger than he attacks him and overcomes him, he takes away his armor in which he trusted and divides his spoil."

### JOHN 10:27–28

My sheep hear My voice, and I know them, and they follow Me. I give them eternal life, and they will never perish, and no one will snatch them out of My hand.

## Additional Readings

1 John 4:1–6; 5:13–21

## Prayers

O Holy Lord, almighty Father, who has sent Your only-begotten Son into the world that He might destroy the works of the devil, speedily hear us we pray. Grant Your servants strength to fight valiantly against the evil one. May the strength of Your right hand make Satan loose Your servant, so that he no longer dares to hold captive him whom You have redeemed in Your Son and washed clean in the waters of Holy Baptism. In the name of Your mighty Son we pray. Amen.

O Lord, mercifully hear our prayers, and having set us free from the bonds of our sins deliver us from every evil; through Jesus Christ, Your Son, our Lord, who lives and reigns with You and the Holy Spirit, one God, now and forever. Amen. (*LSB Altar Book*, 576)

*For additional prayers, see Section IV, p. 225*

## Hymnody

A mighty fortress is our God,
A trusty shield and weapon;
He helps us free from ev'ry need
That hath us now o'ertaken.
The old evil foe
Now means deadly woe;
Deep guile and great might
Are his dread arms in fight;
On earth is not his equal.

With might of ours can naught be done,
Soon were our loss effected;
But for us fights the valiant One,
Whom God Himself elected.
Ask ye, Who is this?
Jesus Christ it is,
Of Sabaoth Lord,
And there's none other God;
He holds the field forever.

Though devils all the world should fill,
All eager to devour us,
We tremble not, we fear no ill;

They shall not overpow'r us.
This world's prince may still
Scowl fierce as he will,
He can harm us none.
He's judged; the deed is done;
One little word can fell him.

The Word they still shall let remain
Nor any thanks have for it;
He's by our side upon the plain
With His good gifts and Spirit.
And take they our life,
Goods, fame, child, and wife,
Though these all be gone,
Our vict'ry has been won;
The Kingdom ours remaineth.

("A Mighty Fortress Is Our God," *LSB* 656)

## *Additional Hymns*

"Lord God, to Thee We Give All Praise" (*LSB* 522); "Triune God, Be Thou Our Stay" (*LSB* 505)

## Nature of Spiritual Warfare

There is a war in heaven between Jesus with His holy angels and the devil with his minions. The defeat of Satan is certain, for he is conquered by the blood of the Lamb and the Word preached by the Church about that very blood. The victory is already ours in Christ and His living Word.

## *Psalmody*

### PSALM 3

O Lord, how many are my foes!
    Many are rising against me;
many are saying of my soul,
    there is no salvation for him in God.

But You, O LORD, are a shield about me,
  my glory, and the lifter of my head.
I cried aloud to the LORD,
  and He answered me from His holy hill.

I lay down and slept;
  I woke again, for the LORD sustained me.
I will not be afraid of many thousands of people
  who have set themselves against me all around.

Arise, O LORD!
  Save me, O my God!
For You strike all my enemies on the cheek;
You break the teeth of the wicked.

Salvation belongs to the LORD;
  Your blessing be on Your people!

**PSALM 21**

O LORD, in Your strength the king rejoices,
  and in Your salvation how greatly he exults!
You have given him his heart's desire
  and have not withheld the request of his lips.
For You meet him with rich blessings;
  You set a crown of fine gold upon his head.
He asked life of You; You gave it to him,
  length of days forever and ever.
His glory is great through Your salvation;
  splendor and majesty You bestow on him.
For You make him most blessed forever;
  You make him glad with the joy of Your presence.
For the king trusts in the LORD,
  and through the steadfast love of the Most High he
  shall not be moved.

Your hand will find out all Your enemies;
  Your right hand will find out those who hate You.
You will make them as a blazing oven
  when You appear.
The LORD will swallow them up in His wrath,
  and fire will consume them.

You will destroy their descendants from the earth,
    and their offspring from among the children of
    man.
Though they plan evil against You,
    though they devise mischief, they will not succeed.
For You will put them to flight;
    You will aim at their faces with Your bows.

Be exalted, O Lord, in Your strength!
    We will sing and praise Your power.

## Additional Psalms

Psalm 10; 12; 21

## Readings

### LUKE 10:17–20

The seventy-two returned with joy, saying, "Lord, even the demons are subject to us in Your name!" And He said to them, "I saw Satan fall like lightning from heaven. Behold, I have given you authority to tread on serpents and scorpions, and over all the power of the enemy, and nothing shall hurt you. Nevertheless, do not rejoice in this, that the spirits are subject to you, but rejoice that your names are written in heaven."

### EPHESIANS 6:10–20

Finally, be strong in the Lord and in the strength of His might. Put on the whole armor of God, that you may be able to stand against the schemes of the devil. For we do not wrestle against flesh and blood, but against the rulers, against the authorities, against the cosmic powers over this present darkness, against the spiritual forces of evil in the heavenly places. Therefore take up the whole armor of God, that you may be able to withstand in the evil day, and having done all, to stand firm. Stand therefore, having fastened on the belt of truth, and having put on the breastplate of righteousness, and, as shoes for your feet, having put on the readiness given by the gospel of peace. In all circumstances take up the shield of faith, with which you can extinguish all the flaming darts of the evil one; and take the helmet of salvation, and the sword of the Spirit, which is the word of God, praying at all times in the Spirit, with all prayer and supplication. To that end keep alert with all perseverance, making supplication for all the saints, and also for me, that words may be given to me in opening my mouth boldly to proclaim the mystery of the gospel, for which I am an ambassador in chains, that I may declare it boldly, as I ought to speak.

**REVELATION 12:7–12**

Now war arose in heaven, Michael and his angels fighting against the dragon. And the dragon and his angels fought back, but he was defeated and there was no longer any place for them in heaven. And the great dragon was thrown down, that ancient serpent, who is called the devil and Satan, the deceiver of the whole world—he was thrown down to the earth, and his angels were thrown down with him. And I heard a loud voice in heaven, saying, "Now the salvation and the power and the kingdom of our God and the authority of His Christ have come, for the accuser of our brothers has been thrown down, who accuses them day and night before our God. And they have conquered him by the blood of the Lamb and by the word of their testimony, for they loved not their lives even unto death. Therefore, rejoice, O heavens and you who dwell in them! But woe to you, O earth and sea, for the devil has come down to you in great wrath, because he knows that his time is short!"

## Additional Readings

James 4:7; Revelation 12:7–12

## Prayers

Jesus Christ, the very Word of God, who gave to Your holy apostles the power to trample underfoot serpents and scorpions, who was pleased to grant them the authority to say, "Depart, you devils!" and by whose might Satan was made to fall from heaven like lightening, I humbly call upon Your name in fear and trembling, asking You to grant this, Your servant, pardon for all sin, steadfast faith, and the power—supported by Your mighty arm—to confront with confidence and resolution the cruel demon; through the same Jesus Christ, our Lord, who is coming to judge both the living and the dead. Amen.

O everlasting God, whose wise planning has ordained and constituted the ministry of men and angels in a wonderful order, mercifully grant that, as Your holy angels always serve You in heaven, so by Your appointment they may also help and defend us here on earth; through Jesus Christ, Your Son, our Lord, who lives and reigns with You and the Holy Spirit, one God, now and forever. Amen.

*For additional prayers, see Section IV, p. 226*

## Hymnody

> Lord Jesus, since You love me,
> Now spread Your wings above me
> And shield me from alarm.
> Though Satan would devour me,
> Let angel guards sing o'er me:
> This child of God shall meet no harm.
>
> My loved ones, rest securely,
> For God this night will surely
> From peril guard your heads.
> Sweet slumbers may He send you
> And bid His hosts attend you
> And through the night watch o'er your beds.

("Now Rest beneath Night's Shadow," *LSB* 880:4–5)

## Additional Hymns

"Be Still, My Soul" (*LSB* 752); "Eternal Father, Strong to Save" (*LSB* 717); "Jesus, Priceless Treasure" (*LSB* 743)

# God's Purpose in Suffering

*For devotions suitable for this topic, see Section II, p. 57*

Suffering is a result of the fall into sin. God uses suffering to bring us closer to Him so that we might trust Him solely, joining us to Jesus Christ and His sufferings on the cross where He died on our behalf. Through our suffering we participate in the sufferings of Jesus.

## *Psalmody*

### PSALM 77:1–15

I cry aloud to God,
   aloud to God, and He will hear me.
In the day of my trouble I seek the Lord;
   in the night my hand is stretched out
      without wearying;
   my soul refuses to be comforted.
When I remember God, I moan;
   when I meditate, my spirit faints.

You hold my eyelids open;
   I am so troubled that I cannot speak.
I consider the days of old,
   the years long ago.
I said, "Let me remember my song in the night;
   let me meditate in my heart."
   Then my spirit made a diligent search:
"Will the Lord spurn forever,
   and never again be favorable?
Has His steadfast love forever ceased?
   Are His promises at an end for all time?
Has God forgotten to be gracious?
   Has He in anger shut up His compassion?"

Then I said, "I will appeal to this,
   to the years of the right hand of the Most High."

I will remember the deeds of the LORD;

yes, I will remember Your wonders of old.
I will ponder all Your work,
   and meditate on Your mighty deeds.
Your way, O God, is holy.
   What god is great like our God?
You are the God who works wonders;
   You have made known Your might
   among the peoples.
You with Your arm redeemed Your people,
   the children of Jacob and Joseph.

**PSALM 121**

I lift up my eyes to the hills.
   From where does my help come?
My help comes from the LORD,
   who made heaven and earth.

He will not let your foot be moved;
   He who keeps you will not slumber.
Behold, He who keeps Israel
   will neither slumber nor sleep.

The LORD is your keeper;
   the LORD is your shade on your right hand.
The sun shall not strike you by day,
   nor the moon by night.

The LORD will keep you from all evil;
   He will keep your life.
The LORD will keep
   your going out and your coming in
   from this time forth and forevermore.

## Additional Psalms

Psalm 30:4–12; 39:7–13; 89:31–34; 126:5–6

## Readings

**GALATIANS 4:13–14**

You know it was because of a bodily ailment that I preached the gospel to you at first, and though my condition was a trial to you, you did not scorn or despise me, but received me as an angel of God, as Christ Jesus.

**HEBREWS 5:7–10**

In the days of His flesh, Jesus offered up prayers and supplications, with loud cries and tears, to Him who was able to save Him from death, and He was heard because of His reverence. Although He was a son, He learned obedience through what He suffered. And being made perfect, He became the source of eternal salvation to all who obey Him, being designated by God a high priest after the order of Melchizedek.

## Additional Readings

Matthew 16:24–25; John 5:1–14; Romans 8:14–17; 1 Peter 4:12–19

## Prayers

Almighty God, Your Son willingly endured the agony and shame of the cross for our redemption. Grant us courage to take up our cross daily and follow Him wherever He leads; through the same Jesus Christ, our Lord, who lives and reigns with You and the Holy Spirit, one God, now and forever. Amen. (*LSB Altar Book*, p. 633)

O God, our refuge and strength, the author of all godliness, hear the devout prayers of Your Church, especially in times of persecution, and grant that what we ask in faith we may obtain; through Jesus Christ, our Lord, who lives and reigns with You and the Holy Spirit, one God, now and forever. Amen. (*LSB Altar Book*, p. 635)

*For additional prayers, see Section IV, p. 227*

## Hymnody

Jesus, priceless treasure,
Fount of purest pleasure,
Truest friend to me,
Ah, how long in anguish

Shall my spirit languish,
Yearning, Lord, for Thee?
Thou art mine,
O Lamb divine!
I will suffer naught to hide Thee;
Naught I ask beside Thee.

In Thine arms I rest me;
Foes who would molest me
Cannot reach me here.
Though the earth be shaking,
Ev'ry heart be quaking,
Jesus calms my fear.
Lightnings flash
And thunders crash;
Yet, though sin and hell assail me,
Jesus will not fail me.

Hence, all fear and sadness!
For the Lord of gladness,
Jesus, enters in.
Those who love the Father,
Though the storms may gather,
Still have peace within.
Yea, whate'er
I here must bear,
Thou art still my purest pleasure,
Jesus, priceless treasure!

("Jesus, Priceless Treasure," *LSB* 743:1–2, 4)

### Additional Hymns

"A Lamb Goes Uncomplaining Forth" (*LSB* 438); "If Thou But Trust in God to Guide Thee" (*LSB* 750); "Lord of Our Life" (*LSB* 659); "O Christ, You Walked the Road" (*LSB* 424); "Why Should Cross and Trial Grieve Me" (*LSB* 756)

# BAPTISMAL IDENTITY—CALL TO REPENTANCE

*For devotions suitable for this topic, see Section II, p. 66*

Repentance must be understood in relation to Holy Baptism. In Baptism, Christians are killed, buried, and raised with Christ in the font of new life. They are a new creation, now living in the eternal eighth day, the day of the resurrection. While it is "today," Christians are called to leave behind their old ways (drown their old Adam) and follow Christ anew. This call to repentance is a Gospel call, making repentance nothing less than a Gospel word.

## *Psalmody*

### PSALM 32

Blessed is the one whose transgression is forgiven,
    whose sin is covered.
Blessed is the man against whom the LORD
    counts no iniquity,
    and in whose spirit there is no deceit.

For when I kept silent, my bones wasted away
    through my groaning all day long.
For day and night Your hand was heavy upon me;
    my strength was dried up as by the heat of summer.

I acknowledged my sin to You,
    and I did not cover my iniquity;
I said, "I will confess my transgressions to the LORD,"
    and You forgave the iniquity of my sin.

Therefore let everyone who is godly
    offer prayer to You at a time
        when You may be found;
    surely in the rush of great waters,
    they shall not reach him.
You are a hiding place for me;
    You preserve me from trouble;
    You surround me with shouts of deliverance.

I will instruct you and teach you
   in the way you should go;
   I will counsel you with My eye upon you.
Be not like a horse or a mule, without understanding,
   which must be curbed with bit and bridle,
   or it will not stay near you.

Many are the sorrows of the wicked,
   but steadfast love surrounds the
      one who trusts in the LORD.
Be glad in the LORD, and rejoice, O righteous,
   and shout for joy, all you upright in heart!

## Additional Psalms

Psalm 23; 51; 139

## Readings

### JEREMIAH 3:12–13

Go, and proclaim these words toward the north, and say, "Return, faithless Israel, declares the LORD. I will not look on you in anger, for I am merciful, declares the LORD; I will not be angry forever. Only acknowledge your guilt, that you rebelled against the LORD your God and scattered your favors among foreigners under every green tree, and that you have not obeyed My voice, declares the LORD."

### ACTS 2:38–39

And Peter said to them, "Repent and be baptized every one of you in the name of Jesus Christ for the forgiveness of your sins, and you will receive the gift of the Holy Spirit. For the promise is for you and for your children and for all who are far off, everyone whom the Lord our God calls to Himself."

### MATTHEW 9:12–13

But when He heard it, He said, "Those who are well have no need of a physician, but those who are sick. Go and learn what this means, 'I desire mercy, and not sacrifice.' For I came not to call the righteous, but sinners."

## Additional Readings

Ezekiel 18:25–32; Matthew 3:1–12; Luke 5:27–32

## *Prayers*

Almighty and everlasting God, You despise nothing You have made and forgive the sins of all who are penitent. Create in us new and contrite hearts that lamenting our sins and acknowledging our wretchedness we may receive from You full pardon and forgiveness; through Jesus Christ, Your Son, our Lord, who lives and reigns with You and the Holy Spirit, one God, now and forever. Amen. (*LSB Altar Book*, p. 578)

O God, whose glory it is always to have mercy, be gracious to all who have gone astray from Your ways and bring them again with penitent hearts and steadfast faith to embrace and hold fast the unchangeable truth of Your Word; through Jesus Christ, Your Son, our Lord, who lives and reigns with You and the Holy Spirit, one God, now and forever. Amen. (*LSB Altar Book*, p. 582)

*For additional prayers, see Section IV, p. 229*

## *Hymnody*

To Thee, omniscient Lord of all,
In grief and shame I humbly call;
I see my sins against Thee, Lord,
The sins of thought and deed and word.
They press me sore; I cry to Thee:
O God, be merciful to me!

O Lord, my God, to Thee I pray:
O cast me not in wrath away!
Let Thy good Spirit ne'er depart,
But let Him draw to Thee my heart
That truly penitent I be:
O God, be merciful to me!

O Jesus, let Thy precious blood
Be to my soul a cleansing flood.
Turn not, O Lord, Thy guest away,
But grant that justified I may

Go to my house at peace with Thee:
O God, be merciful to me!

("To Thee, Omniscient Lord of All," *LSB* 613)

## Additional Hymns

"Savior, When in Dust to Thee" (*LSB* 419); "Upon the Cross Extended" (*LSB* 453)

# BAPTISMAL IDENTITY—FORGIVENESS AND RECONCILIATION

*For devotions suitable for this topic, see Section II, p. 68*

No greater need exists among human beings than the need for forgiveness and reconciliation. To be forgiven is to be set free from the bondage of sin; to be reconciled to God is to live in His presence without fear. That is why our life with God begins in holy water where we are washed clean by Word and Spirit, forgiven and reconciled forever.

## Psalmody

**PSALM 32**

Blessed is the one whose transgression is forgiven,
    whose sin is covered.
Blessed is the man against whom
      the LORD counts no iniquity,
    and in whose spirit there is no deceit.

For when I kept silent, my bones wasted away
    through my groaning all day long.
For day and night Your hand was heavy upon me;
    my strength was dried up as by the heat of summer.

I acknowledged my sin to You,
    and I did not cover my iniquity;
I said, "I will confess my transgressions to the LORD,"
    and You forgave the iniquity of my sin.

Therefore let everyone who is godly
  offer prayer to You at a time when You may be
    found;
  surely in the rush of great waters,
  they shall not reach him.
You are a hiding place for me;
  You preserve me from trouble;
  You surround me with shouts of deliverance.

I will instruct you and teach you
  in the way you should go;
  I will counsel you with My eye upon you.
Be not like a horse or a mule, without understanding,
  which must be curbed with bit and bridle,
  or it will not stay near you.

Many are the sorrows of the wicked,
  but steadfast love surrounds the
    one who trusts in the LORD.
Be glad in the LORD, and rejoice, O righteous,
  and shout for joy, all you upright in heart!

## Additional Psalms

Psalm 38; 40; 41; 51

## Reading

### LUKE 23:32–47

Two others, who were criminals, were led away to be put to death with Him. And when they came to the place that is called The Skull, there they crucified Him, and the criminals, one on His right and one on His left. And Jesus said, "Father, forgive them, for they know not what they do." And they cast lots to divide His garments. And the people stood by, watching, but the rulers scoffed at Him, saying, "He saved others; let Him save Himself, if He is the Christ of God, His Chosen One!" The soldiers also mocked Him, coming up and offering Him sour wine and saying, "If You are the King of the Jews, save Yourself!" There was also an inscription over Him, "This is the King of the Jews."

One of the criminals who were hanged railed at Him, saying, "Are You not the Christ? Save Yourself and us!" But the other rebuked him, saying, "Do you not fear God, since you are under the same sentence of condemnation? And we indeed justly, for we are receiving the due reward of our deeds; but this man has done nothing wrong." And he said, "Jesus, remember me when You come into Your kingdom." And He said to him, "Truly, I say to you, today you will be with Me in Paradise."

It was now about the sixth hour, and there was darkness over the whole land until the ninth hour, while the sun's light failed. And the curtain of the temple was torn in two. Then Jesus, calling out with a loud voice, said, "Father, into Your hands I commit My spirit!" And having said this He breathed His last. Now when the centurion saw what had taken place, he praised God, saying, "Certainly this man was innocent!"

### Additional Readings

Genesis 50:15–21; Exodus 12:1–28; John 7:53–8:11; Acts 7:54–60; Ephesians 2:1–10

### Prayers

O blessed Jesus Christ, You are the manifestation of God's love; please give to us the same to exhibit Your work of mercy to the poor and weak, and the sick and dying, for Your name's sake. Amen.

O Jesus Christ, You are the Life of the living, help us to remember that there is no life apart from Yours, and grant that today we would live Your life of love, for Your mercy's sake. Amen.

Merciful heavenly Father, who graciously loved the world that did not love Him in return, forgive us our sin and give to us Your life and salvation so that we may join with You in the same so that the world may see Your light in Jesus Christ, in whose name we pray. Amen.

O almighty Father, it is according to Your desire that You love us, give us this same so that we turn our eyes away from our sinful self and fix them upon Your Son who freely forgives, revealing Your will of reconciling the world back to You. Give us Your joy so that we may endure the path set before us, and grant us peace in the last, through Jesus Christ, who lives and reigns with You and the Holy Spirit, one God, now and forever. Amen.

*For additional prayers, see Section IV, p. 229*

## Hymnody

My song is love unknown,
My Savior's love to me,
Love to the loveless shown
That they might lovely be.
Oh, who am I
That for my sake
My Lord should take
Frail flesh and die?

("My Song Is Love Unknown," *LSB* 430:1)

## Additional Hymns

"Chief of Sinners Though I Be" (*LSB* 611); "From Depths of Woe I Cry to Thee" (*LSB* 607); "God's Own Child, I Gladly Say It" (*LSB* 594); "O Lord, How Shall I Meet You" (*LSB* 334:4); "O Sacred Head, Now Wounded" (*LSB* 449); "Thanks to Thee, O Christ, Victorious" (*LSB* 548)

## BAPTISMAL IDENTITY—PEACE

*For devotions suitable for this topic, see Section II, p. 77*

Many things can disrupt the peace that the world gives. In Baptism we have received a new identity, a new name upon us, and in that name we now stand by faith. Jesus is a rock that cannot be moved. In the midst of circumstance, emotion, uncertainty, others

come alongside us to point to and remind us where
peace is to be found without fail.

## *Psalmody*

### PSALM 71:1–3

In You, O Lord, do I take refuge;
    let me never be put to shame!
In Your righteousness deliver me and rescue me;
    incline Your ear to me, and save me!
Be to me a rock of refuge,
    to which I may continually come;
You have given the command to save me,
    for You are my rock and my fortress.

### PSALM 118:4–9

Let those who fear the Lord say,
    "His steadfast love endures forever."

Out of my distress I called on the Lord;
    the Lord answered me and set me free.
The Lord is on my side; I will not fear.
    What can man do to me?
The Lord is on my side as my helper;
    I shall look in triumph on those who hate me.

It is better to take refuge in the Lord
    than to trust in man.
It is better to take refuge in the Lord
    than to trust in princes.

## *Additional Psalms*

Psalm 18:1–6, 16–18; 27; 31; 37; 46; 91

## *Readings*

### JOHN 16:33

I have said these things to you, that in Me you may have
peace. In the world you will have tribulation. But take heart;
I have overcome the world.

**MARK 4:37–40**

And a great windstorm arose, and the waves were breaking into the boat, so that the boat was already filling. But He was in the stern, asleep on the cushion. And they woke Him and said to Him, "Teacher, do You not care that we are perishing?" And He awoke and rebuked the wind and said to the sea, "Peace! Be still!" And the wind ceased, and there was a great calm. He said to them, "Why are you so afraid? Have you still no faith?"

**JOHN 14:27**

Peace I leave with you; My peace I give to you. Not as the world gives do I give to you. Let not your hearts be troubled, neither let them be afraid.

### Additional Readings

Isaiah 9:2–7; 52:7–10; Romans 5:1–11; Ephesians 2:13–22; Philippians 4:4–9

### Prayers

Almighty and most merciful God, in this earthly life we endure sufferings and death before we enter into eternal glory. Grant us grace at all times to subject ourselves to Your holy will and to continue steadfast in the true faith to the end of our lives that we may know the peace and joy of the blessed hope of the resurrection of the dead and the glory of the world to come; through Jesus Christ, our Lord. Amen. (*LSB*, p. 317)

Visit, O Lord, the homes in which Your people dwell, and keep all harm and danger far from them. Grant that we may dwell together in peace under the protection of Your holy angels, sharing eternally in Your blessings; through Jesus Christ, our Lord. Amen. (*LSB*, p. 315)

*For additional prayers, see Section IV, p. 232*

### Hymnody

Though Satan should buffet, though trials
should come,
Let this blest assurance control,

That Christ hath regarded my helpless estate
And hath shed His own blood for my soul.

And, Lord, haste the day when our faith shall be
    sight,
The clouds be rolled back as a scroll,
The trumpet shall sound and the Lord shall
    descend;
Even so it is well with my soul.

("When Peace, like a River," *LSB* 763:2, 4)

## Additional Hymn

"Be Still, My Soul" (*LSB* 752)

## Baptismal Identity—Thanksgiving

*For devotions suitable for this topic, see Section II, p. 80*

God the Father is the giver of gifts, including the gift of His Son, Jesus Christ, whose bodily presence among us through the preaching of the Gospel, Baptism, and the Lord's Supper gives us the gifts of forgiveness, life, and salvation in Him. We receive these gifts in faith—another gift given by God—and we respond in Christ with love and thanksgiving. The Lord's Supper is also called the "Eucharist," which means thanksgiving, because as the baptized we are continually giving thanks to God for His gifts.

## Psalmody

### PSALM 28:6–9

Blessed be the LORD!
    for He has heard the voice of
        my pleas for mercy.
The LORD is my strength and my shield;
    in Him my heart trusts, and I am helped;
    my heart exults,
    and with my song I give thanks to Him.

The Lord is the strength of His people;
  He is the saving refuge of His anointed.
Oh, save Your people and bless Your heritage!
  Be their shepherd and carry them forever.

**PSALM 100**

Make a joyful noise to the Lord, all the earth!
  Serve the Lord with gladness!
  Come into His presence with singing!

Know that the Lord, He is God!
  It is He who made us, and we are His;
  we are His people, and the sheep of His pasture.

Enter His gates with thanksgiving,
  and His courts with praise!
  Give thanks to Him; bless His name!

For the Lord is good;
  His steadfast love endures forever,
  and His faithfulness to all generations.

## Additional Psalms

Psalm 8; 30; 34:1–8; 36; 65; 92; 98; 100; 103:1–5, 19–22;
145; 150

## Readings

**1 CHRONICLES 29:10–13**

Therefore David blessed the Lord in the presence of all
the assembly. And David said: "Blessed are You, O Lord, the
God of Israel our father, forever and ever. Yours, O Lord, is
the greatness and the power and the glory and the victory
and the majesty, for all that is in the heavens and in the
earth is Yours. Yours is the kingdom, O Lord, and You are
exalted as head above all. Both riches and honor come from
You, and You rule over all. In Your hand are power and
might, and in Your hand it is to make great and to give
strength to all. And now we thank You, our God, and praise
Your glorious name."

**1 PETER 1:3–9**

Blessed be the God and Father of our Lord Jesus Christ! According to His great mercy, He has caused us to be born again to a living hope through the resurrection of Jesus Christ from the dead, to an inheritance that is imperishable, undefiled, and unfading, kept in heaven for you, who by God's power are being guarded through faith for a salvation ready to be revealed in the last time. In this you rejoice, though now for a little while, if necessary, you have been grieved by various trials, so that the tested genuineness of your faith—more precious than gold that perishes though it is tested by fire—may be found to result in praise and glory and honor at the revelation of Jesus Christ. Though you have not seen Him, you love Him. Though you do not now see Him, you believe in Him and rejoice with joy that is inexpressible and filled with glory, obtaining the outcome of your faith, the salvation of your souls.

## Additional Readings

1 Chronicles 16:8–24; Jonah 2; Philippians 4:6–7

## Prayers

O Eternal and merciful God, Father, Son, and Holy Spirit, I give you humble thanks. In the washing of Holy Baptism, you cleansed me from all sin, received me into the covenant of grace, and made me an heir of eternal life. Your mercy is far greater than any praise I could render. Through Baptism I have been washed and purified from all my impurities. Everything that Christ merited by His holy obedience and by the shedding of His holy precious blood He entrusts to the saving font of Baptism. Thus the precious blood of Christ cleanses me from all sins and makes me whiter than snow in God's sight. I give to You, my God, eternal thanks for this immeasurable kindness. (Adapted from "Thanksgiving for Holy Baptism," *Meditations on Divine Mercy*, trans. M. C. Harrison, pp. 83–84.)

Merciful Father, You have given Your only Son as the sacrifice for sinners. Grant us grace to receive the fruits of

His redeeming work with thanksgiving and daily to follow in His way; through Jesus Christ, our Lord, who lives and reigns with You and the Holy Spirit, one God, now and forever. Amen. (*LSB Altar Book*, p. 712)

*For additional prayers, see Section IV, p. 233*

### *Hymnody*

> All who believe and are baptized
> Shall see the Lord's salvation;
> Baptized into the death of Christ,
> They are a new creation.
> Through Christ's redemption they shall stand
> Among the glorious, heav'nly band
> Of ev'ry tribe and nation.
>
> With one accord, O God, we pray:
> Grant us Your Holy Spirit.
> Help us in our infirmity
> Through Jesus' blood and merit.
> Grant us to grow in grace each day
> That by this sacrament we may
> Eternal life inherit.

("All Who Believe and Are Baptized," *LSB* 601)

### *Additional Hymns*

"All Glory Be to God on High" (*LSB* 947); "Come, Thou Almighty King" (*LSB* 905); "Open Now Thy Gates of Beauty" (*LSB* 901); "Sing, My Tongue, the Glorious Battle" (*LSB* 454); "The Lord Is My Light" (*LSB* 723); "To Jordan Came the Christ, Our Lord" (*LSB* 406); "Water, Blood, and Spirit Crying" (*LSB* 597)

## Baptismal Identity—Trust in God

*For devotions suitable for this topic, see Section II, p. 83*

To trust God means to rest solely on Him for our life and our salvation. This is not possible by our human effort, but only in Christ. His faithfulness unto death, even death on a cross, makes our trust in Him possible. This trust begins in Baptism and is nurtured throughout our life by listening to Jesus' voice and feasting upon His body and blood where His faithfulness to us is given in this Holy Meal.

## *Psalmody*

### PSALM 63

O God, You are my God; earnestly I seek You;
> my soul thirsts for You;
> my flesh faints for You,
>> as in a dry and weary land
>> where there is no water.
So I have looked upon You in the sanctuary,
> beholding Your power and glory.
Because Your steadfast love is better than life,
> my lips will praise You.
So I will bless You as long as I live;
> in Your name I will lift up my hands.
My soul will be satisfied as with fat and rich food,
> and my mouth will praise You with joyful lips,
> when I remember You upon my bed,
> and meditate on You in the watches of the night;
> for You have been my help,
> and in the shadow of Your wings I will sing for joy.
My soul clings to You;
> Your right hand upholds me.

But those who seek to destroy my life
> shall go down into the depths of the earth;
> they shall be given over to the power of the sword;
> they shall be a portion for jackals.
But the king shall rejoice in God;
> all who swear by Him shall exult,
> for the mouths of liars will be stopped.

## *Additional Psalms*

9:9–10; 13; 33:18; 42; 43; 62

## Readings

### JEREMIAH 29:10–14

For thus says the LORD: When seventy years are completed for Babylon, I will visit you, and I will fulfill to you My promise and bring you back to this place. For I know the plans I have for you, declares the LORD, plans for wholeness and not for evil, to give you a future and a hope. Then you will call upon Me and come and pray to Me, and I will hear you. You will seek Me and find Me. When you seek Me with all your heart, I will be found by you, declares the LORD, and I will restore your fortunes and gather you from all the nations and all the places where I have driven you, declares the LORD, and I will bring you back to the place from which I sent you into exile.

### MATTHEW 7:7–11

Ask, and it will be given to you; seek, and you will find; knock, and it will be opened to you. For everyone who asks receives, and the one who seeks finds, and to the one who knocks it will be opened. Or which one of you, if his son asks him for bread, will give him a stone? Or if he asks for a fish, will give him a serpent? If you then, who are evil, know how to give good gifts to your children, how much more will your Father who is in heaven give good things to those who ask Him!

## Additional Readings

Proverbs 1:33; Nahum 1:7; Matthew 24:13; Luke 11:5–13

## Prayers

O Lord, our dwelling place and our peace, who has pity on our weakness, put far from us all worry and fearfulness that, having confessed our sins and commending ourselves to Your gracious mercy, we may commit ourselves, our work, and all we love into Your keeping, receiving from You the gift of contentment; through Jesus Christ our Lord. Amen. (Adapted from *LW*, pp. 232–33)

Almighty and ever-living God, You have given exceedingly great and precious promises to those who trust in You. Grant us so firmly to believe in Your Son Jesus that our faith may never be found wanting; through the same Jesus Christ, our Lord, who lives and reigns with You and the Holy Spirit, one God, now and forever. Amen. (*LSB Altar Book*, p. 740)

*For additional prayers, see Section IV, p. 233*

## Hymnody

Rely on God your Savior
And find your life secure.
Make His work your foundation
That your work may endure.
No anxious thought, no worry,
No self-tormenting care
Can win your Father's favor;
His heart is moved by prayer.

Leave all to His direction;
His wisdom rules for you
In ways to rouse your wonder
At all His love can do.
Soon He, His promise keeping,
With wonder-working pow'rs
Will banish from your spirit
What gave you troubled hours.

("Entrust Your Days and Burdens," *LSB* 754:2, 4)

## Additional Hymns

"I Leave All Things to God's Direction" (*LSB* 719); "The King of Love My Shepherd Is" (*LSB* 709)

## RECOVERY FROM SICKNESS

*For devotions suitable for this topic, see Section II, p. 99*

Everyone has been ill at one time or another. Those who experience severe suffering and life-threatening illness rejoice with great thanksgiving when they are healed of sickness and their suffering is relieved. Such healing is a glimpse of the eternal healing of our bodies and souls in Holy Baptism and how the Lord's Supper is the medicine of immortality.

## *Psalmody*

### PSALM 30

I will extol You, O LORD, for You have drawn me up
    and have not let my foes rejoice over me.
O LORD my God, I cried to You for help,
    and You have healed me.
O LORD, You have brought up my soul from Sheol;
    You restored me to life from
        among those who go down to the pit.

Sing praises to the LORD, O you His saints,
    and give thanks to His holy name.
For His anger is but for a moment,
    and His favor is for a lifetime.
Weeping may tarry for the night,
    but joy comes with the morning.

As for me, I said in my prosperity,
    "I shall never be moved."
By Your favor, O LORD,
    You made my mountain stand strong;
You hid Your face;
    I was dismayed.

To You, O LORD, I cry,
    and to the Lord I plead for mercy:
"What profit is there in my death,
    if I go down to the pit?
Will the dust praise You?
    Will it tell of Your faithfulness?
Hear, O LORD, and be merciful to me!
    O LORD, be my helper!"

You have turned for me my mourning into dancing;
    You have loosed my sackcloth

and clothed me with gladness,
that my glory may sing Your praise and not be silent.
O Lord my God, I will give thanks to You forever!

## *Additional Psalms*

103; 145

## *Readings*

### ACTS 3:1–10

Now Peter and John were going up to the temple at the hour of prayer, the ninth hour. And a man lame from birth was being carried, whom they laid daily at the gate of the temple that is called the Beautiful Gate to ask alms of those entering the temple. Seeing Peter and John about to go into the temple, he asked to receive alms. And Peter directed his gaze at him, as did John, and said, "Look at us." And he fixed his attention on them, expecting to receive something from them. But Peter said, "I have no silver and gold, but what I do have I give to you. In the name of Jesus Christ of Nazareth, rise up and walk!" And he took him by the right hand and raised him up, and immediately his feet and ankles were made strong. And leaping up he stood and began to walk, and entered the temple with them, walking and leaping and praising God. And all the people saw him walking and praising God, and recognized him as the one who sat at the Beautiful Gate of the temple, asking for alms. And they were filled with wonder and amazement at what had happened to him.

### PHILIPPIANS 2:25–30

I have thought it necessary to send to you Epaphroditus my brother and fellow worker and fellow soldier, and your messenger and minister to my need, for he has been longing for you all and has been distressed because you heard that he was ill. Indeed he was ill, near to death. But God had mercy on him, and not only on him but on me also, lest I should have sorrow upon sorrow. I am the more eager to send him, therefore, that you may rejoice at seeing him again, and that I may be less anxious. So receive him in the

Lord with all joy, and honor such men, for he nearly died for the work of Christ, risking his life to complete what was lacking in your service to me.

### MARK 5:34

And He said to her, "Daughter, your faith has made you well; go in peace, and be healed of your disease."

### Additional Readings

Job 42:10–17; Isaiah 38:9–20; 40:29, 31; Luke 8:39

### Prayers

God, the Giver of life, of health, of safety, and of strength, we bless You for having granted to Your servant *name* recovery from *his/her* bodily sickness. Fill *his/her* heart with daily remembrance of Your great goodness that *he/she* may serve You with a holy and obedient life; through Jesus Christ, our Lord. Amen. (*LW Little Agenda*, p. 101)

Almighty and gracious God, we give thanks that You have restored the health of Your servant, on whose behalf we praise Your name. Grant that *he/she* may continue the mission You have given *him/her* in this world and also share in eternal glory at the appearing of Your Son, Jesus Christ, our Lord. Amen. (*LW Agenda*, p. 369)

*[For a child]* Gracious God, our Father, we thank and praise You for blessing this child with recovery from sickness and pain. Continue to strengthen *him/her* in body, mind, and soul; grant *him/her* an increase and continuance of well-being; and bless *him/her* with all things necessary to grow and to maintain the health You give. Grant this for the sake of Jesus Christ, our Lord. Amen. (*LW Agenda*, p. 368)

*For additional prayers, see Section IV, p. 237*

### Hymnody

God loved the world so that He gave
His only Son the lost to save,
That all who would in Him believe
Should everlasting life receive.

God would not have the sinner die;
His Son with saving grace is nigh;
His Spirit in the Word declares
How we in Christ are heaven's heirs.

If you are sick, if death is near,
This truth your troubled heart can cheer:
Christ Jesus saves your soul from death;
That is the firmest ground of faith.

("God Loved the World So That He Gave," *LSB* 571:1, 3, 5)

### Additional Hymns

"O Son of God, in Galilee" (*LSB* 841); "Your Hand, O Lord, in Days of Old" (*LSB* 846)

## MINISTRY TO A SICK PERSON

*For devotions suitable for this topic, see Section II, p. 102*

One of the greatest fears of anyone is being alone, especially in times of sickness and suffering. To comfort the terrified conscience, sick people need to know that while they suffer, they are not alone but are joined to the suffering of Christ. Moreover, when their suffering is over, their end will be the same as His: eternal glory.

### Psalmody

**PSALM 22:14–15, 19**

I am poured out like water,
   and all My bones are out of joint;
My heart is like wax;
   it is melted within My breast;
My strength is dried up like a potsherd,
   and My tongue sticks to My jaws;
You lay Me in the dust of death.

But You, O LORD, do not be far off!
   O You My help, come quickly to My aid!

## *Psalm 23*

The LORD is my shepherd; I shall not want.
　　He makes me lie down in green pastures.
He leads me beside still waters.
　　He restores my soul.
He leads me in paths of righteousness
　　for His name's sake.

Even though I walk through the
　　　　valley of the shadow of death,
　　I will fear no evil,
　　for You are with me;
　　Your rod and Your staff,
　　they comfort me.

You prepare a table before me
　　in the presence of my enemies;
You anoint my head with oil;
　　my cup overflows.
Surely goodness and mercy shall follow me
　　　all the days of my life,
　　and I shall dwell in the house of the LORD
　　　forever.

## *Additional Psalms*

31; 34:15–22; 43; 46; 73:21–28; 90; 139

## *Readings*

### LAMENTATIONS 3:31–33

For the Lord will not cast off forever, but, though He cause grief, He will have compassion according to the abundance of His steadfast love; for He does not willingly afflict or grieve the children of men.

### LUKE 17:11–19

On the way to Jerusalem He was passing along between Samaria and Galilee. And as He entered a village, He was met by ten lepers, who stood at a distance and lifted up their voices, saying, "Jesus, Master, have mercy on us." When He saw them He said to them, "Go and show yourselves to the priests." And as they went they were cleansed. Then one of them, when he saw that he was healed, turned back, praising God with a loud voice; and he fell on his face at Jesus' feet, giving Him thanks. Now he was a Samaritan. Then Jesus answered, "Were not ten cleansed? Where are the nine? Was no one found to return and give praise to God except this foreigner?" And He said to him, "Rise and go your way; your faith has made you well."

**2 TIMOTHY 2:8–13**

Remember Jesus Christ, risen from the dead, the offspring of David, as preached in my gospel, for which I am suffering, bound with chains as a criminal. But the word of God is not bound! Therefore I endure everything for the sake of the elect, that they also may obtain the salvation that is in Christ Jesus with eternal glory. The saying is trustworthy, for:

If we have died with Him, we will also live with Him; if we endure, we will also reign with Him; if we deny Him, He also will deny us; if we are faithless, He remains faithful— for He cannot deny Himself.

### Additional Readings

Isaiah 35:1–10; 38:16–17; Matthew 15:29–31; Luke 9:1–7; Romans 8:18–39; Hebrews 12:1–13; James 5:10–20

### Prayers

O Lord, look down from heaven, behold, visit, and relieve Your servant for whom we offer our supplications; look upon *him/her* with the eyes of Your mercy; give *him/her* comfort and sure confidence in You, defend *him/her* from the danger of the enemy, and keep *him/her* in perpetual peace and safety; through Jesus Christ, our Lord. Amen.

Almighty, everlasting God, the eternal salvation of them that believe, hear our prayers on behalf of Your servant who is sick, for whom we implore Your mercy, that, being restored to health, *he/she* may render thanks to You in Your Church; through Jesus Christ, our Lord. Amen.

O God, by the patient suffering of Your only-begotten Son You have beaten down the pride of the old enemy. Now help us, we humbly pray, rightly to reassure in our hearts all that our Lord has of His goodness borne for our sake that after His example we may bear with patience all that is adverse to us; through Jesus Christ, our Lord. (*LW*, p. 125)

*For additional prayers, see Section IV, p. 238*

## Hymnody

> In suff'ring be Thy love my peace,
> In weakness be Thy love my pow'r;
> And when the storms of life shall cease,
> O Jesus, in that final hour,
> Be Thou my rod and staff and guide,
> And draw me safely to Thy side!

("Jesus, Thy Boundless Love to Me," *LSB* 683:4)

~

> If you are sick, if death is near,
> This truth your troubled heart can cheer:
> Christ Jesus saves your soul from death;
> That is the firmest ground of faith.

("God Loved the World So That He Gave," *LSB* 571:5)

~

> Lord, who once came to bring,
> On Your redeeming wing,
> Healing and sight,
> Health to the sick in mind,
> Sight to the inly blind:
> Oh, now to humankind
> Let there be light!

("God, Whose Almighty Word," *LSB* 979:2; available through *Lutheran Service Builder*)

## Additional Hymns

"Baptized into Your Name Most Holy" (*LSB* 590); "From Depths of Woe I Cry to Thee" (*LSB* 607); "Jesus,

Refuge of the Weary" (*LSB* 423); "O Little Flock, Fear Not the Foe" (*LSB* 666); "Praise the One Who Breaks the Darkness" (*LSB* 849)

## COMFORT AND CONSOLATION

*For devotions suitable for this topic, see Section II, p. 113*

No greater comfort and consolation may be given to those who are grieving over sin, suffering, and death than the assurance that in Christ all these things have been conquered by His blood shed on the cross. That blood washes us clean and makes us whole in Baptism, enters our mouths and bodies in the Holy Supper, joining us to Him forever. This is not only our comfort but our hope.

### *Psalmody*

**PSALM 119:49–56**

Remember Your word to Your servant,
    in which You have made me hope.
This is my comfort in my affliction,
    that Your promise gives me life.
The insolent utterly deride me,
    but I do not turn away from Your law.
When I think of Your rules from of old,
    I take comfort, O LORD.
Hot indignation seizes me because of the wicked,
    who forsake Your law.
Your statutes have been my songs
    in the house of my sojourning.
I remember Your name in the night, O LORD,
    and keep Your law.
This blessing has fallen to me,
    that I have kept Your precepts.

**PSALM 130:1–5**

Out of the depths I cry to You, O Lord!
O Lord, hear my voice!
Let Your ears be attentive
to the voice of my pleas for mercy!

If You, O Lord, should mark iniquities,
O Lord, who could stand?
But with You there is forgiveness,
that You may be feared.

I wait for the Lord, my soul waits,
and in His word I hope.

## Additional Psalms

Psalm 38:9, 21–22; 139:1–12, 23–24

## Readings

**LAMENTATIONS 3:22–26**

The steadfast love of the Lord never ceases; His mercies
never come to an end; they are new every morning; great is
Your faithfulness. "The Lord is my portion, says my soul,
"therefore I will hope in Him." The Lord is good to those
who wait for Him, to the soul who seeks Him. It is good that
one should wait quietly for the salvation of the Lord.

**2 CORINTHIANS 1:3–7**

Blessed be the God and Father of our Lord Jesus Christ,
the Father of mercies and God of all comfort, who comforts
us in all our affliction, so that we may be able to comfort
those who are in any affliction, with the comfort with which
we ourselves are comforted by God. For as we share abundantly in Christ's sufferings, so through Christ we share
abundantly in comfort too. If we are afflicted, it is for your
comfort and salvation; and if we are comforted, it is for your
comfort, which you experience when you patiently endure
the same sufferings that we suffer. Our hope for you is
unshaken, for we know that as you share in our sufferings,
you will also share in our comfort.

**HEBREWS 12:1–4**

Therefore, since we are surrounded by so great a cloud of witnesses, let us also lay aside every weight, and sin which clings so closely, and let us run with endurance the race that is set before us, looking to Jesus, the founder and perfecter of our faith, who for the joy that was set before Him endured the cross, despising the shame, and is seated at the right hand of the throne of God.

Consider Him who endured from sinners such hostility against Himself, so that you may not grow weary or faint-hearted. In your struggle against sin you have not yet resisted to the point of shedding your blood.

### Additional Readings

Job 36:15; Hosea 6:1; John 3:17; 6:37b; Romans 5:8–9; James 5:14–15

### Prayers

Almighty and everlasting God, the consolation of the sorrowful and the strength of the weak, may the prayers of those who in any tribulation or distress cry to You graciously come before You, so that in all their necessities they may mark and receive Your manifold help and comfort; through Jesus Christ, our Lord. Amen. (*LW Agenda*, p. 370)

O Father of mercies and God of all comfort, our only help in time of need, look with favor upon Your servant. Assure *him/her* of Your mercy, comfort *him/her* with the awareness of Your goodness, preserve *him/her* from the temptations of the evil one, and give *him/her* patience in *his/her* tribulation. If it please You, restore *him/her* to health or give *him/her* grace to accept this affliction; through Jesus Christ, our Lord. Amen. (*LW Agenda*, p. 367)

*For additional prayers, see Section IV, p. 241*

### Hymnody

"Come unto Me, ye weary,
And I will give you rest."
O blessed voice of Jesus,
Which comes to hearts oppressed!

It tells of benediction,
Of pardon, grace, and peace,
Of joy that hath no ending,
Of love that cannot cease.

"Come unto Me, ye fainting,
And I will give you life."
O cheering voice of Jesus,
Which comes to aid our strife!
The foe is stern and eager,
The fight is fierce and long;
But Thou hast made us mighty
And stronger than the strong.

"And whosoever cometh,
I will not cast him out."
O patient love of Jesus,
Which drives away our doubt,
Which, though we be unworthy
Of love so great and free,
Invites us very sinners
To come, dear Lord, to Thee!

("Come Unto Me, Ye Weary," *LSB* 684:1, 3, 4)

### Additional Hymns

"Have No Fear, Little Flock" (*LSB* 735); "Through Jesus' Blood and Merit" (*LSB* 746)

## PROLONGED RECOVERY/LINGERING ILLNESS

*For devotions suitable for this topic, see Section II, p. 115*

Many prayers in the Church for those who are sick petition for a quick and speedy recovery. Yet sometimes the suffering of the faithful lingers. Perseverance in suffering is an act of great faith, for as the apostle Paul acknowledges, suffering produces endurance, endurance character, and character hope, and hope never disappoints.

## *Psalmody*

### PSALM 17:1–9

Hear a just cause, O LORD; attend to my cry!
  Give ear to my prayer from lips free of deceit!
From Your presence let my vindication come!
  Let Your eyes behold the right!

You have tried my heart, You have
      visited me by night,
  You have tested me, and You will find nothing;
  I have purposed that my mouth will not transgress.
With regard to the works of man,
      by the word of Your lips
  I have avoided the ways of the violent.
My steps have held fast to Your paths;
  my feet have not slipped.

I call upon You, for You will answer me, O God;
  incline Your ear to me; hear my words.
Wondrously show Your steadfast love,
  O Savior of those who seek refuge
  from their adversaries at Your right hand.

Keep me as the apple of Your eye;
  hide me in the shadow of Your wings,
  from the wicked who do me violence,
  my deadly enemies who surround me.

### PSALM 40:1–4

I waited patiently for the LORD;
  He inclined to me and heard my cry.
He drew me up from the pit of destruction,
  out of the miry bog,
  and set my feet upon a rock,
  making my steps secure.
He put a new song in my mouth,
  a song of praise to our God.
Many will see and fear,
  and put their trust in the LORD.

Blessed is the man who makes
   the Lord his trust,
   who does not turn to the proud,
   to those who go astray after a lie!

## Readings

### JEREMIAH 31:2–4A

Thus says the Lord: "The people who survived the sword found grace in the wilderness; when Israel sought for rest, the Lord appeared to him from far away. I have loved you with an everlasting love; therefore I have continued My faithfulness to you. Again I will build you, and you shall be built, O virgin Israel!"

### JAMES 1:2–4, 12

Count it all joy, my brothers, when you meet trials of various kinds, for you know that the testing of your faith produces steadfastness. And let steadfastness have its full effect, that you may be perfect and complete, lacking in nothing. . . . Blessed is the man who remains steadfast under trial, for when he has stood the test he will receive the crown of life, which God has promised to those who love Him.

## Prayers

O Lord God, most merciful Father, through Christ, Your Son, You have bestowed on me Your grace, and in Your Word and through Your Sacraments, You have assured me that Your kindness shall not be removed and the promise of Your Son shall not depart from me. I often forget and neglect Your will, yet You never forget me and graciously receive me anew. Have mercy on me; comfort my heart with the assurance that in sickness and distress I am still Your dear child. Grant me steadfastness to believe that Christ bears my burdens, even while I endure these sufferings. Let Jesus, my God, be my comfort in life and death. Amen.

Lord Jesus, my dear Savior, how graciously You call those that labor and are heavy laden. Behold, I am one that labors and has been heavy laden with sickness and misery.

Fulfill Your promise and give me rest. Take away my pain and restlessness and heal me. Refresh my soul with the forgiveness of sins. Take away from me the burden of my sins, and strengthen in me the faith that You have redeemed and have reconciled me to my heavenly Father, so that I may partake of everlasting rest before Your throne. Amen.

*For additional prayers, see Section IV, p. 242*

## Hymnody

What God ordains is always good:
His loving thought attends me;
No poison can be in the cup
That my physician sends me.
My God is true;
Each morning new
I trust His grace unending,
My life to Him commending.

("What God Ordains Is Always Good," *LSB* 760:3)

## Additional Hymn

"When in the Hour of Deepest Need" (*LSB* 615)

## MINISTRY TO A DYING PERSON

*For devotions suitable for this topic, see Section II, p. 117*

As people near death, they need the assurance that the Lord has not forgotten them but has remembered them in His mercy. The Lord's remembrance evokes blessing and gift—the blessing and gift of being remembered in paradise with Christ.

## Psalmody

**PSALM 31:5–8**

Into Your hand I commit my spirit;
    You have redeemed me, O LORD, faithful God.

I hate those who pay regard to worthless idols,
    but I trust in the LORD.

I will rejoice and be glad in Your steadfast love,
    because You have seen my affliction;
    You have known the distress of my soul,
    and You have not delivered me
    into the hand of the enemy;
    You have set my feet in a broad place.

### PSALM 116:15–19

Precious in the sight of the LORD
    is the death of His saints.
O LORD, I am Your servant;
    I am Your servant, the son of Your maidservant.
    You have loosed my bonds.
I will offer to You the sacrifice of thanksgiving
    and call on the name of the LORD.
I will pay my vows to the LORD
    in the presence of all His people,
    in the courts of the house of the LORD,
    in your midst, O Jerusalem.
Praise the LORD!

## Additional Psalms

23:4; 31:5; 46; 79:9; 102:11–13

## Readings

### ISAIAH 25:7–8; 35:10

[The LORD] will swallow up on this mountain the covering that is cast over all peoples, the veil that is spread over all nations. He will swallow up death forever; and the Lord GOD will wipe away tears from all faces, and the reproach of His people He will take away from all the earth, for the LORD has spoken. . . . And the ransomed of the LORD shall return and come to Zion with singing; everlasting joy shall be upon their heads; they shall obtain gladness and joy, and sorrow and sighing shall flee away.

### JOHN 6:40

For this is the will of My Father, that everyone who looks on the Son and believes in Him should have eternal life, and I will raise him up on the last day.

### HEBREWS 4:9–10, 14–16

So then, there remains a Sabbath rest for the people of God, for whoever has entered God's rest has also rested from his works as God did from His. . . . Since then we have a great high priest who has passed through the heavens, Jesus, the Son of God, let us hold fast our confession. For we do not have a high priest who is unable to sympathize with our weaknesses, but one who in every respect has been tempted as we are, yet without sin. Let us then with confidence draw near to the throne of grace, that we may receive mercy and find grace to help in time of need.

### REVELATION 7:9–17

After this I looked, and behold, a great multitude that no one could number, from every nation, from all tribes and peoples and languages, standing before the throne and before the Lamb, clothed in white robes, with palm branches in their hands, and crying out with a loud voice, "Salvation belongs to our God who sits on the throne, and to the Lamb!" And all the angels were standing around the throne and around the elders and the four living creatures, and they fell on their faces before the throne and worshiped God, saying, "Amen! Blessing and glory and wisdom and thanksgiving and honor and power and might be to our God forever and ever!"

Then one of the elders addressed me, saying, "Who are these, clothed in white robes, and from where have they come?" I said to him, "Sir, you know." And he said to me, "These are the ones coming out of the great tribulation. They have washed their robes and made them white in the blood of the Lamb.

"Therefore they are before the throne of God, and serve Him day and night in His temple; and He who sits on the throne will shelter them with His presence. They shall hunger no more, neither thirst anymore; the sun shall not strike them, nor any scorching heat. For the Lamb in the midst of the throne will be their shepherd, and He will guide them to springs of living water, and God will wipe away every tear from their eyes."

### Additional Readings

Isaiah 41:10; John 3:16; 8:51; 14:18–19; 20:1–18; Romans 8:35; 1 Thessalonians 4:17; 1 John 5:20

### Prayers

Eternal Father, You alone make the decisions about life and death. We ask You to show mercy to Your servant *name*, whose departure seems near. If it be Your gracious will, restore *him/her* and lengthen *his/her* earthly life; if not, O Father, keep *him/her* in *his/her* baptismal grace and prepare *him/her* to commit *himself/herself* to Your eternal care and keeping. Give *him/her* a truly repentant heart, firm faith, and lively hope. Let not the pain or fear of death cause *him/her* to waver in confidence and trust. Grant *him/her* a peaceful departure and a joyous entrance into everlasting life with the glorious company of all Your saints; through Jesus Christ, our Savior. Amen. (*LW Little Agenda*, p. 103)

Almighty and eternal God, faithful heavenly Father, comfort Your servant, strengthen *him/her*, spare *him/her* through Your great mercy. Help *him/her* out of all agony and distress. Release *him/her* in Your grace. Take *him/her* to You, into Your kingdom. Into Your hands we commit *his/her* soul. You have redeemed *him/her*, O faithful God, through the blood of Jesus Christ, our only Savior and Lord. Amen.

*For additional prayers, see Section IV, p. 242*

### Hymnody

> The King of love my shepherd is,
> Whose goodness faileth never;
> I nothing lack if I am His
> And He is mine forever.
>
> Where streams of living water flow,
> My ransomed soul He leadeth
> And, where the verdant pastures grow,
> With food celestial feedeth.

Perverse and foolish oft I strayed,
But yet in love He sought me
And on His shoulder gently laid
And home rejoicing brought me.

In death's dark vale I fear no ill
With Thee, dear Lord, beside me,
Thy rod and staff my comfort still,
Thy cross before to guide me.

Thou spreadst a table in my sight;
Thine unction grace bestoweth;
And, oh, what transport of delight
From Thy pure chalice floweth!

And so through all the length of days
Thy goodness faileth never;
Good Shepherd, may I sing Thy praise
Within Thy house forever!

("The King of Love My Shepherd Is," *LSB* 709)

### Additional Hymns

"Abide with Me" (*LSB* 878); "I Know My Faith Is Founded" (*LSB* 587); "In Peace and Joy I Now Depart" (*LSB* 938); "My Hope Is Built on Nothing Less" (*LSB* 575)

## ACCEPTANCE OF INEVITABLE DEATH

*For devotions suitable for this topic, see Section II, p. 127*

Everyone knows that death is inevitable, but when the moment comes, it always seems to take us by surprise. It is a good thing to fight death, for death is not how God wanted it to be. But when the death of the faithful is inevitable, to rest in Jesus eternally is a blessed relief and the final goal of our baptismal promises.

## *Psalmody*

### PSALM 34:12, 17–19

What man is there who desires life
  and loves many days, that he may see good?

When the righteous cry for help,
    the LORD hears
  and delivers them out of all their troubles.
The LORD is near to the brokenhearted
  and saves the crushed in spirit.

Many are the afflictions of the righteous,
  but the LORD delivers him out of them all.

### PSALM 73:26–28

My flesh and my heart may fail,
  but God is the strength of my heart
    and my portion forever.
For behold, those who are far
    from You shall perish;
  You put an end to everyone
    who is unfaithful to You.
But for me it is good to be near God;
  I have made the Lord God my refuge,
    that I may tell of all Your works.

## *Additional Psalms*

16; 23; 90

## *Readings*

### ROMANS 14:7–9

None of us lives to himself, and none of us dies to himself. If we live, we live to the Lord, and if we die, we die to the Lord. So then, whether we live or whether we die, we are the Lord's. For to this end Christ died and lived again, that He might be Lord both of the dead and of the living.

### 1 CORINTHIANS 10:13

No temptation has overtaken you that is not common to man. God is faithful, and He will not let you be tempted beyond your ability, but with the temptation He will also provide the way of escape, that you may be able to endure it.

**2 TIMOTHY 4:6–8**

I am already being poured out as a drink offering, and the time of my departure has come. I have fought the good fight, I have finished the race, I have kept the faith. Henceforth there is laid up for me the crown of righteousness, which the Lord, the righteous judge, will award to me on that Day, and not only to me but also to all who have loved His appearing.

**REVELATION 2:10–11**

Do not fear what you are about to suffer. Behold, the devil is about to throw some of you into prison, that you may be tested. . . . Be faithful unto death, and I will give you the crown of life. He who has an ear, let him hear what the Spirit says to the churches. The one who conquers will not be hurt by the second death.

## *Prayers*

Eternal Father, You alone make the decisions about life and death. We ask You to show mercy to Your servant, whose departure seems near. If it be Your gracious will, restore *him/her* and lengthen *his/her* earthly life; if not, O Father, keep *him/her* in *his/her* baptismal grace and prepare *him/her* to commit *himself/herself* to Your eternal care and keeping. Give *him/her* a truly repentant heart, firm faith, and lively hope. Let not the pain or fear of death cause *him/her* to waver in confidence and trust. Grant *him/her* a peaceful departure and a joyous entrance into everlasting life with the glorious company of all Your saints; through Jesus Christ, our Savior. Amen. (*LW Agenda*, p. 370)

O God, whose days are without end and whose mercies cannot be numbered, we implore You to make us deeply aware of the shortness and uncertainty of life. Let Your Holy Spirit lead us in faith, in holiness, and in righteousness all our days that, when we have served You in our generation, we may be gathered unto our fathers; through Jesus Christ, our Lord. Amen. (*LW Agenda*, p. 370–71)

You alone, O Lord, make the decisions of life and death, reminding us that You are the one who holds our life in Your hands. By this knowledge teach us holy fear of You, to repent of our sin, and to worship You in humble trust. But especially make known to us through Your servants the meritorious sufferings and death of Your Son, Jesus Christ, by whom the effect of death is cancelled. You take away, O Lord, because of our sin, but You give life because of Christ. Blessed be Your name. Keep us ever confident in Jesus through our Baptism and His holy body and blood, that we may depart this vale of tears and enter into Your heavenly kingdom. Amen.

*For additional prayers, see Section IV, p. 243*

## *Hymnody*

> In the midst of death's dark vale
> Pow'rs of hell o'ertake us.
> Who will help when they assail,
> Who secure will make us?
> Thou only, Lord, Thou only!
> Thy heart is moved with tenderness,
> Pities us in our distress.
> Holy and righteous God!
> Holy and mighty God!
> Holy and all-merciful Savior!
> Eternal Lord God!
> Save us from the terror
> Of the fiery pit of hell.
> Have mercy, O Lord!
>
> ("In the Very Midst of Life," *LSB* 755:2)

## *Additional Hymns*

"Abide with Me" (*LSB* 878); "Holy God, We Praise Thy Name" (*LSB* 940); "O Holy Spirit, Grant Us Grace" (*LSB* 693); "The Lord's My Shepherd, I'll Not Want" (*LSB* 710); "There Is a Time for Everything" (*LSB* 762)

# COMMENDATION OF THE DYING

*See also Section V, p. 260*
*For devotions suitable for this topic, see Section II, p. 129*

The opening versicles of the service of Compline declare, "The Lord almighty grant us a quiet night and peace at the last." Peace at the last is the commendation for all who are ready to depart this life and join their Lord with His saints and angels.

## *Psalmody*

### PSALM 16

Preserve me, O God, for in You I take refuge.
I say to the LORD, "You are my Lord;
   I have no good apart from You."

As for the saints in the land, they
     are the excellent ones,
   in whom is all my delight.

The sorrows of those who run
     after another god shall multiply;
   their drink offerings of blood I will not pour out
   or take their names on my lips.

The LORD is my chosen portion and my cup;
   You hold my lot.
The lines have fallen for me in pleasant places;
   indeed, I have a beautiful inheritance.

I bless the LORD who gives me counsel;
   in the night also my heart instructs me.
I have set the LORD always before me;
   because He is at my right hand,
     I shall not be shaken.

Therefore my heart is glad, and
     my whole being rejoices;
   my flesh also dwells secure.
For You will not abandon my soul to Sheol,
   or let Your holy one see corruption.

You make known to me the path of life;
in Your presence there is fullness of joy;
at Your right hand are pleasures forevermore.

**PSALM 23**

The LORD is my shepherd; I shall not want.
He makes me lie down in green pastures.
He leads me beside still waters.
He restores my soul.
He leads me in paths of righteousness
for His name's sake.

Even though I walk through the
valley of the shadow of death,
I will fear no evil,
for You are with me;
Your rod and Your staff,
they comfort me.

You prepare a table before me
in the presence of my enemies;
You anoint my head with oil;
my cup overflows.
Surely goodness and mercy shall follow me
all the days of my life,
and I shall dwell in the house of the LORD
forever.

## Additional Psalms

34:12, 17–19; 73:26–28; 90

## Readings

**JOHN 3:16–21**

For God so loved the world, that He gave His only Son, that whoever believes in Him should not perish but have eternal life. For God did not send His Son into the world to condemn the world, but in order that the world might be saved through Him. Whoever believes in Him is not condemned, but whoever does not believe is condemned already, because he has not believed in the name of the only Son of God. And this is the judgment: the light has come into the world, and people loved the darkness rather than the light because their deeds were evil. For everyone who does wicked things hates the light and does not come to the light, lest his deeds should be exposed. But whoever does what is true comes to the light, so that it may be clearly seen that his deeds have been carried out in God.

**REVELATION 7:9–12**

After this I looked, and behold, a great multitude that no one could number, from every nation, from all tribes and peoples and languages, standing before the throne and before the Lamb, clothed in white robes, with palm branches in their hands, and crying out with a loud voice, "Salvation belongs to our God who sits on the throne, and to the Lamb!" And all the angels were standing around the throne and around the elders and the four living creatures, and they fell on their faces before the throne and worshiped God, saying, "Amen! Blessing and glory and wisdom and thanksgiving and honor and power and might be to our God forever and ever! Amen."

## Additional Readings

Mark 16:1–8; John 20:1–18

## Prayers

O Lord, support us all the day long of this troubled life, until the shadows lengthen and the evening comes and the busy world is hushed, the fever of life is over, and our work is done. Then, Lord, in Your mercy, grant us a safe lodging, and a holy rest, and peace at the last; through Jesus Christ our Lord. Amen. (*Occasional Services, LBW,* 107)

*Name,* our *brother/sister* in the faith, we entrust you to God who created you. May you return to the one who formed us out of the dust of the earth. Surrounded by the angels and triumphant saints, may Christ come to meet you as you go forth from this life.

Christ, the Lord of glory, who was crucified for you, bring you freedom and peace.

Christ, the High Priest, who has forgiven all your sins, keep you among His people.

Christ, the Son of God, who died for you, show you the glories of His eternal kingdom.

Christ, the Good Shepherd, enfold you with His tender care. May you see your Redeemer face to face and enjoy the sight of God forever. Amen. (*Occasional Services, LBW*, 106)

*For additional prayers, see Section IV, p. 244*

## Hymnody

> Lord, let at last thine angels come,
> To Abram's bosom bear me home,
> That I may die unfearing;
> And in its narrow chamber keep
> My body safe in peaceful sleep
> Until Thy reappearing.
> And then from death awaken me
> That these mine eyes with joy may see,
> O Son of God, Thy glorious face,
> My Savior and my Fount of grace.
> Lord Jesus Christ, my prayer attend, my prayer
>     attend,
> And I will praise Thee without end.

("Lord, Thee I Love with All My Heart," *LSB* 708:3)

## Additional Hymns

"I Know My Faith Is Founded" (*LSB* 587); "I'm but a Stranger Here" (*LSB* 748); "In Peace and Joy I Now Depart" (*LSB* 938); "Oh, What Their Joy" (*LSB* 675)

# SECTION IV

*Visitation Prayers*

# ANGER, BITTERNESS, SELF-PITY, TURMOIL

*For additional resources, see Section III, p. 135*
*For devotions suitable for this topic, see Section II, p. 41*

Gracious God, our heavenly Father, Your mercy attends us all our days. Be our strength and support amid the wearisome changes of this world, and at life's end grant us Your promised rest and the full joys of Your salvation; through Jesus Christ, Your Son, our Lord, who lives and reigns with You and the Holy Spirit, one God, now and forever. Amen. (*LSB Altar Book*, p. 623)

Gracious God, You gave Your Son into the hands of sinful men who killed Him. Forgive us when we reject Your unfailing love, and grant us the fullness of Your salvation; through Jesus Christ, Your Son, our Lord, who lives and reigns with You and the Holy Spirit, one God, now and forever. Amen. (*LSB Altar Book*, p. 639)

Lord, Jesus, You are the Good Shepherd, without whom nothing is secure. Rescue and preserve us that we may not be lost forever but follow You, rejoicing in the way that leads to eternal life; for You live and reign with the Father and the Holy Spirit, one God, now and forever. Amen. (*LSB Altar Book*, p. 825)

~

# ANXIETY, APPREHENSION, FEAR

*For additional resources, see Section III, p. 138*
*For devotions suitable for this topic, see Section II, p. 42*

Merciful and everlasting God, You did not spare Your only Son but delivered Him up for us all to bear our sins on the cross. Grant that our hearts may be so fixed with steadfast faith in Him that we fear not the power of sin, death, and the devil; through the same Jesus Christ, our Lord, who lives and reigns with You and the Holy Spirit, one God, now and forever. Amen. (*LSB Altar Book*, p. 589)

Almighty and most merciful God, preserve us from all harm and danger that we, being ready in both body and soul, may cheerfully accomplish what You want done; through Jesus Christ, Your Son, our Lord, who lives and reigns with You and the Holy Spirit, one God, now and forever. Amen. (*LSB Altar Book*, p. 630)

Almighty and everlasting Father, You give Your children many blessings even though we are undeserving. In every trial and temptation grant us steadfast confidence in Your loving-kindness and mercy; through Jesus Christ, Your Son, our Lord, who lives and reigns with You and the Holy Spirit, one God, now and forever. Amen. (*LSB Altar Book*, p. 631)

O Lord, grant us wisdom to recognize the treasures You have stored up for us in heaven, that we may never despair but always rejoice and be thankful for the riches of Your grace; through Jesus Christ, Your Son, our Lord, who lives and reigns with You and the Holy Spirit, one God, now and forever. Amen. (*LSB Altar Book*, p. 818)

~

## Guilt

*For additional resources, see Section III, p. 142*
*For devotions suitable for this topic, see Section II, p. 44*

O Lord, absolve Your people from their guilt that from the bonds of our sins, which by reason of our frailty we have brought upon ourselves, we may be delivered by Your bountiful goodness; through Jesus Christ, Your Son, our Lord, who lives and reigns with You and the Holy Spirit, one God, now and forever. Amen. (Adapted from *LSB Altar Book*, p. 936)

Lord of all power and might, author and giver of all good things, graft into our hearts the love of Your name and nourish us with all goodness that we may love and serve our neighbor; through Jesus Christ, Your Son, our Lord, who lives and reigns with You and the Holy Spirit, one God, now and forever. Amen. (*LSB Altar Book*, p. 812)

~

## IMPATIENCE, BOREDOM, RESTLESSNESS

*For additional resources, see Section III, p. 147*
*For devotions suitable for this topic, see Section II, p. 45*

Lord Jesus Christ, our support and defense in every need, continue to preserve Your Church in safety, govern her by Your goodness, and bless her with Your peace; for You live and reign with the Father and the Holy Spirit, one God, now and forever. Amen. (*LSB Altar Book*, p. 730)

O Lord of grace and mercy, teach us by Your Holy Spirit to follow the example of Your Son in true humility, that we may withstand the temptations of the devil and with pure hearts and minds avoid ungodly pride; through the same Jesus Christ, our Lord, who lives and reigns with You and the Holy Spirit, one God, now and forever. Amen. (*LSB Altar Book*, p. 823)

Heavenly Father, who sent His Son to help all of Abraham's children, to be their life and praise, give to us that life of Your Son so that our soul may live forever with You, praising Your name, through Jesus Christ, who lives and reigns with You and the Holy Spirit, one God, now and forever. Amen.

Almighty and everlasting God, who joyfully created us, stir up in us that same joy of life so that we may reflect Your glory even in times of restlessness, through Jesus Christ, who lives with You and the Holy Spirit, one God, now and forever. Amen.

## ADDICTION

*For additional resources, see Section III, p. 150*
*For devotions suitable for this topic, see Section II, p. 47*

O God, our Maker and Redeemer, You wonderfully created us and in the incarnation of Your Son yet more wondrously restored our human nature. Grant that we may ever be alive in Him who made Himself to be like us; through Jesus Christ, our Lord, who lives and reigns with You and the Holy Spirit, one God, now and forever. Amen. (*LSB Altar Book*, p. 563)

Almighty God, grant that in the midst of our failures and weaknesses we may be restored through the passion and intercession of Your only-begotten Son, who lives and reigns with You and the Holy Spirit, one God, now and forever. Amen. (*LSB Altar Book*, p. 587)

O God, Your divine wisdom sets in order all things in heaven and on earth. Put away from us all things hurtful and give us those things that are beneficial for us; through Jesus Christ, Your Son, our Lord, who lives and reigns with You and the Holy Spirit, one God, now and forever. Amen. (*LSB Altar Book*, p. 736)

Lord Jesus Christ, in Your deep compassion You rescue us from whatever may hurt us. Teach us to love You above all things and to love our neighbors as ourselves; for You live and reign with the Father and the Holy Spirit, one God, now and forever. Amen. (*LSB Altar Book*, p. 814)

O Lord, keep Your Church in Your perpetual mercy; and because without You we cannot but fall, preserve us from all things hurtful, and lead us to all things profitable to our salvation; through Jesus Christ, Your Son, our Lord, who lives and reigns with You and the Holy Spirit, one God, now and forever. Amen. (*LSB Altar Book*, p. 826)

Almighty God, our heavenly Father, because of Your

tender love toward us sinners You have given us Your Son that, believing in Him, we might have everlasting life. Continue to grant us Your Holy Spirit that we may remain steadfast in this faith to the end and finally come to life everlasting; through Jesus Christ, our Lord. Amen.

~

## LONELINESS

*For additional resources, see Section III, p. 153*
*For devotions suitable for this topic, see Section II, p. 49*

Almighty God, grant that those who live alone may not be lonely but find fulfillment in loving You and their neighbors as they follow in the footsteps of Jesus Christ, our Lord. Amen. (*LW Little Agenda*, p. 103)

O God, the helper of all who call on You, have mercy on us and give us eyes of faith to see Your Son that we may follow Him on the way that leads to eternal life; through the same Jesus Christ, Your Son, our Lord, who lives and reigns with You and the Holy Spirit, one God, now and forever. Amen. (*LSB Altar Book*, p. 737)

O Lord, Father of all mercy and God of all comfort, You always go before and follow after us. Grant that we may rejoice in Your gracious presence and continually be given to all good works; through Jesus Christ, Your Son, our Lord, who lives and reigns with You and the Holy Spirit, one God, now and forever. Amen. (*LSB Altar Book*, p. 808)

~

## OLD AGE

*For additional resources, see Section III, p. 157*
*For devotions suitable for this topic, see Section II, p. 51*

O Lord Jesus Christ, my own Savior, who does not spurn the sighs of the miserable or despise the longing of grieving hearts, to You I cry from the depths of great sorrow that in these latter years of my life I find myself alone. I feel so alone and miserable that I have become estranged from my friends and relatives. My friends have forgotten me, and my neighbors have drawn themselves away from me. To You I humbly pray, that in grace You would look upon my misery and stand by me, not like the world that so exults in the strength and vigor of youth and leaves the old to their loneliness, but according to Your sure promise. Lord, were I to have You alone, I would have no need to desire anything else in heaven or on earth. And were all the world to forget me, yet You remain my heart's only comfort, then I have a certain and faithful friend in life and death. My hope is placed in You, O Lord; leave me in ruin nevermore! Amen. (*LBP*, p. 224)

Lord God, heavenly Father, send forth Your Son to lead home His bride, the Church, that with all the company of the redeemed we may finally enter into His eternal wedding feast; through the same Jesus Christ, our Lord, who lives and reigns with You and the Holy Spirit, one God, now and forever. Amen. (*LSB Altar Book*, p. 645)

Eternal God, merciful Father, You have appointed Your Son as judge of the living and the dead. Enable us to wait for the day of His return with our eyes fixed on the kingdom prepared for Your own from the foundation of the world; through Jesus Christ, our Lord, who lives and reigns with You and the Holy Spirit, one God, now and forever. Amen. (*LSB Altar Book*, p. 648)

Almighty God, whom to know is everlasting life, grant us to know Your Son, Jesus, to be the way, the truth, and the life, that we may steadfastly follow His steps in the way that leads to life eternal; through Jesus Christ, our Lord, who lives and reigns with You and the Holy Spirit, one God, now and forever. Amen. (*LSB Altar Book*, p. 726)

Lord Jesus Christ, You reign among us by the preaching of Your cross. Forgive Your people their offenses that we, being governed by Your bountiful goodness, may enter at last into Your eternal paradise; for You live and reign with the Father and the Holy Spirit, one God, now and forever. Amen. (*LSB Altar Book*, p. 837)

~

## POOR AND NEEDY

*For additional resources, see Section III, p. 160*
*For devotions suitable for this topic, see Section II, p. 53*

Lord Jesus Christ, whose grace always precedes and follows us, help us to forsake all trust in earthly gain and to find in You our heavenly treasure; for You live and reign with the Father and the Holy Spirit, one God, now and forever. Amen. (*LSB Altar Book*, p. 735)

O Lord, grant us the Spirit to hear Your Word and know the one thing needful that by Your Word and Spirit we may live according to Your will; through Jesus Christ, Your Son, our Lord, who lives and reigns with You and the Holy Spirit, one God, now and forever. Amen. (*LSB Altar Book*, p. 816)

~

## SPIRITUAL OPPRESSION

*For additional resources, see Section III, p. 164*
*For devotions suitable for this topic, see Section II, p. 54*

Almighty and most merciful God, the protector of all who trust in You, strengthen our faith and give us courage to believe that in Your love You will rescue us from all adversities; through Jesus Christ, Your Son, our Lord, who lives and reigns with You and the Holy Spirit, one God, now and forever. Amen. (*LSB Altar Book*, p. 722)

O God, You have prepared for those who love You such good things as surpass our understanding. Cast out all sins and evil desires from us, and pour into our hearts Your Holy Spirit to guide us into all blessedness; through Jesus Christ,

Your Son, our Lord, who lives and reigns with You and the Holy Spirit, one God, now and forever. Amen. (*LSB Altar Book*, p. 811)

Almighty God, You have built Your Church on the foundation of the apostles and prophets with Christ Jesus Himself as the cornerstone. Continue to send Your messengers to preserve Your people in true peace that, by the preaching of Your Word, Your Church may be kept free from all harm and danger; through Jesus Christ, Your Son, our Lord, who lives and reigns with You and the Holy Spirit, one God, now and forever. Amen. (*LSB Altar Book*, p. 813)

O Lord, merciful Father, who delivered us from sin and death, continue to rescue us from the snare of the devil and the world so that we live to tell the story of Jesus Christ, through whose name we pray. Amen.

~

## NATURE OF SPIRITUAL WARFARE

*For additional resources, see Section III, p. 167*

Everlasting God, You have ordained and constituted the service of angels and men in a wonderful order. Mercifully grant that, as Your holy angels always serve and worship You in heaven, so by Your appointment they may also help and defend us here on earth; through Jesus Christ, Your Son, our Lord, who lives and reigns with You and the Holy Spirit, one God, now and forever. Amen. (*LSB Altar Book*, p. 978)

Almighty and eternal God, Your Son Jesus triumphed over the prince of demons and freed us from bondage to sin. Help us to stand firm against every assault of Satan, and enable us always to do Your will; through Jesus Christ, our Lord, who lives and reigns with You and the Holy Spirit, one God, now and forever. Amen. (*LSB Altar Book*, p. 714)

Lord, we implore You, grant Your people grace to withstand the temptations of the devil and with pure hearts and minds to follow You, the only God; through Jesus Christ, Your Son, our Lord, who lives and reigns with You and the Holy Spirit, one God, now and forever. Amen. (*LSB Altar Book*, p. 928)

Almighty God, You know we live in the midst of so many dangers that in our frailty we cannot stand upright. Grant strength and protection to support us in all dangers and carry us through all temptations; through Jesus Christ, Your Son, our Lord, who lives and reigns with You and the Holy Spirit, one God, now and forever. Amen. (*LSB Altar Book*, p. 571)

Almighty and ever-living God, You have given exceedingly great and precious promises to those who trust in You. Dispel from us the works of darkness and grant us to live in the light of Your Son, Jesus Christ, that our faith may never be found wanting; through the same Jesus Christ, our Lord, who lives and reigns with You and the Holy Spirit, one God, now and forever. Amen. (*LSB Altar Book*, p. 646)

~

## God's Purpose in Suffering

*For additional resources, see Section III, p. 172*
*For devotions suitable for this topic, see Section II, p. 57*

O Lord, You granted Your prophets strength to resist the temptations of the devil and courage to proclaim repentance. Give us pure hearts and minds to follow Your Son faithfully even into suffering and death; through the same Jesus Christ, our Lord, who lives and reigns with You and the Holy Spirit, one God, now and forever. Amen. (*LSB Altar Book*, p. 720)

O merciful Lord, You did not spare Your only Son but delivered Him up for us all. Grant us courage and strength to take up the cross and follow Him, who lives and reigns with You and the Holy Spirit, one God, now and forever. Amen. (*LSB Altar Book*, p. 824)

Heavenly Father, in the midst of our sufferings for the sake of Christ grant us grace to follow the example of the first martyrs, that we also may look to the One who suffered and was crucified on our behalf and pray for those who do us wrong; through Jesus Christ, Your Son, our Lord, who lives and reigns with You and the Holy Spirit, one God, now and forever. Amen. (*LSB Altar Book*, p. 946)

Almighty God, the martyred innocents of Bethlehem showed forth Your praise not by speaking but by dying. Put to death in us all that is in conflict with Your will that our lives may bear witness to the faith we profess with our lips; through Jesus Christ, Your Son, our Lord, who lives and reigns with You and the Holy Spirit, one God, now and forever. Amen. (*LSB Altar Book*, p. 948)

Almighty God, grant that we, who have died and risen with Christ in Holy Baptism, may daily repent of our sins, patiently suffer for the sake of the truth, and fearlessly bear witness to His victory over death; through the same Jesus Christ, our Lord, who lives and reigns with You and the Holy Spirit, one God, now and forever. Amen. (*LSB Altar Book*, p. 974)

Merciful God, Your Son, Jesus Christ, was lifted high upon the cross that He might bear the sins of the world and draw all people to Himself. Grant that we who glory in His death for our redemption may faithfully heed His call to bear the cross and follow Him, who lives and reigns with You and the Holy Spirit, one God, now and forever. Amen. (*LSB Altar Book*, p. 976)

# BAPTISMAL IDENTITY—CALL TO REPENTANCE

*For additional resources, see Section III, p. 176*
*For devotions suitable for this topic, see Section II, p. 66*

O God, for our redemption You gave Your only-begotten Son to the death of the cross and by His glorious resurrection delivered us from the power of the enemy. Grant that all our sin may be drowned through daily repentance and that day by day we may arise to live before You in righteousness and purity forever; through Jesus Christ, our Lord, who lives and reigns with You and the Holy Spirit, one God, now and forever. Amen. (*LSB Altar Book*, p. 596)

O God, Your almighty power is made known chiefly in showing mercy. Grant us the fullness of Your grace that we may be called to repentance and made partakers of Your heavenly treasures; through Your Son, Jesus Christ, our Lord, who lives and reigns with You and the Holy Spirit, one God, now and forever. Amen. (*LSB Altar Book*, p. 719)

Almighty and everlasting God, You desire not the death of a sinner but that all would repent and live. Hear our prayers as we come before You in sorrow for our sins and faith to believe that You forgive even the most heinous sins. Take away our iniquity, and turn us from those things that entangle us and lead us away from You, the living and true God. Gather us into Your holy Church to the glory of Your name; through Jesus Christ, our Lord. Amen. (Adapted from *LSB*, p. 305)

~

# BAPTISMAL IDENTITY—FORGIVENESS AND RECONCILIATION

*For additional resources, see Section III, p. 179*
*For devotions suitable for this topic, see Section II, p. 68*

Almighty God, in Your mercy so guide the course of this world that we may forgive as we have been forgiven and joyfully serve You in godly peace and quietness; through Jesus Christ, Your Son, our Lord, who lives and reigns with You and the Holy Spirit, one God, now and forever. Amen. (*LSB Altar Book*, p. 806)

Almighty and everlasting God, increase in us Your gifts of faith, hope, and love that we may receive the forgiveness You have promised and love what You have commanded; through Jesus Christ, Your Son, our Lord, who lives and reigns with You and the Holy Spirit, one God, now and forever. Amen. (*LSB Altar Book*, p. 809)

O almighty Father, it is according to Your desire that You love us, give us this same love so that we turn our eyes away from our sinful self and fix them upon Your Son, who freely forgives, revealing Your will of reconciling the world back to You. Give us Your joy so that we may endure the path set before us, and grant us peace in the last, through Jesus Christ, who lives and reigns with You and the Holy Spirit, one God, now and forever. Amen.

O Jesus Christ, You are the Life of the living, help us to remember that there is no life apart from Yours, and grant that today we would live Your life of love, for Your mercy's sake. Amen.

Merciful Father, You gave Your Son Jesus as the heavenly bread of life. Grant us faith to feast on Him in Your Word and Sacraments that we may be nourished unto life everlasting; through the same Jesus Christ, our Lord, who lives and reigns with You and the Holy Spirit, one God, now and forever. Amen. (*LSB Altar Book*, p. 724)

Lord Jesus Christ, our great High Priest, cleanse us by the power of Your redeeming blood that in purity and peace we may worship and adore Your holy name; for You live and reign with the Father and the Holy Spirit, one God, now and forever. Amen. (*LSB Altar Book*, p. 739)

O Lord, by Your bountiful goodness release us from the bonds of our sins, which by reason of our weakness we have brought upon ourselves, that we may stand firm until the day of our Lord Jesus Christ, who lives and reigns with You and the Holy Spirit, one God, now and forever. Amen. (*LSB Altar Book*, p. 741)

Almighty God, whose compassion never fails and who invites us to call upon You in prayer, hear the heartfelt confession of our sins and receive our humble supplication for Your mercy. Spare us from the just punishment of sin, which our Lord Jesus Christ has borne for us, and enable us to serve You in holiness and purity of life; through Jesus Christ, Your Son, our Lord, who lives and reigns with You and the Holy Spirit, one God, now and forever. Amen. (*LSB Altar Book*, p. 992)

~

## Baptismal Identity—Gratitude

*For devotions suitable for this topic, see Section II, p. 74*

Almighty God, our heavenly Father, Your mercies are new every morning; and though we deserve only punishment, You receive us as Your children and provide for all our needs of body and soul. Grant that we may heartily acknowledge Your merciful goodness, give thanks for all Your benefits, and serve You in willing obedience; through Jesus Christ, Your Son, our Lord, who lives and reigns with You and the Holy Spirit, one God, now and forever. Amen. (*LSB Altar Book*, p. 583)

Almighty and gracious God, we give thanks that You have restored the health of Your servant, *name,* on whose behalf we bless and praise Your name. Grant that *he/she* may continue the mission You have given *him/her* in this world and also share in eternal glory at the appearing of Your Son, Jesus Christ our Lord. Amen. (*Occasional Services*, p. 52)

O Lord our God, source of life and wholeness: Gladly we thank You that You hear our prayers for *name,* and that You are turning *his/her* sickness into health and *his/her* weakness into strength; through Jesus Christ our Lord. Amen. (*Occasional Services*, p. 52)

~

## Baptismal Identity—Peace

*For additional resources, see Section III, p. 182*
*For devotions suitable for this topic, see Section II, p. 77*

Almighty and everlasting God, who governs all things in heaven and on earth, mercifully hear the prayers of Your people and grant us Your peace through all our days; through Jesus Christ, Your Son, our Lord, who lives and reigns with You and the Holy Spirit, one God, now and forever. Amen. (*LSB Altar Book*, p. 568)

Almighty God, through the resurrection of Your Son You have secured peace for our troubled consciences. Grant us this peace evermore that trusting in the merit of Your Son we may come at last to the perfect peace of heaven; through the same Jesus Christ, Your Son, our Lord, who lives and reigns with You and the Holy Spirit, one God, now and forever. Amen. (*LSB Altar Book*, p. 598)

Almighty God, in Your mercy guide the course of this world so that Your Church may joyfully serve You in godly peace and quietness; through Jesus Christ, Your Son, our Lord, who lives and reigns with You and the Holy Spirit, one God, now and forever. Amen. (*LSB Altar Book*, p. 716)

O Lord, grant that the course of this world may be so peaceably ordered by Your governance that Your Church may joyfully serve You in all godly quietness; through Jesus Christ, our Lord, who lives and reigns with You and the Holy Spirit, one God, now and forever. Amen. (*LSB Altar Book*, p. 912)

# BAPTISMAL IDENTITY—THANKSGIVING

*For additional resources, see Section III, p. 185*
*For devotions suitable for this topic, see Section II, p. 80*

Almighty God, You show mercy to Your people in all their troubles. Grant us always to recognize Your goodness, give thanks for Your compassion, and praise Your holy name; through Jesus Christ, Your Son, our Lord, who lives and reigns with You and the Holy Spirit, one God, now and forever. Amen. (*LSB Altar Book*, p. 830)

Almighty God, Your mercies are new every morning and You graciously provide for all our needs of body and soul. Grant us Your Holy Spirit that we may acknowledge Your goodness, give thanks for Your benefits, and serve You in willing obedience all our days; through Jesus Christ, Your Son, our Lord, who lives and reigns with You and the Holy Spirit, one God, now and forever. Amen. (*LSB Altar Book*, p. 991)

~

# BAPTISMAL IDENTITY—TRUST IN GOD

*For additional resources, see Section III, p. 188*
*For devotions suitable for this topic, see Section II, p. 83*

Jesus Christ, Light of life, who illuminates our world with Your truth, reveal to us Your saving will and work in us to trust in Your purpose of eternal life, for Your mercy's sake. Amen.

Lord God, heavenly Father, since we cannot stand before You relying on anything we have done, help us trust in Your abiding grace and live according to Your Word; through Jesus Christ, Your Son, our Lord, who lives and reigns with You and the Holy Spirit, one God, now and forever. Amen. (*LSB Altar Book*, p. 636–37)

Almighty God, You invite us to trust in You for our salvation. Deal with us not in the severity of Your judgment but by the greatness of Your mercy; through Jesus Christ, Your Son, our Lord, who lives and reigns with You and the Holy Spirit, one God, now and forever. Amen. (*LSB Altar Book*, p. 640)

O God, the protector of all who trust in You, have mercy on us that with You as our rule and guide we may so pass through things temporal that we lose not the things eternal; through Jesus Christ, Your Son, our Lord, who lives and reigns with You and the Holy Spirit, one God, now and forever. Amen. (*LSB Altar Book*, p. 641)

O God, You are the strength of all who trust in You, and without Your aid we can do no good thing. Grant us the help of Your grace that we may please You in both will and deed; through Jesus Christ, Your Son, our Lord, who lives and reigns with You and the Holy Spirit, one God, now and forever. Amen. (*LSB Altar Book*, p. 828)

O Lord, almighty and ever-living God, You have given exceedingly great and precious promises to those who trust in You. Rule and govern our hearts and minds by Your Holy Spirit that we may live and abide forever in Your Son, who lives and reigns with You and the Holy Spirit, one God, now and forever. Amen. (*LSB Altar Book*, p. 836)

O God, the strength of all who trust in You, mercifully accept our prayers; and because through the weakness of our mortal nature we can do no good thing, grant us Your grace to keep Your commandments that we may please You in both will and deed; through Jesus Christ, Your Son, our Lord, who lives and reigns with You and the Holy Spirit, one God, now and forever. Amen. (*LSB Altar Book*, p. 908)

O God, the protector of all who trust in You, without whom nothing is strong and nothing is holy, multiply Your mercy on us that, with You as our ruler and guide, we may so pass through things temporal that we lose not the things eternal; through Jesus Christ, Your Son, our Lord, who lives and reigns with You and the Holy Spirit, one God, now and forever. Amen. (*LSB Altar Book*, p. 910)

~

## CHILDBIRTH—BEFORE CHILDBIRTH

*For devotions suitable for this topic, see Section II, p. 88*

Lord God, heavenly Father, as You protected Mary during the birth of the infant Jesus, so now watch over this mother and her unborn child as she is about to give birth. May her anticipation over the joy at the birth of this child give her strength to endure these next hours of struggle; through Jesus Christ, our Lord. Amen.

O God, the creator and sustainer of life, graciously preserve and protect *name* during childbirth, and safely bring forth in health and wholeness the infant whom You have created; through Jesus Christ our Lord. Amen. (*Occasional Services*, p. 53)

O Lord our God, creator of all that exists: We thank You for the joy of watching new life begin and for the privilege of sharing with You in Your continuing creation. In Your mercy grant that these blessings may continue to us and even to our children's children, that generations yet unborn may bless Your holy name; through Jesus Christ our Lord. Amen. (*Occasional Services*, p. 53)

~

## CHILDBIRTH—FOLLOWING CHILDBIRTH

*For devotions suitable for this topic, see Section II, p. 90*

Heavenly Father, You sent Your own Son into this world as the child of Mary and Joseph. We thank You for the life of this child, *name*, entrusted to our care. Help us to remember that we are all Your children, and so to love and nurture *him/her* that *he/she* may attain to that full stature intended for *him/her* in Your eternal kingdom; for the sake of Jesus Christ, Your Son and our Lord. Amen. (*Occasional Services*, p. 54)

O gracious God, we give You thanks and praise that You have preserved Your servant, *name,* through the anxiety of childbirth. Enable her to live faithfully according to Your will and finally to partake of everlasting glory; through Jesus Christ our Lord. Amen. (*Occasional Services*, p. 53)

∽

## CHILDBIRTH—FOR STILLBORN, DEATH SHORTLY AFTER BIRTH, OR MISCARRIAGE

*For devotions suitable for this topic, see Section II, p. 94*

O Lord God, your ways are often hidden, unsearchable, and beyond our understanding. For reasons beyond our knowing You have turned the hopes of these parents from joy to sadness, and now You desire that in humble faith we bow before Your ordering of these events. You are the Lord. You do what You know to be good. In their hour of sorrow, comfort them with Your life-giving Word, for the sake of Jesus Christ, Your Son, our Lord. Amen. (*LW Little Agenda*, p. 106–7)

∽

## BEFORE SURGERY

*For devotions suitable for this topic, see Section II, p. 95*

Almighty God, our heavenly Father, graciously protect *name* in *his/her* surgery. Fill *his/her* heart with confidence that, though *he/she* may be anxious, *he/she* may put *his/her* trust in You; through Jesus Christ our Lord. Amen. (*Occasional Services*, p. 74)

Strengthen Your servant, *name*, O God, to do what *he/she* must do and bear what *he/she* must bear; that, accepting Your healing gifts through the skill of the medical staff, *he/she* may be restored to health; through Jesus Christ our Lord. Amen. (*Occasional Services*, p. 74)

Loving God, hold *name* in Your care. Give wisdom and skill to *his/her* doctors and nurses, and enable them to serve Your purposes of love and healing; through Jesus Christ our Lord. Amen. (*Occasional Services*, p. 74)

Almighty and gracious God, we give You thanks that You have protected *name* during surgery. Enable *him/her* to trust in Your goodness, to find comfort in Your abiding presence, and to praise Your holy name; through Jesus Christ our Lord. Amen. (*Occasional Services*, p. 75)

~

## RECOVERY FROM SICKNESS

*For additional resources, see Section III, p. 191*
*For devotions suitable for this topic, see Section II, p. 99*

Gracious Father, Your blessed Son came down from heaven to be the true bread that gives life to the world. Grant that the Christ, the bread of life, may live in us and we in Him, who lives and reigns with You and the Holy Spirit, one God, now and forever. Amen. (*LSB Altar Book*, p. 725)

Almighty God, Your Son, Jesus Christ restored many to health and called them to be witnesses of Your mercy. Heal us from all our infirmities and call us to know You in the power of Your Son's unending life; through the same Jesus Christ, our Lord, who lives and reigns with You and the Holy Spirit, one God, now and forever. Amen. (Adapted from *LSB Altar Book*, p. 970)

## Ministry to a Sick Person

*For additional resources, see Section III, p. 195*
*For devotions suitable for this topic, see Section II, p. 102*

Lord God, Your Son, Jesus Christ, bore all our sickness and sin in His body on the cross. In our suffering, help us never to forget that You are our God and that only in You is there health and wholeness; through Jesus Christ, our Lord. Amen.

Almighty and most merciful God, we humbly confess that we have justly deserved Your chastening for our sins, but we implore You of Your boundless goodness to grant us repentance, graciously forgive our sins, and strengthen us by Your grace, that as obedient children we may bear our afflictions in patience; through Jesus Christ, our Lord. Amen.

Lord Jesus, who has given to Your servant to bear the cross, give *him/her* also an obedient and submissive heart, that *he/she* joyfully take Your yoke upon *him/her* and willingly follow You in every affliction, confessing that You restore *him/her* finally to perfect health in body and soul according to Your promise. Amen.

O Father of mercies and God of all comfort, our only help in time of need, look with favor upon Your servant, *name*. Assure *him/her* of Your mercy, comfort *him/her* with the awareness of Your goodness, preserve *him/her* from the temptations of the evil one, and give *him/her* patience in *his/her* tribulation. If it please You, restore *him/her* to health or give *him/her* grace to accept this affliction; through Jesus Christ, our Lord. Amen. (*LW Little Agenda*, p. 98)

O Lord, You are the great Physician of soul and body; You chasten and You heal. We beg You to show mercy to Your servant *name*. Spare *his/her* life, we pray, and restore *his/her* strength. Because You gave Your Son to bear our infirmities and sicknesses, deal compassionately with Your servant, and bless *him/her* with Your healing power. We commit *him/her* to Your gracious mercy and protection; through Jesus Christ, our Lord. Amen. (*LW Little Agenda*, p. 98)

O Lord God, by the example of Your blessed Son, grant us grace to take joyfully the sufferings of the present time in full assurance of the glory that shall be revealed to us; through Jesus Christ, our Lord. Amen. (*LW Little Agenda*, pp. 98–99)

O Lord our heavenly might, You rule over the bodies and souls of men, and in Your Son, our Savior, Jesus Christ, You healed all manner of infirmities and cured all manner of diseases. Mercifully help Your servant *name* in body and soul and, if it be Your will, free *him/her* from *his/her* sickness that, restored to health, *he/she* may with a thankful heart bless Your holy name; through Jesus Christ, our Lord. Amen. (*LW Little Agenda*, p. 99)

O Lord, visit and restore Your servant for whom we offer our prayers. Look upon *him/her* in Your mercy; give *him/her* comfort and sure confidence in You; defend *him/her* from danger and harm; and keep *him/her* in perpetual peace and safety; through Your Son, Jesus Christ our Lord. Amen. (*Occasional Services*, p. 50)

O God, the strength of the weak and the comfort of sufferers: Mercifully hear our prayers and grant to Your servant, *name*, the help of Your power, that *his/her* sickness may be turned into health and our anxiety into joy; through Jesus Christ our Lord. Amen. (*Occasional Services*, p. 51)

O God of power and love, be present with *name*, that *his/her* weakness may be overcome and *his/her* strength restored; and that, *his/her* health being renewed *he/she* may bless Your holy name; through Jesus Christ our Lord. Amen. (*Occasional Services*, p. 51)

Heavenly Father, giver of life and health; Comfort and relieve Your servant, *name,* and give Your power of healing to those who minister to *his/her* needs, that *he/she* may be strengthened in *his/her* weakness and have confidence in Your loving care; through Jesus Christ our Lord. Amen. (*Occasional Services,* p. 51)

O Lord, look upon Your servant, *name.* Touch *him/her* with Your healing hand and let Your life-giving power flow into every cell of *his/her* body and into the depths of *his/her* soul, restoring *him/her* to wholeness and strength for service in Your kingdom; through Jesus Christ our Lord. Amen. (*Occasional Services,* p. 51)

Almighty and everlasting God, mercifully look upon the infirmities and stretch forth the hand of Your majesty to heal and defend us; through Jesus Christ, Your Son, our Lord, who lives and reigns with You and the Holy Spirit, one God, now and forever. Amen. (*LSB Altar Book,* p. 569)

Heavenly Father, during His earthly ministry Your Son Jesus healed the sick and raised the dead. By the healing medicine of the Word and Sacraments pour into our hearts such love toward You that we may live eternally; through the same Jesus Christ, our Lord, who lives and reigns with You and the Holy Spirit, one God, now and forever. Amen. (*LSB Altar Book,* p. 718)

∼

## MINISTRY TO A SICK CHILD/THE PARENTS

*For devotions suitable for this topic, see Section II, p. 109*

O almighty God, our Father in heaven, take pity on *name,* now afflicted with sickness. Mercifully spare, we pray, the life you have given and, as the only Help of the helpless, relieve the pains of this child. Direct the ministry of healing for *his/her* recovery, and revive *his/her* spirit that the frailty of the body may pass away. Renew *his/her* strength, and grant to *him/her* many years of life to serve you faithfully. Yet, O Father, whatever Your will may be concerning this child, we trust that *he/she* is in Your keeping, and we pray that *his/her* soul may be Yours now and forever; through Jesus Christ, our Lord. Amen. (*LW Little Agenda*, p. 99)

~

## RECOVERY FROM SICKNESS OF A SICK CHILD

Gracious God, our Father, we thank and praise You for blessing *name* with recovery from sickness and pain. Continue to strengthen *him/her* in body, mind, and soul; grant *him/her* an increase and continuance of well-being; and bless *him/her* with all things necessary to grow and to maintain the health You give. Grant this for the sake of Jesus Christ, our Lord. Amen. (*LW Little Agenda*, p. 101)

~

## COMFORT AND CONSOLATION

*For additional resources, see Section III, p. 199*
*For devotions suitable for this topic, see Section II, p. 113*

O God, You once taught the hearts of Your faithful people by sending them the light of Your Holy Spirit. Grant us by the same Spirit to have a right understanding in all things and evermore to rejoice in His holy consolation; through Jesus Christ, Your Son, our Lord, who lives and reigns with You and the Holy Spirit, one God, now and forever. Amen. (Adapted from *LSB Altar Book*, p. 611)

Eternal God, Your Son Jesus Christ is our true Sabbath rest. Help us to keep each day holy by receiving His Word of comfort that we may find our rest in Him, who lives and reigns with You and the Holy Spirit, one God, now and forever. Amen. (*LSB Altar Book*, p. 713)

## Prolonged Recovery/Lingering Illness

*For additional resources, see Section III, p. 202*
*For devotions suitable for this topic, see Section II, p. 115*

Dear heavenly Father, remind me of Your grace, keeping my eyes fixed on Jesus, the Author and Finisher of my faith. You have promised that You will not impose upon Your children more than we can endure, and I know the truth of this word. However, I remain weak and days of full health and renewed vigor seem far away. I know not if I am closer to the beginning or the end of this trial. Lead me through the wilderness of testing for the sake of Your Son, Jesus, who knows my pain and weakness through His own temptation and passion. Amen. (Adapted from *LBP*, p. 174)

Lord Jesus Christ, give me at all times a patient spirit, willing and ready to wait and pray, that I may not be weary of Your chastening, but cast my care upon You with all cheerfulness and confidence and ever hope for the best from You, for You bear me up with all my sins and infirmities, bestow upon me Your own strength in Your body and blood, and give eternal life through Baptism. May these always remain my hope and consolation. Amen.

～

## Ministry to a Dying Person

*For additional resources, see Section III, p. 205*
*For devotions suitable for this topic, see Section II, p. 117*

O true Savior, Jesus Christ, You are the Lamb of God that takes away the sin of the world and have washed and cleansed Your servant in Your blood. We beseech You of Your bitter Passion, and especially by Your meritorious death, have mercy upon *his/her* soul in the hour of *his/her* departure and bring *him/her* to life everlasting, where You live and reign with the Father and the Holy Spirit, God forever. Amen.

Gracious and merciful God, by the bitter suffering and death of Jesus Christ and by the ministry of the holy angels guide Your servant into Abraham's bosom, into our eternal home, that *he/she* may live there with all the redeemed in unspeakable joy and bliss. Lord Jesus Christ, be with *him/her* to protect, refresh, lead, and bless *him/her* here in time and hereafter in eternity, for You live and reign with the Father and the Holy Spirit, one God, now and forever. Amen.

~

## ACCEPTANCE OF INEVITABLE DEATH

*For additional resources, see Section III, p. 209*
*For devotions suitable for this topic, see Section II, p. 127*

Almighty and everlasting God, the consolation of the sorrowful and the strength of the weak, may the prayers of those who in any tribulation or distress cry to You graciously come before You, so that in every situation they may recognize and receive Your gracious help, comfort, and peace; through Jesus Christ, our Lord. Amen. (*LSB Altar Book*, p. 464)

Heavenly Father, because of our sin You cause men to die and return to dust. Teach us to number our days. Grant us a true faith in Your only-begotten Son, Jesus Christ, who was delivered for our offenses, raised again for our justification, and reigns to all eternity. Prepare us for a peaceful departure and receive our souls unto Yourself, and grant that at last our bodies may rise again from the grave unto everlasting life; through the same Jesus Christ, our Lord. Amen.

## COMMENDATION OF THE DYING

*See also Section V, p. 260*
*For additional resources, see Section III, p. 213*
*For devotions suitable for this topic, see Section II, p. 129*

O Lord, our shepherd, lead Your sheep in goodness and mercy as we pass with You through the valley of the shadow of death to Your eternal home, where You live and reign with the Father and the Holy Spirit, one God, now and forever. Amen. (*LSB Agenda*, 89)

O Lord, let Your ears be attentive to the voice of our cry, for there is forgiveness with You that You may be feared. By Your unfailing love deliver us from all our sin that our hope may be in You and in Your full redemption; through Jesus Christ, Your Son, our Lord, who lives and reigns with You and the Holy Spirit, one God, now and forever. (*LSB Agenda*, 90)

Almighty God, You breathed life into Adam and have given earthly life also to *name*, Your dear child and servant. With faith in Your power to heal and save, we commend *him/her* to You; through Jesus Christ, Your Son, our Lord, who lives and reigns with You and the Holy Spirit, one God, now and forever. (*LSB Agenda*, 94)

O God the Father, fountain and source of all blessings, we give thanks that You have kept our *brother/sister name* in the faith and have now taken *him/her* to Yourself. Comfort us with Your holy Word, and give us strength that when our last hour comes we may peacefully fall asleep in You; through Jesus Christ, our Lord. (*LSB Agenda*, 96)

Lord Jesus Christ, deliver Your servant, *name,* from all evil and set *him/her* free from every bond, that *he/she* may join all Your saints in the eternal courts of heaven, where with the Father and the Holy Spirit You live and reign, one God, now and forever. (*Occasional Services*, 105)

God of compassion and love, You have breathed into us the breath of life and have given us the exercise of our minds and wills. In our frailty we surrender all life to You from whom it came, trusting in Your gracious promises; through Jesus Christ our Lord. (*Occasional Services*, 106)

Into Your hand, O merciful Savior, we commend Your servant, *name.* Acknowledge, we humbly beseech You, a sheep of Your own fold, a lamb of Your own flock, a sinner of Your own redeeming. Receive *him/her* into the arms of Your mercy, into the blessed rest of everlasting peace, and into the glorious company of the saints in light. (*Occasional Services*, 107)

~

## DEATH OF A CHILD

*For devotions suitable for this topic, see Section II, p. 131*

Almighty and everlasting God, You give and You take away according to Your wisdom and grace. We give thanks for all the mercies granted to this child, *name,* during *his/her* short life on earth and for taking *him/her* to Yourself. Enable *his/her* parents to accept Your holy will that they may be comforted with the assurance that through the power of Holy Baptism their beloved child was delivered from sin and has been received among the saints in glory. Keep all of us in Your grace that when our last hour comes we may depart in peace; through Jesus Christ, Your Son, our Lord and Savior. (*LW Little Agenda*, 106)

O God our Father, Your beloved Son took children into His arms and blessed them. Give us grace, we pray, that we may entrust *name* to Your never-failing care and love, and bring us all to Your heavenly kingdom; through Your Son our Lord. (*Occasional Services*, 111)

# Section V

## Visitation Orders

# HOLY BAPTISM
## *In Cases of Emergency*

*In urgent situations, in the absence of the pastor, any Christian may administer Holy Baptism.*

*If time permits, the following may precede the Baptism.*

> Jesus said, "Assuredly, I say to you, whoever does not receive the kingdom of God as a little child will by no means enter it." And He took them up in His arms, put His hands on them, and blessed them. *Mark 10:15–16 NKJV*
>
> Eternal God, Father of our Lord Jesus Christ, give ___name(s)___ Your grace through rebirth by the Holy Spirit. Receive ___him/her/them___ according to Your promise: "Ask, and it will be given to you; seek, and you will find; knock, and it will be opened to you," that through this heavenly washing ___he/she/they___ may receive the gift of the Holy Spirit and the forgiveness of all ___his/her/their___ sins and come to the eternal kingdom which You have prepared for ___him/her/them___; through Jesus Christ, our Lord. Amen. (508) *Matthew 7:7*

Lord's Prayer

Apostles' Creed

*Take water, call the child or adult by name, and pour or sprinkle the water on the head of the candidate while saying:*

> ___Name___, I baptize you in the name of the Father and of the Son and of the Holy Spirit. Amen.

*Holy Baptism administered by a layperson shall immediately be reported to the pastor for its recognition by the congregation.*

*Holy Baptism administered by the pastor in cases of emergency shall also be recognized by the congregation. See* LSB Agenda, *pages 18–21.*

# VISITING THE SICK AND DISTRESSED

*As he enters the house or room, the pastor speaks this greeting:*

Peace be to this house (place).          *Luke 10:5*

**Amen.**

*The pastor may read an appropriate portion of Holy Scripture according to the circumstance. He will then instruct the person patiently to trust God's holy will, confident that, according to His gracious promise, in all things He works for the good of those who love Him. The pastor may also sing an appropriate hymn.*

*The confession of sins may follow one of the forms below. In the case of individual confession, the pastor assures the confidentiality of the confession by requesting others present to leave the room or by taking other appropriate measures.*

## General Confession

O almighty God, merciful Father, I, a poor, miserable sinner, confess unto You all my sins and iniquities with which I have ever offended You and justly deserved Your temporal and eternal punishment. But I am heartily sorry for them and sincerely repent of them, and I pray You of Your boundless mercy and for the sake of the holy, innocent, bitter sufferings and death of Your beloved Son, Jesus Christ, to be gracious and merciful to me, a poor, sinful being.

*OR*

## Individual Confession

Pastor, please hear my confession and pronounce forgiveness in order to fulfill God's will.
Proceed.

I, a poor sinner, plead guilty before God of all sins. I have lived as if God did not matter and as if I mattered most. My

## Question Form

Do you confess to almighty God that you are a poor, miserable sinner?
Yes.

Do you confess to our merciful Father that you have sinned against Him in thought, word, and deed?
Yes.

Lord's name I have not honored as I should; my worship and prayers have faltered. I have not let His love have its way with me, and so my love for others has failed. There are those whom I have hurt, and those whom I have failed to help. My thoughts and desires have been soiled with sin.

What troubles me particularly is that . . .

*The penitent confesses whatever he has done against the commandments of God, according to his place in life. Then he concludes by saying:*

I am sorry for all of this and ask for grace. I want to do better.

God be merciful to you and strengthen your faith.
**Amen.**

Do you believe that my forgiveness is God's forgiveness?
**Yes.**

Do you confess that you justly deserve His temporal and eternal punishment?
**Yes.**

Do you believe that our Lord Jesus Christ died for you and shed His blood for you on the cross for the forgiveness of all your sins?
**Yes.**

Do you pray God, for the sake of the holy, innocent, bitter sufferings and death of His beloved Son, to be gracious and merciful to you?
**Yes.**

Finally, do you believe that my forgiveness is God's forgiveness?
**Yes.**

Let it be done for you as you believe.

*The pastor places his hands on the head of the penitent and says:*

In the stead and by the command of my Lord Jesus Christ I forgive you all your sins in the name of the Father and of the ☩ Son and of the Holy Spirit.

**Amen.**

*When Individual Confession and Absolution is concluded, the pastor invites the family and loved ones to return.*

*When a sick person is to be anointed with oil, the following passage from Holy Scripture is read:*

Is anyone among you sick? Let him call for the elders[1] of the church, and let them pray over him, anointing him with oil in the name of the Lord. And the prayer of faith will save the one who is sick, and the Lord will raise him up. And if he has committed sins, he will be forgiven. Therefore, confess your sins to one another and pray for one another, that you may be healed. The effective prayer of a righteous person has great power.

*James 5:14–16*

[1] The Greek word for "elders," *presbyteroi*, in the reading from James refers to pastors and not lay elders.

___Name___ , you have confessed your sins and received Holy Absolution. In remembrance of the grace of God given by the Holy Spirit in the waters of Holy Baptism, I will anoint you with oil. Confident in our Lord and in love for you, we also pray for you that you will not lose faith. Know that in godly patience the Church endures with you and supports you during this affliction. We firmly believe that this illness is for the glory of God and that the Lord will both hear our prayer and work according to His good and gracious will.     *[John 11:4]*

*Using his right thumb, the pastor anoints the sick person on the forehead while saying:*

Almighty God, the Father of our Lord Jesus Christ, who has given you the new birth of water and the Spirit and has forgiven you all your sins, strengthen you with His grace to life ✠ everlasting.

**Amen.**

*The pastor leads those gathered in the following prayers.*

**Lord, have mercy upon us.**
**Christ, have mercy upon us.**
**Lord, have mercy upon us.**

**Our Father who art in heaven,**
    **hallowed be Thy name,**
    **Thy kingdom come,**
    **Thy will be done on earth as it is in heaven;**
    **give us this day our daily bread;**

**and forgive us our trespasses**
**as we forgive those who trespass against us;**
**and lead us not into temptation,**
**but deliver us from evil.**
**For Thine is the kingdom and the power and the glory**
**forever and ever. Amen.** *Matthew 6:9–13*

*The pastor and those gathered pray the Prayer Sentences (Preces).*
*Circumstances may require that the pastor read them by himself.*

O Lord, save your servant __name__,
**who trusts in You.** *Psalm 86:2*

Send __him/her__ help from the sanctuary
**and strength from Your holy dwelling.** *Psalm 20:2*

Look upon __his/her__ affliction and pain,
**and forgive all __his/her__ sins.** *Psalm 25:18*

O Lord, hear our prayer,
**and let our cry come to You.** *Psalm 39:12*

The Lord be with you. *2 Timothy 4:22*
**And also with you.**

Let us pray.

O Lord, look down from heaven; behold, visit, and relieve Your servant __name__, for whom we pray. Look upon __him/her__ with the eyes of Your mercy, and give __him/her__ comfort and sure confidence in You. Defend __him/her__ from every danger to body and soul, and keep __him/her__ in peace and safety; through Jesus Christ, Your Son, our Lord, who lives and reigns with You and the Holy Spirit, one God, now and forever. (518)

Father of all mercy, You never fail to help those who call upon You in faith. Give strength and confidence to Your servant __name__ in __his/her__ time of affliction. Grant that __he/she__ may know that You are near, and that underneath __him/her__ are Your everlasting arms. Grant that __he/she__, resting on Your protection, may fear no evil, for You are with __him/her__ to comfort and deliver __him/her__; through Jesus Christ, Your Son, our Lord, who lives and reigns with You and the Holy Spirit, one God, now and forever. (519)

**Amen.**

*If the Lord's Supper is not to be received, the service concludes with the Blessing on page 255.*

It is truly good, right, and salutary that we should at all times and in all places give thanks to You, O Lord, holy Father, almighty and everlasting God, for the countless blessings You so freely bestow on us and all creation. Above all, we give thanks for Your boundless love shown to us when You sent Your only-begotten Son, Jesus Christ, into our flesh and laid on Him our sin, giving Him into death that we might not die eternally. Because He is now risen from the dead and lives and reigns to all eternity, all who believe in Him will overcome sin and death and will rise again to new life.

Our Lord Jesus Christ, on the night when He was betrayed, took bread, and when He had given thanks, He broke it and gave it to the disciples and said: "Take, eat; this is My ✠ body, which is given for you. This do in remembrance of Me."

In the same way also He took the cup after supper, and when He had given thanks, He gave it to them, saying: "Drink of it, all of you; this cup is the new testament in My ✠ blood, which is shed for you for the forgiveness of sins. This do, as often as you drink it, in remembrance of Me."

*Matthew 26:26–28; Mark 14:22–24*
*Luke 22:19–20; 1 Corinthians 11:23–25*

*It is appropriate that the pastor receive the body and blood of the Lord with the sick or distressed person, together with those present who have previously been admitted to the Lord's Table. During the Distribution, the pastor says:*

Take, eat; this is the true body of our Lord and Savior Jesus Christ, given into death for your sins.
Take, drink; this is the true blood of our Lord and Savior Jesus Christ, shed for the forgiveness of your sins.

*After all have communed, the pastor says:*

The body and blood of our Lord Jesus Christ strengthen and preserve you in body and soul to life everlasting. Depart in peace.
**Amen.**

O God the Father, the fountain and source of all goodness, who in loving-kindness sent Your only-begotten Son into the flesh, we thank You that for His sake You have given us pardon and peace in this Sacrament, and we ask You not to forsake Your children but always to rule our hearts and minds by Your Holy Spirit that we may be enabled constantly to serve You; through Jesus Christ, Your Son, our Lord, who lives and reigns with You and the Holy Spirit, one God, now and forever. (403)
**Amen.**

*The pastor speaks one of the following blessings:*

God our Father grant you His wholeness and peace so that you may remain constant in faith and call upon His holy name. The Lord Jesus Christ grant you the joy of His countenance and a new, steadfast spirit. The Holy Spirit generously pour upon you His mercy and grace, that He would fill you inwardly and outwardly, surround you, and be with you always. The blessing of almighty God, the Father, the ✛ Son, and the Holy Spirit, be and remain with you now and forever.

**Amen.**

The Lord bless you and
   keep you.
The Lord make His face
   shine upon you and be
   gracious unto you. .
The Lord lift up His countenance upon you and ✛
   give you peace.
**Amen.**          *Numbers 6:24–26*

# BRIEF SERVICE OF THE WORD

## INVOCATION

**P** In the name of the Father and of the ☩ Son and of the Holy
Spirit.                                                     *Matthew 28:19b*

**C** **Amen.**

## PSALMODY

*One or more psalms are spoken or sung.*

## READING FROM HOLY SCRIPTURE

*One or more readings from Holy Scripture are read. Each is intro-
duced as follows:*

**P** A reading from _____ , chapter _____ .

*Each reading may conclude:*

**P** This is the Word of the Lord.

**C** **Thanks be to God.**

## SERMON OR MEDITATION

*The APOSTLES' CREED may be confessed.*

## HYMN

## PRAYERS

**Collect of the Day**

**Intercessions and Thanksgivings**

## LORD'S PRAYER

*Matthew 6:9–13*

**P** Taught by our Lord and trusting His promises, we are bold to pray:

**C** Our Father who art in heaven,
hallowed be Thy name,
Thy kingdom come,
Thy will be done on earth as it is in heaven;
give us this day our daily bread;
and forgive us our trespasses
as we forgive those who trespass against us;
and lead us not into temptation,
but deliver us from evil.
For Thine is the kingdom and the power and the glory
forever and ever. Amen.

## BLESSING

*2 Corinthians 13:14*

**P** The grace of our Lord ✛ Jesus Christ and the love of God and the communion of the Holy Spirit be with you all.

**C** Amen.

# BLESSING OF A MOTHER AFTER CHILDBIRTH

In the name of the Father and of the ✛ Son and of the Holy
   Spirit.

**Amen.**                                                            *Matthew 28:19b*

*The psalm may be sung by whole verse or spoken by half verse.*

This woman cried out and the Lord ǀ heard her,*
   and saved her out of all her ǀ troubles.                     *Liturgical text*
I will bless the Lord at ǀ all times;*
   his praise shall continually be ǀ in my mouth.
My soul makes its boast ǀ in the Lord;*
   let the humble hear ǀ and be glad.
Oh, magnify the ǀ Lord with me,*
   and let us exalt his name to- ǀ gether!
I sought the Lord, and he ǀ answered me*
   and delivered me from ǀ all my fears.
When the righteous cry for help, the ǀ Lord hears*
   and delivers them out of all their ǀ troubles.
Many are the afflictions of the ǀ righteous,*
   but the Lord delivers him out ǀ of them all.   *Psalm 34:1–4, 17, 19*
**Glory be to the Father and ǀ to the Son***
   **and to the Holy ǀ Spirit;**
as it was in the be- ǀ ginning,*
   **is now, and will be forever. ǀ Amen.**
This woman cried out and the Lord ǀ heard her,*
   and saved her out of all her ǀ troubles.                     *Liturgical text*

Taught by our Lord and trusting His promises, we are bold to
    pray:

**Our Father who art in heaven,**
    **hallowed be Thy name,**
**Thy kingdom come,**
**Thy will be done on earth as it is in heaven;**
**give us this day our daily bread;**
**and forgive us our trespasses**
    **as we forgive those who trespass against us;**
**and lead us not into temptation,**
    **but deliver us from evil.**
**For Thine is the kingdom and the power and the glory**
    **forever and ever. Amen.**                    *Matthew 6:9–13*

The Lord be with you.                             *2 Timothy 4:22*
**And also with you.**

Let us pray.
Almighty and everlasting God, who turns the pains of the
faithful into joy at childbirth, we praise You for the great
mercy which You have shown to _name of mother_ and her
child(ren), _name of child(ren)_. Keep them always in Your
fatherly care, and grant that her _child/children_ may be
brought to the waters of Holy Baptism and grow up in true
fear, love, and trust of You; through Jesus Christ, Your Son,
our Lord, who lives and reigns with You and the Holy Spirit,
one God, now and forever. (523)
**Amen.**

The blessing of almighty God, the Father, the ☩ Son, and
the Holy Spirit be and remain with you always.
**Amen.**

# COMMENDATION OF THE DYING

## WHEN A PASTOR IS NOT PRESENT

**L**  In the name of the Father and of the ✝ Son and of the
Holy Spirit.                                                       *Matthew 28:19b*

**C**  *Amen.*

**L**  Let us pray.

> Lord God, heavenly Father, look with favor upon Your
> child, ___*name*___, forgive ___*him/her*___ all ___*his/her*___ sins,
> and comfort ___*him/her*___ with the promise of resurrection
> to life everlasting; through Your Son, Jesus Christ, our
> Lord, who lives and reigns with You and the Holy Spirit,
> one God, now and forever. (533)

**R**  *Amen.*

**L**  Let us confess our sins.

**L**  O almighty God,
merciful Father,

**R**  *I, a poor, miserable sin-*
*ner, confess unto You all*
*my sins and iniquities*
*with which I have ever*
*offended You and justly*
*deserved Your temporal*
*and eternal punishment.*
*But I am heartily sorry*
*for them and sincerely*
*repent of them, and I*
*pray You of Your bound-*
*less mercy and for the*
*sake of the holy, inno-*
*cent, bitter sufferings and*
*death of Your beloved*
*Son, Jesus Christ, to be*
*gracious and merciful to*
*me, a poor, sinful being.*

**L**  Do you confess to
almighty God that you
are a poor, miserable
sinner?

**R**  *Yes.*

**L**  Do you confess to our
merciful Father that
you have sinned
against Him in
thought, word, and
deed?

**R**  *Yes.*

**L**  Do you confess that
you justly deserve His
temporal and eternal
punishment?

**R**  *Yes.*

**L** Do you believe that our Lord Jesus Christ died for you and shed His blood for you on the cross for the forgiveness of all your sins?

**R** *Yes.*

**L** Do you pray God, for the sake of the holy, innocent, bitter sufferings and death of His beloved Son, to be gracious and merciful to you?

**R** *Yes.*

**L** In the mercy of almighty God, Jesus Christ was given to die for us, and for His sake God forgives us all our sins. To those who believe in Jesus Christ He gives the power to become the children of God and bestows on them the Holy Spirit. May the Lord, who has begun this good work in us, bring it to completion in the day of our Lord Jesus Christ.

**R** *Amen.*

*One of the following psalms is prayed. When copies of the rite are provided to those present, all may join in as the psalm is sung by whole verse or spoken by half verse. After the psalm and a time of silence, the psalm collect may be spoken. The use of one or more penitential psalms (6, 32, 38, 51, 102, 130, 143) is customary and appropriate when death is near.*

*Sola Gratia*

GRACE ALONE

## Psalm 23

*English Standard Version*

The LORD is my | shepherd;*
    I | shall not want.
He makes me lie down in
green | pastures.*
      He leads me beside
      still | waters.
He re- | stores my soul.*
      He leads me in paths
      of righteousness for
      his | name's sake.
Even though I walk
through the valley of the
shadow of death, I will fear
no evil, for you are | with
me;*
      your rod and your staff,
      they | comfort me.
You prepare a table before
me in the presence of my |
enemies;*
      you anoint my head
      with oil; my cup | over-
      flows.
Surely goodness and mercy
shall follow me all the
days | of my life,*
      and I shall dwell in the
      house of the LORD for- |
      ever.
**Glory be to the Father and | to
the Son***
      **and to the Holy | Spirit;**
**as it was in the be- | ginning,***
      **is now, and will be for**
      **ever. | Amen.**

*King James Version*

The LORD is my | shepherd;*
    I | shall not want.
He maketh me to lie down
in green | pastures:*
      he leadeth me beside
      the still | waters.
He restoreth | my soul:*
      he leadeth me in the
      paths of righteousness
      for his | name's sake.
Yea, though I walk through
the valley of the shadow of
death, I will fear no evil:
for thou art | with me;*
      thy rod and thy staff
      they | comfort me.
Thou preparest a table before
me in the presence of mine |
enemies:*
      thou anointest my head
      with oil; my cup runneth
      | over.
Surely goodness and mercy
shall follow me all the days
| of my life:*
      and I will dwell in the
      house of the LORD for- |
      ever.
**Glory be to the Father and | to
the Son***
      **and to the Holy | Spirit;**
**as it was in the be- | ginning,***
      **is now, and will be for-**
      **ever. | Amen.**

L  O Lord, our shepherd, lead Your sheep in goodness and mercy as we pass with You through the valley of the shadow of death to Your eternal home, where You live and reign with the Father and the Holy Spirit, one God, now and forever. (534)

R  *Amen.*

## Psalm 130

Out | of the depths\*
    I cry to you, | O Lord!
O Lord, | hear my voice!\*
    Let your ears be attentive to the voice of my pleas for | mercy!
If you, O Lord, should mark in- | iquities,\*
    O Lord, | who could stand?
But with you there is for- | giveness,\*
    that you | may be feared.
I wait for the Lord, my | soul waits,\*
    and in his | word I hope;
my soul waits for the Lord more than watchmen for the | morning,\*
    more than watchmen for the | morning.
O Israel, hope in the Lord! For with the Lord there is | steadfast love,\*
    and with him is plentiful re- | demption.
And he will redeem | Israel\*
    from all his in- | iquities.
**Glory be to the Father and | to the Son**\*
    **and to the Holy | Spirit;**
**as it was in the be- | ginning,**\*
    **is now, and will be forever. | Amen.**

L  O Lord, let Your ears be attentive to the voice of our cry, for there is forgiveness with You that You may be feared. By Your unfailing love deliver us from all our sin that our hope may be in You and in Your full redemption; through Jesus Christ, Your Son, our Lord, who lives and reigns with You and the Holy Spirit, one God, now and forever. (535)

R  *Amen.*

*One or more of the following passages from Holy Scripture may be read.*

### My sheep hear My voice

[Jesus said:] "My sheep hear my voice, and I know them, and they follow me. I give them eternal life, and they will never perish, and no one will snatch them out of my hand. My Father, who has given them to me, is greater than all, and no one is able to snatch them out of the Father's hand."

*John 10:27–29*

### Into Your hand I commit my spirit

Into your hand I commit my spirit;
you have redeemed me, O LORD, faithful God.  *Psalm 31:5*

### I will give you rest

[Jesus said:] "Come to me, all who labor and are heavy laden, and I will give you rest. Take my yoke upon you, and learn from me, for I am gentle and lowly in heart, and you will find rest for your souls. For my yoke is easy, and my burden is light."  *Matthew 11:28–30*

### God so loved the world

[Jesus said:] "For God so loved the world, that he gave his only Son, that whoever believes in him should not perish but have eternal life. For God did not send his Son into the world to condemn the world, but in order that the world might be saved through him. Whoever believes in him is not condemned, but whoever does not believe is condemned already, because he has not believed in the name of the only Son of God. And this is the judgment: the light has come into the world, and people loved the darkness rather than the light because their deeds were evil. For everyone who does wicked things hates the light and does not come to the light, lest his deeds should be exposed. But whoever does what is true comes to the light, so that it may be clearly seen that his deeds have been carried out in God."  *John 3:16–21*

## The crucifixion of our Lord

Then the soldiers of the governor took Jesus into the governor's headquarters, and they gathered the whole battalion before him. And they stripped him and put a scarlet robe on him, and twisting together a crown of thorns, they put it on his head and put a reed in his right hand. And kneeling before him, they mocked him, saying, "Hail, King of the Jews!" And they spit on him and took the reed and struck him on the head. And when they had mocked him, they stripped him of the robe and put his own clothes on him and led him away to crucify him. As they went out, they found a man of Cyrene, Simon by name. They compelled this man to carry his cross.

And when they came to a place called Golgotha (which means Place of a Skull), they offered him wine to drink, mixed with gall, but when he tasted it, he would not drink it. And when they had crucified him, they divided his garments among them by casting lots. Then they sat down and kept watch over him there. And over his head they put the charge against him, which read, "This is Jesus, the King of the Jews." Then two robbers were crucified with him, one on the right and one on the left. And those who passed by derided him, wagging their heads and saying, "You who would destroy the temple and rebuild it in three days, save yourself! If you are the Son of God, come down from the cross." So also the chief priests, with the scribes and elders, mocked him, saying, "He saved others; he cannot save himself. He is the King of Israel; let him come down now from the cross, and we will believe in him. He trusts in God; let God deliver him now, if he desires him. For he said, 'I am the Son of God.'" And the robbers who were crucified with him also reviled him in the same way.

Now from the sixth hour there was darkness over all the land until the ninth hour. And about the ninth hour Jesus cried out with a loud voice, saying, "Eli, Eli, lema sabachthani?" that is, "My God, my God, why have you forsaken me?" And some of the bystanders, hearing it, said, "This man is calling Elijah." And one of them at once ran and took a sponge, filled it with sour wine, and put it on a reed and gave it to him to drink. But the others said, "Wait, let us see whether Elijah will come to save him." And Jesus cried out again with a loud voice and yielded up his spirit. And behold, the curtain of the temple was torn in two, from top to bottom. And the earth shook, and the rocks were split. The tombs also were opened. And many bodies of the saints who had fallen asleep were raised, and coming out of the tombs after his resurrection they went into the holy city and appeared to many. When the centurion and those who were with him, keeping watch over Jesus, saw the earthquake and what took place, they were filled with awe and said, "Truly this was the Son of God!"     *Matthew 27:27–54*

## The resurrection of our Lord

Now on the first day of the week Mary Magdalene came to the tomb early, while it was still dark, and saw that the stone had been taken away from the tomb. So she ran and went to Simon Peter and the other disciple, the one whom Jesus loved, and said to them, "They have taken the Lord out of the tomb, and we do not know where they have laid him." So Peter went out with the other disciple, and they were going toward the tomb. Both of them were running together, but the other disciple outran Peter and reached the tomb first. And stooping to look in, he saw the linen cloths lying there, but he did not go in. Then Simon Peter came, following him, and went into the tomb. He saw the linen cloths lying there, and the face cloth, which had been on Jesus' head, not lying with the linen cloths but folded up in a place by itself. Then the other disciple, who had reached the tomb first, also went in, and he saw and believed; for as yet they did not understand the Scripture, that he must rise from the dead. Then the disciples went back to their homes.

But Mary stood weeping outside the tomb, and as she wept she stooped to look into the tomb. And she saw two angels in white, sitting where the body of Jesus had lain, one at the head and one at the feet. They said to her, "Woman, why are you weeping?" She said to them, "They have taken away my Lord, and I do not know where they have laid him." Having said this, she turned around and saw Jesus standing, but she did not know that it was Jesus. Jesus said to her, "Woman, why are you weeping? Whom are you seeking?" Supposing him to be the gardener, she said to him, "Sir, if you have carried him away, tell me where you have laid him, and I will take him away." Jesus said to her, "Mary." She turned and said to him in Aramaic, "Rabboni!" (which means Teacher). Jesus said to her, "Do not cling to me, for I have not yet ascended to the Father; but go to my brothers and say to them, 'I am ascending to my Father and your Father, to my God and your God.'" Mary Magdalene went and announced to the disciples, "I have seen the Lord"—and that he had said these things to her.

*John 20:1–18*

## Standing before the throne and the Lamb

After this I looked, and behold, a great multitude that no one could number, from every nation, from all tribes and peoples and languages, standing before the throne and before the Lamb, clothed in white robes, with palm branches in their hands, and crying out with a loud voice, "Salvation belongs to our God who sits on the throne, and to the Lamb!" And all the angels were standing around the throne and around the elders and the four living creatures, and they fell on their faces before the throne and worshiped God, saying, "Amen! Blessing and glory and wisdom and thanksgiving and honor and power and might be to our God forever and ever! Amen."

Then one of the elders addressed me, saying, "Who are these, clothed in white robes, and from where have they come?" I said to him, "Sir, you know." And he said to me, "These are the ones coming out of the great tribulation. They have washed their robes and made them white in the blood of the Lamb.

"Therefore they are before the throne of God,
    and serve him day and night in his temple;
    and he who sits on the throne will shelter them with his presence.
They shall hunger no more, neither thirst anymore;
    the sun shall not strike them,
    nor any scorching heat.

For the Lamb in the midst of the throne will be their shepherd, and he will guide them to springs of living water, and God will wipe away every tear from their eyes."

*Revelation 7:9–17*

*The CREED is confessed.*

I believe in God, the Father Almighty,
    maker of heaven and earth.
And in Jesus Christ, His only Son, our Lord,
    who was conceived by the Holy Spirit,
    born of the virgin Mary,
    suffered under Pontius Pilate,
    was crucified, died and was buried.
    He descended into hell.
    The third day He rose again from the dead.
    He ascended into heaven
    and sits at the right hand of God the Father Almighty.
    From thence He will come to judge the living and the dead.
I believe in the Holy Spirit,
    the holy Christian Church,
        the communion of saints,
    the forgiveness of sins,
    the resurrection of the body,
    and the life ☩ everlasting. Amen.

    *Christian:* the ancient text reads "catholic," meaning the whole Church as it confesses the wholeness of Christian doctrine.

*The Litany for the Dying may be prayed, either responsively or alone by the leader.*

| | |
|---|---|
| O Lord, | have mercy. |
| O Christ, | have mercy. |
| O Lord, | have mercy. |
| God the Father in heaven, | have mercy on us. |
| God the Son, Redeemer of the world, | have mercy on us. |
| God the Holy Spirit, | have mercy on us. |
| Be gracious to us. | Spare us, good Lord. |
| Be gracious to us. | Help us, good Lord. |
| From all sin, from all evil, from all suffering, | good Lord, deliver us. |

By Your incarnation, by Your cross
    and suffering, by Your death
    and burial,                **help us, good Lord.**
By Your resurrection and ascension,
    by the coming of Your Holy Spirit,    **help us, good Lord.**
We poor sinners implore You    **to hear us, good Lord.**
That You deliver Your servant
    _name_ from all evil and from
    eternal death,               **we implore You to hear us,**
                                  **good Lord.**

That You forgive all _his/her_ sins,    **we implore You to hear us,**
                                  **good Lord.**

That You give _him/her_
    refreshment and everlasting
    blessing,                   **we implore You to hear us,**
                                  **good Lord.**

That You give _him/her_ joy and glad-
    ness in heaven with Your saints,    **we implore You to hear us,**
                                  **good Lord.**

Christ, the Lamb of God,
    who takes away the sin of the world,    **have mercy on us.**
Christ, the Lamb of God,
    who takes away the sin of the world,    **have mercy on us.**
Christ, the Lamb of God,
    who takes away the sin of the world,    **grant us Your peace.**
O Lord,    **have mercy.**
O Christ,    **have mercy.**
O Lord,    **have mercy.**

*The leader then prays:*

L  Almighty God, You breathed life into Adam and have
    given earthly life also to _name_, Your dear child and
    servant. With faith in Your power to heal and save, we
    commend _him/her_ to You; through Jesus Christ, Your
    Son, our Lord, who lives and reigns with You and the Holy
    Spirit, one God, now and forever. (536)

R  *Amen.*

*The Lord's Prayer is then prayed.*

**Our Father who art in heaven,**
**hallowed be Thy name,**
**Thy kingdom come,**
**Thy will be done on earth as it is in heaven;**
**give us this day our daily bread;**
**and forgive us our trespasses**
**as we forgive those who trespass against us;**
**and lead us not into temptation,**
**but deliver us from evil.**
**For Thine is the kingdom and the power and the glory**
**forever and ever. Amen.** *Matthew 6:9–13*

**Ⓛ** *Name*, go in peace. May God the Father, who created you, may God the ✝ Son, who redeemed and saved you with His blood, may God the Holy Spirit, who sanctified you in the water of Holy Baptism, receive you into the company of saints and angels to await the resurrection and live in the light of His glory forevermore.

**Ⓡ** *Amen.*

*The Nunc Dimittis is spoken or sung.*

**Lord, now You let Your servant go in peace;**
**Your word has been fulfilled.**
**My own eyes have seen the salvation**
**which You have prepared in the sight of every people:**
**a light to reveal You to the nations**
**and the glory of Your people Israel.** *Luke 2:29–32*
**Glory be to the Father and to the Son and to the Holy Spirit;**
**as it was in the beginning, is now, and will be forever. Amen.**

*The following hymn stanza may be sung or spoken:*

Lord, let at last Thine angels come,
To Abr'ham's bosom bear me home,
    That I may die unfearing;
And in its narrow chamber keep
My body safe in peaceful sleep
    Until Thy reappearing.
And then from death awaken me,
That these mine eyes with joy may see,
    O Son of God, Thy glorious face,
    My Savior and my fount of grace.
Lord Jesus Christ,
    My prayer attend,
    My prayer attend,
    And I will praise Thee without end.

*Hymn 708:3*

*Should death occur, the following prayer is said.*

Ⓛ O God the Father, fountain and source of all blessings, we give thanks that You have kept our __brother/sister name__ in the faith and have now taken __him/her__ to Yourself. Comfort us with Your holy Word, and give us strength that when our last hour comes we may peacefully fall asleep in You; through Jesus Christ, our Lord. (537)

Ⓡ *Amen.*

*The rite concludes concludes with the blessing.*

Ⓛ The almighty and merciful Lord, the Father, the ✝ Son, and the Holy Spirit, bless us and keep us.

Ⓡ *Amen.*

# Topical Index